GAMBLING WITH VIOLENCE

Dispossession without Development
Michael Levien

The Other One Percent
Sanjoy Chakravorty, Devesh Kapur, and Nirvikar Singh

Social Justice through Inclusion
Francesca R. Jensenius

The Man Who Remade India
Vinay Sitapati

GAMBLING WITH VIOLENCE

STATE OUTSOURCING OF WAR IN PAKISTAN AND INDIA

YELENA BIBERMAN

OXFORD
UNIVERSITY PRESS

OXFORD
UNIVERSITY PRESS

Oxford University Press is a department of the University of Oxford. It furthers
the University's objective of excellence in research, scholarship, and education
by publishing worldwide. Oxford is a registered trade mark of Oxford University
Press in the UK and certain other countries.

Published in the United States of America by Oxford University Press
198 Madison Avenue, New York, NY 10016, United States of America.

Library of Congress Cataloging-in-Publication Data
Names: Biberman, Yelena, author.
Title: Gambling with violence: state outsourcing of war in Pakistan and India /
Yelena Biberman.
Description: New York : Oxford University Press, 2019. |
Includes bibliographical references and index.
Identifiers: LCCN 2018029520 | ISBN 9780190929978 (paperback : alkaline paper) |
ISBN 9780190929961 (hardback : alkaline paper)
Subjects: LCSH: Counterinsurgency—Pakistan. | Counterinsurgency—India. |
Non-state actors (International relations)—South Asia. | Civil war—South
Asia. | South Asia—Politics and government. | Alliances.
Classification: LCC DS341 .B55 2019 | DDC 355.02/180954—dc23
LC record available at https://lccn.loc.gov/2018029520

For Mom, Jane, and Bas'ka

CONTENTS

Acknowledgments xi

1

INTRODUCTION 1

Why Study State-Nonstate Alliances in Civil War? 3

Why South Asia? 6

Existing Research and Book's Contribution 7

State Alliances 8

Rebel Alliances 9

Militias 11

The Argument 11

Book Plan 12

2

STATE-NONSTATE ALLIANCES IN CIVIL WAR:
A NEW BALANCE-OF-INTERESTS THEORY 14

A Typology of Nonstate Allies 15

Auxiliary 20

Proxy 21

Freelancer 22

Potential Explanations Suggested in the Existing Literature 23

A New Balance-of-Interests Framework 24

Scope Conditions 30

Cases, Data, and Research Methods 32

Research Design and Case Selection 32

Data Collection 34

3

SAVING THE HOUSE OF ISLAM: PAKISTAN'S "VOLUNTEERS" IN
THE WAR OF 1971 37

Pakistan Regains Control in East Pakistan, March–May 1971 41

From State Control to Parity, May–June 1971 47

Alliance between Pakistan and Razakar Opportunists 51

From Parity to Insurgent Dominance, June–December 1971 54

Alliance between Pakistan and al-Badr Activists 56

Conclusion 59

4

"GUNS PLUS INTEREST": RENEGADES AND VILLAGERS IN INDIA'S
KASHMIR WAR 64

From Insurgent Control to Parity in Kashmir Valley, 1989–1993 67

From Parity to India's Control in Kashmir Valley, 1993–1996 72

Alliance between India and Ikhwan-ul-Muslimoon Opportunists 73

Alliance between India and Muslim Mujahideen Opportunists 82

1996 Elections Mark a Turning Point 88

New Theater of War in Jammu 92

Alliance between India and Village Defense Committee Activists 92

Conclusion 94

5

TRIBAL "AWAKENINGS" IN PAKISTAN AND INDIA 97

Anti-Taliban "Awakening" in Pakistan 100

Pakistan's Interests in Context 101

*Misalignment of Interests and Weak Alliance between Pakistan and
Lashkars 106*

Anti-Naxalite "Awakening" in India 112

Background of Naxalite (a.k.a. Maoist) Insurgency 113

India's Interests in Context 115

From India's Weakness to Parity in Chhattisgarh 117

Alliance between India and Salwa Judum Opportunists 119

Conclusion 127

6

ALL THE STATE'S PROXIES IN TURKEY AND RUSSIA 129

Turkey's War against Kurdish Rebels 133

Alliance between Turkey and Kurdish Clans 135

Alliance between Turkey and Kurdish Hizbullah 140

Russia's First War in Chechnya 143

Russia's Second War in Chechnya 149

Alliance between Russia and Gantamirovtsy 152

Alliance between Russia and Kadyrovtsy 153

Conclusion 155

7

CONCLUSION 157

Policy Recommendations 161

Directions for Future Research 165

Implications for South Asian Security 168

Notes 171

Index 209

ACKNOWLEDGMENTS

When conceiving this project over eight years ago, I could have hardly imagined how many people and institutions would help me carry it out. I begin by thanking those who took the time to share their experiences and thoughts with me in Islamabad, Srinagar, New Delhi, Dhaka, Diyarbakır, Ankara, Moscow, London, and Washington, DC.

I owe a most profound debt to my mentor and dissertation advisor, Ashutosh Varshney. His brilliance, boldness, passion, and extraordinarily generous support at every step of the process inspired me to produce my very best work. His example emboldened me to take intellectual risks and conquer new territories.

Peter Andreas has not only been my advisor as a graduate student and mentor thereafter but also a role model of intrepid and ground-breaking research on illicit state behavior. The journey I embarked on over eight years ago that culminates in this book is unimaginable without the wise and cheerful counsel of Pauline Jones.

I am very grateful to the Center for Contemporary South Asia at the Watson Institute for International and Public Affairs at Brown University for hosting a day-long workshop devoted to my book manuscript and to the workshop participants—Fotini Christia, Christopher Clary, Christine Fair, Dipali Mukhopadhyay, and Vipin Narang—for their extensive and valuable feedback.

Brown University and the Watson Institute provided me with an extraordinarily rich learning environment that fostered exploration and creativity over narrow notions of success. The late Alan Zuckerman's "boot camp" for first-year graduate students instilled fidelity to rigor. Richard Snyder's survey of the diverse paths taken by some of the most prominent scholars in comparative politics broadened my image of what it means to be a political scientist, helped me recognize the enduring importance of "big questions," and created an appetite for fieldwork.

Skidmore College regularly reminds of me why I became an academic in the first place. It has become my new intellectual home, where I can focus on creative research projects. My students keep me inspired to pursue new questions and share what I learn in an environment that values both teaching and research. The exceptional friendliness and support of my colleagues in the Department of Political Science, as well as the college as a whole, has made these early years as a professor uniquely gratifying. For this, I am particularly grateful to Roy Ginsberg and Kirsten Mishkin, Kate Graney, Steven Hoffmann, Christopher Mann, Barbara McDonough, Ron Seyb and Grace Burton, Natalie Taylor and Flagg Taylor, Bob Turner, and Aldo Vacs, as well as Michael Arnush and Leslie Mechem, Beau Breslin, Margaret Greaves, Eliza Kent, and Mahesh Shankar. A special thanks to my talented research assistants Trevor Cloen, Zewen Hu, Jan Janiszewski, Gage Willand, and Mende Yangden.

My work has benefited from the feedback it received at the Massachusetts Institute of Technology Strategic Use of Force Working Group, American Institute of Pakistan Studies Junior Scholars Conference, Modern South Asia Workshop at Yale University, and Olympia Summer Seminars, as well as at the International Studies Association, American Political Science Association, Conference on South Asia, Association for the Study of Nationalities, and New England Political Science Association annual meetings.

The research I conducted for this book was also enriched by the comments I received at the National Police Academy in Islamabad, Institute of Kashmir Studies at the University of Kashmir, Observer Research Foundation in New Delhi, Center for International Politics,

Organization and Disarmament at Jawaharlal Nehru University, Nelson Mandela Centre for Peace and Conflict Resolution at Jamia Millia Islamia, Diplomatic Academy of the Ministry of Foreign Affairs of the Russian Federation, and National Ground Intelligence Center of the US Army Intelligence and Security Command. So too was highly instructive my participation in the Raisina Dialogue in New Delhi, US Army War College National Security Seminar, Philip Merrill Center for Strategic Studies Basin Harbor Workshop, United States Institute of Peace Jennings Randolph Senior Fellows and Peace Scholars Workshop, and Summer Workshop on Analysis of Military Operations and Strategy at Cornell University.

I am indebted to colleagues and friends for their contributions to this project. Some of them supported me during fieldwork, others commented on countless presentations and drafts, or provided moral support. Many have helped sharpen my ideas. Thank you: Malik Hammad Ahmad, Ariel Ahram, Belgin Şan Akça, Azhar Ali, Michele Angrist, Ekim and Eren Arbatli, Ana Arjona, Victor Asal, Bilal Baloch, Regina Bateson, Maria Angelica Bautista, Abu Syed Muhammad Belal, Samir Ahmad Bhat, Stephen Biddle, Gavril Bilev, Filly and Lawson Brown, Erica De Bruin, Charles Burnett, Ahsan Butt, Melani Cammett, Rachel Castellano, Uday Chandra, Stephen P. Cohen, Brian Dudley, Sumit Ganguly, Robert Gerwarth, Larry Goodson, Bharath Gopalaswamy, Philip Hultquist, Oleg Ivanov, Corinna Jentzsch, Stathis Kalyvas, Nickolas Katsakis, Bettina Koch, Walter Ladwig, Sameer Lalwani, Anatol Lieven, Romain Malejacq, Kimberly Marten, Katya Mellott, Raja Mohan, Shivaji Mukherjee, Shuja Nawaz, T.V. Paul, Roger Petersen, Srinath Raghavan, Muhibbur Rahman, Sadia Saeed, Lee J. M. Seymour, Swaran Singh, Paul Staniland, Niloufer Siddiqui, Shawn Tabankin, Megan Turnbull, Andrey Turovsky, Michael Weintraub, and Farhan Zahid.

Archival research was indispensable to my findings and so was the help of Nuzhat Khatoon at the Asia Division of the Library of Congress, Thomas Lannon at the Manuscripts and Archives Division of the New York Public Library, and Andrea Singer at the Indiana University-Bloomington Library. I am also grateful to the librarians at the Liberation

War Museum Archives in Dhaka, University of Kashmir Library, Nehru Memorial and Library Archives in New Delhi, Defence Studies and Analyses Library in New Delhi, British Library—Asia, Pacific, and Africa Collections (formerly the India Office Library), British National Archives at Kew, King's College London Archives, US National Archives at College Park, Human Rights Association office in Diyarbakır, and Columbia University Rare Book and Manuscript Library (Human Rights Watch Collection).

This book has benefited a great deal from the research I conducted for my dissertation, which was generously supported by the United States Institute of Peace Jennings Randolph Peace Scholar Dissertation Fellowship, American Institute of Pakistan Studies Junior Fellowship, Smith Richardson Foundation World Politics and Statecraft Fellowship, Horowitz Foundation for Social Policy Research Grant (Special Recognition: John L. Stanley Award), New York Public Library Short-Term Research Fellowship, Brown University Graduate School Internal Dissertation Fellowship, and Brown University Office of International Affairs, as well as Graduate School Research Travel Grants. My study of Urdu language at the South Asia Summer Language Institute (SASLI) was made possible by the Foreign Language and Area Studies Summer Fellowship. Further research for this book was generously supported by the Atlantic Council US-Pakistan Exchange Fellowship, Judith Johns Carrico Faculty Grant, and Skidmore College Faculty Development Grant.

One of the real pleasures of producing this book has been working with Dave McBride, my editor at Oxford University Press. I owe him a great debt not only for being interested in my manuscript but also for all the work he put into enhancing it through incredibly insightful and thorough feedback, for which I am also very grateful to my reviewers.

A special thanks to my brother, Aleksandr, sister-in-law, Rachel Casseus, and cousins, Yan and Sammy Shurin, for their cheer and moral support. My family has been, and always will be, my main reason for it all. This book is for and because of them. Like so many others before and after us, we arrived in the United States as refugees fleeing persecution and violence. From where we came discussing politics, even at home, could get one into serious trouble. I am grateful to my family for making it possible for me to talk about and to study politics, and especially to study persecution and violence.

My husband, Feryaz Ocakli, deserves more credit than I can ever convey for helping and bolstering me through it all. That he has maintained high spirits despite reading nearly all of my drafts is a testament to his resilience and devotion. Our shared love of what we do and, of course, our new son, Timur, are my greatest treasures. I am grateful to my Turkish family, and especially the late Bedri Ocakli as well as Ayşe, Fevzi, Pelin, and Beste Ocakli, for my comrade in arms.

GAMBLING WITH VIOLENCE

INTRODUCTION

As anyone who has ever been in combat will tell you, the last thing you want is a fair fight.[1]

By 1999, the Clinton Administration wanted Osama bin Laden dead. The bombing of two US embassies in East Africa made obvious the al-Qaeda leader's intention to attack the United States worldwide. His shopping list included nuclear material. But who could get the mission accomplished? Bin Laden was effectively out of reach of the United States and its state allies. He was in Afghanistan, under the protection of the Taliban. So the US Central Intelligence Agency (CIA) turned to nonstate actors: paid "tribal assets" in Afghanistan. "From the American President down to the average man on the street, we want him [bin Laden] stopped," a CIA field officer instructed the tribals. Their response, however, caught the agency off guard. The tribals agreed to capture bin Laden but refused to kill or harm him. They explained that their actions were constrained by their "beliefs and laws we have to respect," and that is what distinguished them from bin Laden. The CIA was "impressed" the tribals were "not in it for the money but as an investment in the future of Afghanistan" and grudgingly acquiesced.[2]

The lesson of this story is twofold. First, militarily superior states are not always capable of tackling insurgents on their own. Sometimes they need the help of nonstate partners. This is especially the case at the local level, or "on the ground," where states' reach may be severely limited. Second, the relationship between states and nonstate actors is far more complex than the existing literature allows. Assets are not mere puppets at the hands of their principals. They have agency and interests of their own. Even those operating in "weak and collapsing states characterized by fluid alignments among armed actors"[3] can be surprisingly nonmaterialistic and farsighted. The aforementioned Afghan tribals were not the ferocious opportunists the CIA assumed they were. They had principles and a long-term outlook.

This book tackles a particularly perplexing and underexplored type of alliance. Much of the existing work focuses on either interstate or interrebel alliances, or on states supporting rebels against rival states.[4] This book explores state-nonstate alliances. Its focus is on counterinsurgency. As Carl von Clausewitz reminds us, to fight any war is to gamble.[5] But to fight a war inside one's borders with nonprofessionals is a particularly dicey proposition. This is not merely because of the questionable loyalty of those driven solely by their own interests that so preoccupied Niccolò Machiavelli,[6] or the inferior proficiency Adam Smith attributed to those for whom war is not "the sole or principal occupation."[7] It is also because, as army commanders George Washington and Leon Trotsky equally observed, arming individuals who are neither professional nor loyal soldiers tends to exacerbate internal problems, thereby strengthening the hands of powerful foreign adversaries.[8]

The phenomenon of governments outsourcing violence to nonstate actors inside their borders is particularly puzzling when we consider states with robust militaries—such as Pakistan and India. Why would these countries' powerful armies share their resources and responsibilities with characters of questionable capability and loyalty? Pakistan's military is so protective of its turf that it barely entrusts domestic security to the police.[9] India prides itself on being the "world's largest democracy." But it has continued to outsource counterinsurgency to nonstate actors despite its Supreme Court's condemnation, which characterized the practice as "tantamount to sowing of suicide pills that could divide and destroy society."[10]

The disturbingly high prevalence of (and marked variation in) Pakistan and India arming their own citizens against insurgents, without fully and formally incorporating them into their security apparatus, offers an opportunity closely and systematically to study the phenomenon. It allows us to generate hypotheses about its causes and mechanisms while controlling for many plausible alternative explanations. It also sheds light on an important but largely overlooked source of human rights violations and states' low infrastructural power in South Asia.

WHY STUDY STATE-NONSTATE ALLIANCES IN CIVIL WAR?

Uprisings in states with robust armed forces are surprisingly common. Eleven of the fifteen states with the world's strongest militaries confronted an insurgency of some magnitude inside their borders in 2000–2015.[11] The global prevalence of state outsourcing of violence is no less astounding. Figure 1.1 displays the geographical distribution of "pro-government militias" between the years 1981 and 2007.[12] At least 64 percent of the 332 identified groups had direct links to a state institution.[13] Given the significant limitations to collecting accurate cross-national data on armed nonstate groups' relationships with state institutions, the figures very likely underestimate the incidence of state outsourcing of violence.

Violence outsourcing is a high-stakes gamble carrying serious political and security risks. In the short run, states chance betrayal and further exacerbating the conflict. The long-term risks of violence outsourcing include loss of local legitimacy and international prestige.[14] Backlash can also be a serious problem: the empowered nonstate groups may turn into their sponsor's gravediggers,[15] or new militant forces may rise in reaction to the abuses perpetrated by the proxies.[16] The ensuing disorder may compel powerful outside actors, such as India in 1971 (see chapter 3), to get involved in the conflict.[17]

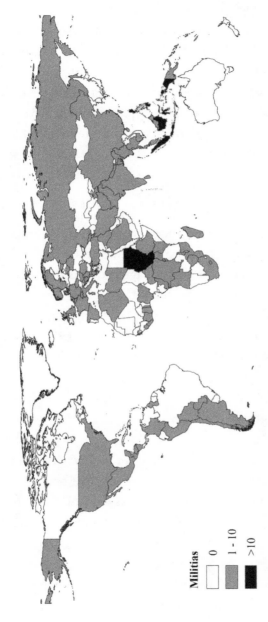

Figure 1.1 Prevalence of Pro-Government Militias, 1981–2007

Source: GIS map created using Carey, Mitchell, and Lowe dataset. Sabine C. Carey, Neil J. Mitchell, and Will Lowe, "States, the Security Sector, and the Monopoly of Violence: A New Database on Pro-Government Militias," *Journal of Peace Research* 50, no. 2 (March 2013): 249–258.

Militias

☐ 0

▨ 1 - 10

■ >10

Cases as diverse as Syria, Guatemala, and Afghanistan remind us of the high costs of violence outsourcing. Syrian President Bashar al-Assad used the notorious *shabiha* (ghosts) forces, comprising racketeers and smugglers, to torture and execute regime opponents in the aftermath of the Arab Spring. The *shabiha* quickly became a symbol of the Syrian regime's brutality and further mobilized domestic and international opposition. What ensued was a full-fledged civil war with a hefty dose of foreign involvement.

During a nearly four-decade-old civil war, the Guatemalan military collaborated with nonstate counterinsurgent groups comprising roughly 1 million peasant farmers. These so-called *Patrullas de Autodefensa Civil* (civil self-defense patrols) committed over 3,000 human rights violations, with some 14,000 victims.[18] Two decades after the end of the civil war, and despite the state's demobilization efforts, the proxies persist, detaining and interrogating "suspicious individuals, who are sometimes punished, tortured, or even lynched."[19]

The Afghan government and its international supporters enlisted the help of tribal fighters against the Taliban-led insurgency as part of the international exit strategy. However, these efforts were frequently "hijacked by local strongmen or by ethnic or political factions, spreading fear, exacerbating local political tensions, fueling vendettas and ethnic conflict, and in some areas even playing into the hands of Taliban insurgents."[20]

The jury is still out on whether nonstate counterinsurgents are actually useful. It might be tempting to conclude that they are. Counterinsurgency is, after all, "an intelligence-driven endeavor" requiring high familiarity with the local context.[21] As insurgents and states compete for local influence, nonstate partners may help states by collecting tactical intelligence, building the state's legitimacy at the local level, making credible threats against civilians in the case of noncooperation, providing plausible deniability, supplying low-cost auxiliary manpower in operations, and carrying out selective violence.[22] However, according to a classified CIA report, nonstate allies often have "a minimal impact on the long-term outcome of a conflict."[23] Moreover, in all the cases closely examined in this book (chapters 3–6), the victories states achieved with the help of nonstate allies were either ephemeral or incomplete.

The usefulness of nonstate counterinsurgents notwithstanding, violence outsourcing violates national and international norms. International humanitarian law requires combatants to be clearly distinguished from civilians and expressly prohibits them from posing as such.[24] State-sponsored nonstate combatants raise a number of legal issues: Does the military's code of conduct apply to them? If captured, do they receive the protections offered to soldiers by the Geneva Conventions? Which courts have jurisdiction over them—military or civil? Can their sponsor be held accountable for their misbehaviors? The irresolution of these questions makes violence outsourcing a deeply controversial subject. Hence, when India's defense minister let it publicly slip that his country should "neutralize terrorists through terrorists only," observers gasped: "Even if you want that as a part of your strategy, you don't say it publicly."[25]

WHY SOUTH ASIA?

South Asia is the ideal setting for exploring the question of state-nonstate alliances for several important reasons. First, although Pakistan is most notorious for using nonstate proxies, the less known instances of India's violence outsourcing offer a rich universe of cases to select those most appropriate for our comparative purposes. Among them are the Ikhwan in Kashmir, the Salwa Judum in Chhattisgarh, the Cats in Punjab, the Tigers and Cobras in Andhra Pradesh, and the SULFA (Surrendered ULFA, or United Liberation Front of Assam) in Assam. Some also see the Bodo Liberation Tigers as a force propped up by the state to counter the National Democratic Front of Bodoland (NDFB) in Assam, or the National Socialist Council of Nagaland-Khaplang (NSCN-K) used as a counterforce to the National Socialist Council of Nagaland-Isak-Muivah NSCN(IM) in Nagaland.[26]

Second, South Asia is a region of high geostrategic importance. This is not only because of its size, location, environmental vulnerability, and economic prospects.[27] It is also because of its high potential for nuclear conflict and the critical role state-nonstate alliances play in either aggravating or lessening that potential.[28]

Finally, much of the existing work on state use of nonstate proxies centers on Latin America, especially Colombia, and the Middle East. This book contributes to a better understanding of state outsourcing of violence as a global phenomenon with cases that have received little accurate in-depth analysis.

EXISTING RESEARCH AND BOOK'S CONTRIBUTION

What distinguishes the modern state from its medieval and early modern predecessors is the possession of an unprecedented resource: the legitimate use of physical force. The state is the only organization that has the widely, if not universally, recognized right to use violence as a means of achieving its goals. No other organization is granted such power over the creation, and destruction, of security. No other organization so jealously guards it.

Warfare is conventionally viewed as the state's quintessential and exclusive domain. Centralization, nationalization, and bureaucratization of violence are deemed necessary for the making and survival of the modern state within the anarchic international system.[29] The standing army is widely acknowledged as "necessary for the constant pacification of large territories as well as for warfare against distant enemies."[30] States that reach beyond it are considered problematic and pathological. Pakistan is a case in point. It has been labeled "an abnormal state" for using "Islamic militants—jihadi groups, nonstate actors—in addition to diplomacy and trade to pursue its defense and foreign policies."[31] Prominent experts describe the country's security policy as emblematic of a "greedy state determined to pursue its revisionism for ideological and even religious goals," and therefore dangerous to the existing world order.[32]

Many believe that violent nonstate actors arise and proliferate because states are too weak to contain them.[33] Currently emerging is a new body of work that recognizes states can play an active role in the rise of armed nonstate groups on their territory. However, it too associates violence outsourcing with military backwardness. Miguel Centeno, for example, proposes that states that have not fought "total wars" (highly destructive wars that require the militarization of the entire society) have failed to undergo the kind of centralization and military development processes necessary to fight in the "regular" style.[34] Following a similar logic, Ariel Ahram links the relationships between postcolonial states and their proxies to an absence of a strong, external competitor that would have compelled the building and centralization of the armed forces.[35] The underlying assumption in the existing scholarship is that states with strong militaries do not outsource violence.

The conventional view that fighting "irregularly" through nonstate proxies necessarily reflects a state's abnormality or failure to build strong conventional forces does not square with the ubiquity of violence outsourcing by militarily superior states. The British army and police in Northern Ireland have colluded with loyalist paramilitaries on targeted killings.[36] China has delegated internal security to "units that are not formally government employees, and probably have little or no legal training."[37] Irregular practices that intentionally straddle the legitimate-illegitimate divide are far more common than their misnomer suggests. Modern states ostensibly exercise a monopoly on legitimate violence, but this does not mean that nonstate actors have a monopoly on illegitimate violence. The state is as capable of illicit behavior as its nonstate counterparts.[38]

The main argument of the book bridges and extends key insights drawn from realist international relations (IR) theory and civil war scholarship. It does this by demonstrating that civil wartime state-nonstate alliances are a product of the local balance of power and actors' interests.

State Alliances

State alliances are "central to the conduct of international politics, and thus the discipline of IR."[39] IR scholarship contains a rich array of theories accounting for alliance patterns across different types of global and regional orders.[40] In Waltz's neorealist tradition, many deem structure (in which a key element, be it power or threat, is distributed) the main driver of alliances. Enter the "neoclassical realist" proposition that different states have different political goals. Some states may prioritize self-preservation (status quo states), while others are "willing to take great risks—even if losing the gamble means extinction—to improve their condition" (revisionist states).[41] Classic examples of revisionist states are Nazi Germany and imperial Japan. Alliances thus likely reflect not a balance of power per se but rather a balance of *interests*. States ally in ways that maximize their interests: some just want to hold onto what they have; others want more.

This book draws on the insights of structural and neoclassical realism to illuminate civil-wartime alliances between states and nonstate actors. In doing so, it builds on the innovative work of Fotini Christia, who uses neorealism's standard emphasis on relative power to explain civil-wartime alliances between nonstate actors.[42] I show that, while relative power is no doubt important, so are the actors' interests. And these interests are not limited to power. This book departs from Christia's approach to alliances between nonstate actors by showing that nonstate actors' interests need not be limited to maintaining or augmenting their influence. Some may be driven primarily by ideational or identity considerations. This book's original contribution is also in distinguishing and taking into account the varied interests of both the state and the nonstate actors.

Rebel Alliances

While the field of IR has characteristically focused on the alliance patterns between states, there is increasing interest in the civil war literature in alliances between nonstate actors, namely rebel groups. The question of whether anarchy is as relentless at the domestic level as it is at the international level underlies much of the debate. Some have shown that it can be.[43] Others have argued that anarchy is not evenly distributed in civil-war-torn states. Territories may, in fact, be governed by the state or a rebel group.[44]

Frequent defections, fractionalization, and alliance reconfigurations among nonstate groups have been shown to prolong civil conflict. This book examines the drivers of an alliance that has, so far, received little theoretical attention. Yet, it is one with the capacity to fundamentally transform and even end a conflict.[45]

The principal question of this book is: What drives state-nonstate alliances? The principal answer: power and interest. But, where does interest come from? Civil war studies have identified two important structural sources: organizational and systemic. Jeremy Weinstein's pioneering work theorizes the former. It identifies two types of rebel: (1) an *opportunist*, who is driven by material and other short-term interests; and (2) an *activist*, who is "willing to invest their time and energy in the hope of reaping large gains in the future."[46] Rebel organizations with significant resources attract opportunists, while their poorer counterparts draw on social ties to make credible promises about the private rewards that will come with victory.[47] The latter attracts highly committed members, while the former succumbs to the so-called "rebel resource curse." At the systemic level, Lee Seymour's work shows that, in weak and collapsing states, short-term horizons dominate alliance-making.[48] Because life is nasty, brutish, and short in collapsing states, immediate payoffs trump long-term oriented activism.

This book builds on the opportunist-activist framework. It treats each condition as sticky but, unlike Weinstein, does not assume it to be fixed. Activists may become disillusioned with their movement or, as Seymour suggests, structurally compelled to forgo farsightedness for pragmatism. Consider one ISIS deserter's account of why he no longer supported an ideology that initially inspired his journey from Virginia to Mosul: "It was pretty hard to live in Mosul. It's not like the Western countries, you know, it's very strict. There's no smoking. I found it hard for everyone there."[49] This book's qualitative methodology is designed precisely to capture unexpected but consequential transformations in individual orientation, which are otherwise easily missed in macro- and micro-level quantitative research.

Militias

There is a marked surge in both scholarly and policy interest in the so-called third actors operating "alongside state security forces or independently of the state."[50] These actors go by different names: "pro-government militia," "paramilitary," "civil defense force," and "self-defense patrol." The existing literature has traced their historical roots,[51] as well as negative[52] and positive effects,[53] on conflict dynamics. However, their relationship with the state, especially in a civil war context, remains little examined and poorly understood. The few accounts that do exist are either state centric or rebel centric. They are also largely functionalist and thus poorly account for variation.

The state-centric approaches emphasize the benefits states reap from militias, such as local knowledge and plausible deniability.[54] The role of ideology has been suggested as important in shaping state-militia relations, but, so far, this research has focused on how ideology influences only the state's choice of nonstate partner.[55] It has neglected to consider the importance of ideology to the nonstate actors. The hereto sole rebel-centric account of state-rebel collaboration posits that the latter turn to the former for protection when a rising insurgent hegemon tries to eliminate them.[56] This book incorporates the interests of both states and nonstate actors, and it brings in the structure and the agency of each to explain state-nonstate alliance patterns.

THE ARGUMENT

Civil wartime state-nonstate alliances are primarily a product of power and interest. The strong cannot always do what they want. A state's military power is relative to the context in which it must be deployed. States with strong armed forces sometimes need nonstate partners for the tactical benefits (e.g., local knowledge, selective violence, force multiplication) they can provide. The nonstate partners have interests of their own. Some (*opportunists*) prioritize the immediate material payoffs of collaboration, be it protection or patronage. Others (*activists*) are more farsighted and play a longer game in the name of ideas.

The proposed "balance-of-interests" theory recognizes the role of both power and interest in state-nonstate alliances, specifies when states seek nonstate allies, and identifies the conditions under which different types of nonstate actors join the counterinsurgency operations.

In a civil war context, the state's main goal is either to reestablish its sovereignty or to preserve the status quo. When the local balance of power is in its favor, it does not need, nor does it wish to bear the costs of, nonstate allies. Nonstate allies are useful to the state when rebels have the upper hand or when the local balance of power is roughly equal. However, this is precisely when it is difficult to find nonstate partners willing to assume the risks of collaboration. *Activists*, for whom ideals or identities rank above survival and enrichment, may be convinced to join the state even when it is losing, so long as they believe the alliance will serve their long-term interests. Making credible promises of future rewards to activists requires cultivating social or ideological links with them: constructing a compelling, even if not altogether earnest, narrative of shared commitments. *Opportunists* prioritize immediate payoffs,[57] and so they may be compelled or co-opted into an alliance with the state when it is doing reasonably well—when the local balance of power with the rebels is roughly equal or favors the state.

To sum up, state-nonstate alliances are balance-of-interests bargains. A state seeking to shift the local balance of power in its favor may enlist activists if it can cultivate social or ideological ties with them. Opportunists are more likely to serve as balance tippers.

BOOK PLAN

This book is organized into three parts: theoretical, empirical, and policy. Chapter 2 offers a novel theoretical framework for understanding state-nonstate alliances in times of civil war. A brief overview of the main concepts and alternative explanations provides the foundation for the arguments introduced here and developed in the rest of the book. The chapter also describes the book's research design and methodologies used for data collection and analysis.

Chapters 3 through 5 trace the main argument with a comparison of four different cases drawn from South Asia: Pakistan's counterinsurgency campaign in East Pakistan/Bangladesh (1971); India's counterinsurgency in Kashmir (1988–2003); Pakistan's counterinsurgency in the Federally Administered Tribal Areas (FATA) and Khyber Pakhtunkhwa Province (2002–2014); and India's counterinsurgency in Chhattisgarh (2004–2015). Chapter 6 evaluates the explanatory power of the argument cultivated in the previous chapters with cases drawn from outside of South Asia, namely Turkey's counterinsurgency against Kurdish rebels (1984–1999) and Russia's two counterinsurgency campaigns in Chechnya (1994–1996 and 1999–2009).

Chapter 7 concludes the book. It summarizes the key findings and considers their policy implications, as well as directions for future research and lessons for South Asian security.

STATE-NONSTATE ALLIANCES IN CIVIL WAR
A New Balance-of-Interests Theory

Nearly two millennia before Niccolò Machiavelli penned what is now widely regarded as the first work of modern political science because of its emphasis on statecraft and empirical knowledge, a far more ambitious king-maker tackled practical statecraft in a treatise entitled *The Arthashastra (The Science of Politics)*. Kautilya, the author in question, advised Chandragupta Maurya on how to rule the Indian subcontinent. That was a time when the region mainly comprised small independent states, and Chandragupta became the first emperor to unify most of India under one administration.

Much of *The Arthashastra* focuses on alliances, and so it is perhaps not surprising that the work is best known for the maxim: "The enemy of my enemy is my friend." Kautilya observed that ideal allies are amenable to control, share a common interest, and are capable of delivering on their promises.[1] *The Arthashastra* also distinguishes between a "natural ally" (one linked through ancestral ties and, therefore, driven by emotion) and an "ally by intent" (one requiring wealth or safety and, therefore, driven by need).[2]

This chapter develops a framework for understanding how states and nonstate actors identify and enlist one another as allies in times of civil unrest. It too distinguishes between those who are driven primarily by need and those driven by emotion. The chapter begins by considering the relevant terms and develops the concepts and categories useful for the study of state-nonstate alliances. A brief overview of the relevant scholarly approaches provides potential explanations as well as the foundation for a new theoretical framework, which is then presented and developed. The chapter also considers the scope of conditions for the argument. It concludes by describing the research design and methodologies used for data collection and analysis.

A TYPOLOGY OF NONSTATE ALLIES

A state may ally with a nonstate actor for a number of reasons. It may ally during war or peace. It may ally in time of an interstate war or a civil war. It may ally against a state or a nonstate rival. The latter may operate primarily outside or inside the territory of the allied state. The focus of this book is on state-nonstate alliances in times of civil war against nonstate rivals operating primarily inside the allied state. It is one of the most underexplored and poorly documented alliances, and this section develops the analytical tools for its study.

This section begins by evaluating the key concepts and terms: the state, violence outsourcing, alliance, militia, and nonstate actor. It then develops a typology of nonstate allies based on their relationship with the state.

To be applicable, a concept must be both precise and useful. It must effectively "carve up" the empirical world while also helping to develop statements of wide explanatory and predictive power.[3] Concepts are essentially theories about "the fundamental constitutive elements of a phenomenon."[4] How we define them directly influences the validity of our causal claims.

The state is conceptualized in Weberian terms: as an organization comprising a centralized set of institutions and personnel exercising, within a given territory, a monopoly on authoritative rule-making that is backed by the exclusive right to use physical force.[5] It is capable of autonomy and having its own distinct interests.[6] The use of the term in this book is not meant to ignore or obfuscate states' potential for engaging in mutually constitutive and transformative relationships with societal actors, as illuminated by the Marxist and "state-in-society" literatures.[7] This book's central focus is on the poorly documented links between states and societal actors. The goal is to give agency to, make legible, and attach accountability to a bureaucratized political force that, unlike any societal actor, possesses the widely recognized right to use violence as a means of achieving its goals.

"Violence outsourcing" refers to a process where a principal (in our case, the state) contracts out to an external provider (a nonstate actor) a function (the use of physical force) which is commonly performed "in-house" (by the national armed forces). The problem with a state outsourcing violence is that, while they may possess a monopoly on the legitimate use of physical force, states do not have a widely recognized right to share that monopoly with nonstate actors.[8] Unlike the outsourcing of customer support or medical diagnostic services by firms, the outsourcing of violence by states is a rejection of international norms—of what it means to play by the ostensible rules of war.

Underlying state outsourcing of violence to nonstate actors are the formation and maintenance of state-nonstate alliances. The concept of alliance is distinct from that of alignment, which is a broader term for an implicit agreement generating expectations about whether one will be "supported or opposed" in "future interactions."[9] As Kautilya reminds us, alliances involve actual, rather than just supposed, cooperation.[10] They entail "some level of commitment and an exchange of benefits" and a cost for "severing the relationship or failing to honor the agreement."[11]

This book focuses on wartime alliances, which are also sometimes referred to as "coalitions." Wartime alliances involve a formal or informal agreement about the use of physical force. The agreement typically covers who should and should not be the target of violence and which forms the violence should and should not take (e.g., assassination, terrorism, sexual violence, genocide). Like most alliances, state-nonstate alliances are not necessarily symmetrical. However, as this book shows, each side has some comparative advantage *at the local level* (i.e., "on the ground") that inspires their existence.

The term "militia" is now very popular in the civil war literature, as well as in policy briefs and news media. There is some overlap in its use, but consensus over what it means has yet to emerge. One influential study describes militias as organized armed groups that are pro-government or government sponsored, and not part of the regular state security apparatus. However, they are not necessarily *nonstate* actors because they could mainly comprise "members of the security forces organized clandestinely as an official or informal group."[12] Salvadoran right-wing death squads, which were manned by Salvadoran military and security personnel, are a case in point.[13] Another important study challenges the proposition that militias require "a recognizable link to the state" by arguing that they can, in effect, "shift their loyalties and may pursue agendas that are at odds with the interests of the state."[14] The study proposes that the fundamental feature of militias is their "anti-rebel dimension."[15] Yet, this conceptualization suffers from precisely the problem it attempts to solve. Just as militias can shift their loyalties against the interests of the state, so too can they shift their loyalties and pursue agendas consistent with the interests of the rebels.[16]

Further obfuscating the concept is the prevalence of organizations called "militia" (e.g., China's People's Liberation Army Militia, New York's Naval Militia) with seemingly little in common.

This book conceptualizes militias as *nonstate actors who are actively collaborating with a state on a military or security assignment.* The term "nonstate actor" refers to an individual or group with no formal, professional ties to the state.[17] These are essentially "societal" actors.[18] Militias are states' nonstate allies in times of armed conflict. As allies, they function as the "irregular forces"—armed individuals or groups who are not members of the regular armed forces, police, or other internal security forces.[19] Members of militias may engage in nonviolent activities, such as spying or serving as local guides. But, they are not mere informants. They are expected, if and when necessary, to use physical force.

Nonstate actors may be referred to as militias as long as they are actively collaborating with a state. When the collaboration ends, the most appropriate term for them would be "militants" (if they remain neutral to the state) or "rebels" (if they turn against the state). Collaboration with a state does not necessarily mean open aggression against all rebel groups. Militias may collaborate simultaneously with a state and select rebels, speculatively or as double agents.

Distinguishing militias from the state's regular armed forces is not the former's unusual repertoire of activities. States' "special forces" often perform the types of unconventional, secret, and controversial tasks for which militias are notorious. For example, Israel Defense Forces' Duvdevan unit engages in kidnappings and targeted assassinations, in addition to high-risk arrests and raids. It operates independently in urban Palestinian areas, and its soldiers are typically disguised in Arab civilian clothes.[20]

Militias occupy a unique position vis-à-vis the state. They work *for* but are not *of* the state. They possess very limited, if any, corporateness— "organic unity and consciousness of themselves as a group apart from laymen."[21] They are typically assembled on an ad hoc basis and receive little, if any, professional training. Their background ranges from that of a battle-hardened rebel to that of an ordinary civilian.[22] When militia units are officially recognized, it is usually through improvised decrees or revival of "traditional" customs of service.[23]

Militias are not exactly "nonstate," nor are they "state" actors. More precisely, they are *liminal* agents, suspended between two conditions: statehood and nonstatehood.[24] Liminality is an anthropological concept originally coined for life's transition periods.[25] It has since expanded to capture "the ambiguous state of being between states of being."[26] Militias occupy an indistinct space between two relatively fixed and stable conditions. We are accustomed to imagine war in vague conventional terms: as open confrontation between well-defined forces. The term "conventional" reflects a standard of conduct codified in The Hague and Geneva Conventions. It generates an image of a "bracketed" type of war.[27] Militias stand outside the proverbial brackets. This book shows how they emerge and function in the extra-bracketed space.

Kautilya reminds us that active collaboration is a key element of an alliance. How and how much states and militias collaborate varies. I disaggregate collaboration into two forms—administrative and operational[28]—in order to make clear what to look for when identifying and measuring specific cases of state-militia collaboration. Administrative collaboration is the sharing of resources or influence over one's internal organization. It includes assistance with recruitment, training, arming, and transportation.[29] Operational collaboration involves sharing command authority: designating an actor's operational objectives and providing direction for accomplishing them through the tactical application of force. Prussian military theorist Carl von Clausewitz emphasized that "[t]he end for which a soldier is recruited, clothed, armed, and trained, the whole object of his sleeping, eating, drinking, and marching *is simply that he should fight at the right place and the right time*."[30] Administrative collaboration is about getting the fighters to the fight. Operational collaboration is about what they do once they get there.

Both administrative and operational collaboration between states and militias require organizational capabilities on the part of the state and nonstate bodies responsible for their implementation. Militias typically work with the army and, sometimes, also the police.[31] Local governments,[32] as well as temporary community organizations sometimes called "peace committees,"[33] may also play a role.

The four different configurations of administrative and operational collaboration translate into three ideal types of militia:[34] proxy, auxiliary, and freelancer. Figure 2.1 displays the relationship between administrative and operational control and militia type.

		Administrative	
		Yes	No
Operational	Yes	Auxiliary	Proxy
	No	Proxy	Freelancer

Figure 2.1 Forms of State-Militia Collaboration and Militia Types

Auxiliary

When states and militias collaborate both administratively and operationally, militias typically take the form of an auxiliary force. This is the most robust form of collaboration. Auxiliary forces usually comprise part-time civilian volunteers. These individuals supplement the regulars by acting as force multipliers. The "alarm companies," established in Germany during the early years of the Second World War to supplement the local defense and security forces, are a case in point. Each was composed of up to 150 civilians who had been previously exempt from military service. They were armed by the army with rifles and light machine guns; monthly training drills were scheduled around their regular work schedules. In case of "commando raids, sabotage, prisoner-of-war or foreign worker uprisings, or even enemy invasion," they were to mobilize and fight under *Wehrkreis* (military district) command.[35]

The People's Liberation Army Militia in China represents a more sizable and enduring example of an auxiliary force. Varying in guise since about the sixth century, the *minbing* was turned by the Chinese Communist Party into a "nationwide civilian mass organization of politically reliable and physically fit men and women under the dual leadership of the CCP [Chinese Communist Party] and the People's Liberation Army."[36] In China, as in the Soviet Union, the irregulars had served as "the organized expression of the revolutionary citizen."[37] However, whereas the Soviet

Union quickly dismantled and incorporated them into the secret police, Mao Zedong appended wartime militias to the country's military system. The modern *minbing* functions as "part-time occupations for otherwise employed workers and peasants."[38] Their military training ranges from several days to two weeks yearly, and the elite among them are armed. In times of war, these units are expected to conduct conventional and guerrilla operations "in coordination with and support" of the regular forces.[39]

The custom of using auxiliaries is millennia old. When the powerful Roman army was unexpectedly massacred by Hannibal's troops in the Battle of Cannae, the Roman Senate famously exiled to Sicily two of the defeated legions and used slaves and even death row inmates to bulk up the military. Auxiliary forces vary in size, structure, and function, depending on the historical and security context in which they originate and operate. Yet, what they all have in common is their strong administrative and operational ties to a central authority.

Proxy

Proxies are militias involved in either administrative or operational collaboration with the state. Some of them may be recruited, trained, and armed by the state. But, once mobilized, they may be largely left on their own. The state does not directly manage or closely monitor their operations. Proxies engaged with the state in administrative collaboration may operate either domestically or abroad. Throughout the Cold War, the United States and the Soviet Union engaged in proxy warfare around the world. The former used proxies in Guatemala in the 1950s to oust a leftist regime, in Angola in the 1970s to prevent a civil war from shifting the country toward communism, and in Afghanistan in the 1980s to give the USSR its own "Vietnam."

Other proxies collaborate with states mostly on an operational basis. Operational collaboration on the side of the state is typically carried out by a small group of embedded regular or special forces. The combination of operational support and a lack of administrative oversight by the state makes these types of proxies especially lethal. An absence of a paper trail and popular belief that the organization is autonomous (or even anti-state) facilitates plausible deniability.

Whereas the state may actively participate in the formation and organization of auxiliaries and administrative proxies, operational proxies are self-formed and self-organized. Military or security personnel may infiltrate an armed group and play an important role in directing its extrajudicial violence. The rank-and-file may not even realize that they are helping the state. For example, the secret Force Research Unit of the British army used Irish republican and Ulster loyalist paramilitary groups as operational proxies by infiltrating them with double agents who assisted in assassinations, including civilians.[40]

Freelancer

Freelancers, such as vigilantes, warlords, street gangs, mafias, and drug syndicates, collaborate with the state neither administratively nor operationally. When states outsource violence to them, it is often by turning a blind eye to their activities.[41] This is the weakest form of collaboration. Freelancers are likely to proliferate on territories of failed states or where the administrative and legal authority of the state is weak, in the so-called brown areas.[42]

Auxiliaries, proxies, and freelancers represent distinct types of non-state allies, or militias. Some of them may fall close to one ideal type but, as their relationship with the state evolves, may transition to another. For example, Lashkar-e-Taiba began as a small but ambitious freelance group in 1990, waging jihad on multiple fronts. But, during 1993 to 1995, the Pakistani state transformed it into a heavyweight proxy battling the Indian government forces and Kashmiri nationalists in India-controlled Kashmir.[43]

The focus of this book is on proxies for two important reasons. First, auxiliaries are best thought of not as allies, but as supplementary troops. They have little agency over their organization and activities, which makes their "alliance" with a state barely a choice. Second, freelancers do not engage in active collaboration with a state, and so their association is best characterized as alignment rather than an alliance. Freelancers are, therefore, not technically allies. They are, at best, prospective allies. Proxy militias have both the agency and the active partnership with a state to be considered its actual allies.

POTENTIAL EXPLANATIONS SUGGESTED IN THE EXISTING LITERATURE

This section identifies the potential explanations for state-nonstate alliances suggested in the existing civil war scholarship. On the part of the state, the literature highlights the importance of political regime type, dependence on aid from a democracy, and ideology. It is divided on whether it is immediate benefits (e.g., protection, patronage) or concern with postwar spoils that drives the alliance choices of nonstate actors.

One important cross-national study conducted at the country-year level argues that weak democracies and recipients of aid from democracies are most likely to use nonstate actors to evade accountability (i.e., in pursuit of plausible deniability) for human rights abuses. The logic is that, in strong democracies, voters can sanction their government for illicit behavior, and secrecy is difficult to maintain due to free speech and open information. In autocracies, citizens have far less access to information and ability to sanction their leaders, and so autocrats do not need nonstate actors to violate human rights. It is the partially democratic states that have the most to gain and least to lose from collaborating with militias. Their only deterrence is reliance on foreign aid from a democracy. However, deterrence works only if the donor democracy can monitor the aid recipient.[44]

While this line of reasoning is intuitively appealing, it does not square with the findings that militias are more likely to violate human rights while working *alongside*, not as substitutes for, the regular forces.[45] Moreover, states need not use nonstate actors to carry out covert operations. They may, for example, use special operations forces, such as the aforementioned Duvdevan unit. And they are increasingly doing so.[46]

An alternative argument contests the ostensibly "apolitical,"[47] or tactics-focused, approach to armed nonstate groups by bringing ideology back in. States are said to be more willing to ally with armed groups that "mobilize symbols, cleavages, and demands that can be easily accommodated within the political arena desired by a regime."[48] The study does not, however, consider whether ideology matters to the armed nonstate groups themselves—that is, whether it drives their alliance decisions.

A prominent study focusing squarely on the armed nonstate groups argues that ideology justifies rather than drives alliance choices. Drawing on evidence from extensive fieldwork in Afghanistan and Bosnia, it contends that armed nonstate groups ally "based on power considerations and then construct justifying narratives, looking to their identity repertoires for characteristics shared with their allies and not share with their foes."[49] The study concludes that, because armed nonstate groups are mainly concerned with postwar spoils, they prefer to ally with the side strong enough to win the war but not so strong as to exploit its allies and then not share the postwar spoils.

This approach is challenged by work that argues that nonstate actors operating in a dangerous environment simply cannot afford a long-term outlook. They will, therefore, seek allies who can offer them immediate material benefits, such as patronage and protection.[50]

A NEW BALANCE-OF-INTERESTS FRAMEWORK

In times of civil conflict, the distribution of power inside the theater of war structures both states' and nonstate actors' incentives for forming alliances. Victorious states make for attractive but reluctant partners. They have the most to offer but least to gain from armed associates. It is when the local distribution of power is balanced or favors their opponents that states need assistance.

Most states seek to reestablish their control over the rebellious region. But, it is important to recognize that states' intentions toward insurgent-controlled territories can vary. There are cases in which states seek merely to preserve the status quo, even if it means allowing the insurgents to maintain territorial control. Consequently, while chapters 3 and 4 deal with the typical former scenario, the two case studies in chapter 5 explore the theoretical implications of the latter.

The interests of nonstate actors also vary. Some may be immediate, others far-reaching. Those who are driven primarily by immediate, short-term concerns are referred to as *opportunists* in this book. These actors' main goals typically involve patronage or protection. There are also those who are farsighted and audacious, interested mostly in matters of ideology or identity. These actors are referred to as *activists*.

Opportunists would prefer to work with the state when it can credibly commit to providing for them: when it is winning. But, this is when the state is least interested in them. They could also be swayed toward an alliance when the local distribution of power between the state and the rebels is roughly equal—when the state is still capable of making some credible commitments and threats. Convincing opportunists to ally with the state under such circumstances often involves offering them basic protection while also turning a blind eye to their economic crimes and human rights violations. Coercion is also common.[51] Some proxies may have little choice but to partner with a state if they are to survive, due to pressure exerted on them by the state or the rebels. But, even in the most desperate of circumstances, proxies do not completely lose their agency at the local level—the level at which the alliances take form (and where the state cannot easily monitor compliance). For example, proxies may merely appear to collaborate while, in effect, tacitly and subtly resisting. Forms of invisible defection include foot dragging, dissimulation, false compliance, pilfering, feigned ignorance, slander, and sabotage.[52] Pakistan's "volunteers" (Razakars) during the 1971 war are a case in point. Most of them had little choice but to join the counterinsurgency operations. Refusal to work with the state typically resulted in death—not only the participants but also their family members were threatened. The Razakars, nonetheless, found ways to exercise their agency outside the state's gaze. One rebel commander recalled, "To my surprise, many Razakars at night gave us information. Many Razakars warned me: 'Sir, don't take your boat under that bridge. They [Pakistani soldiers] will kill you.' Otherwise, I would have already been killed many times."[53]

Activists may find it more convenient to join forces with the state when it is winning or, at least, when the local distribution of power is roughly equal. But, unlike opportunists, they could also be persuaded to ally with the state when the local power balance favors the insurgents. Their goals may be lofty, but they need not behave less pragmatically than their opportunistic counterparts. What distinguishes them, due to their prioritization of ideological or identity goals over immediate material returns, is their significantly higher threshold for risk-taking. They are more audacious gamblers.

Recruiting activists is no more straightforward than recruiting opportunists. It requires making credible "appeals around ethnic, religious, cultural, or ideological claims."[54] It involves convincing them that the risk of allying with the state is worthwhile. In order to do that, states must evoke prior or build new socio-ideological links with the prospective activist group. Their ability and willingness to do so is shaped by the distinct historical and social conditions underlying the conflict. For example, a state would have a difficult time enlisting activist proxies from a group that it had previously tried to deport.[55] A historic example of a state building effective socio-ideological links with a population, and consequently the first mass army, is that of revolutionary France: the "citizen-soldiers of the French Revolution identified their interests with those of the nation; consequently, obedience within the army rested primarily on the soldier's willing agreement rather than force or material rewards."[56] The building of socio-ideological links in this case involved stressing "the equality and community of all Frenchmen" while also spreading literacy among the prospective soldiers.[57]

Figure 2.2 summarizes the argument.

States' alliances with opportunists are largely *transactional*, characterized by pragmatic quid-pro-quo agreements. State-activist alliances are typically *relational*, involving the cultivation of loyalty and even emotional attachment. Socio-ideological links are the connections actors form based not on material factors (e.g., economic or security), but on

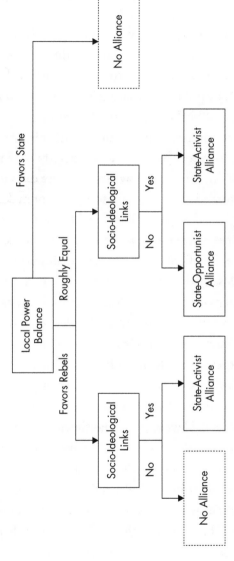

Figure 2.2 Local Power Balance, Socio-Ideological Links, and State-Nonstate Alliance Outcomes

a shared social identity or creed. Measuring them requires closely examining how actors reach out to each other and relate to one another.

The socio-ideological links underlying relational alliances take time and effort to develop. This is the case even when the actors already seem to have much in common. For example, as chapter 3 shows, it took nearly six months for the Pakistani army, which customarily used Islamic symbolism,[58] to build an alliance with Islamists during the 1971 war. The army had to make a credible commitment not just to Islam but also to Islamism. It did this by publicly declaring its allegiance to Islamism while also actually giving political power to the Islamists.

Whether the state prefers activists or opportunists as allies depends on their cost and, therefore, the context. Activists may make for more loyal and daring allies,[59] but they may also be more difficult to recruit for a state that, for historical or political reasons, cannot make credible ideological or identity-based appeals. They also tend to be scarce. Military historian Roger Reese observes that individuals who are "intrinsically motivated to serve and fight and who can maintain their morale and motivation regardless of their social or physical environment will always represent a minority of any population."[60] Opportunists may be easier to buy or coerce into an alliance, but their allegiance requires constant payments and pressure. In sum, alliances with activists may be cheap to maintain but expensive to form. Alliances with opportunists may be cheap to form but expensive to maintain.

Civil-wartime alliances between states and nonstate actors are rarely symmetrical. At the local level (i.e., in the theater of war), the latter typically enjoy tactical advantages—which is why they are recruited in the first place. States with strong modern armies usually exhibit conventional superiority, a blunt but not altogether useless asset. What makes state-nonstate alliances work, however, is a "balance" of interests. In her study of the relationship between the Afghan state and warlords, Dipali Mukhopadhyay describes this as "alignment of incentives."[61] Each actor satisfies, though not necessarily shares, the other's needs.

The proposed framework builds on the novel insights of neoclassical realism, an international relations (IR) theory that combines neorealism's emphasis on the structuring role of relative power distribution in an anarchic system with classical realism's appreciation of actors' divergent interests and agency.[62]

How do we know ex ante whether an actor is an opportunist or an activist? Interests, even one's driving interests, vary. They are a product of both structure and agency, and require close investigation that takes both into account while allowing for the possibility of change across time. This does not mean taking the actors' words at face value. It does mean tracing over time their prior behavioral patterns and the social contexts that engendered them, then contrasting the resultant expectations with the actors', or their close observers',[63] claims. It requires in-depth qualitative analysis.

Civil-wartime alliances between states and nonstate actors form and endure because of the structural incentives and individual preferences each actor brings to the arrangement. Neorealism, with its emphasis on security and survival, may explain long-term systemic patterns. But, by recognizing that actors have interests beyond survival, and that some are more risk-taking than others,[64] neoclassical realism helps to better understand tactical behaviors.[65] These include wartime alliances. The distribution of power still matters because it generates the "pressures and possibilities" for behavior, but it "cannot tell us just how, and how effectively, the units of the system will respond" to them.[66]

Operationalizing power has been "a consistent problem" for civil war scholarship.[67] Over the past decade, there has been growing realization in both academic and policy circles that civil wars are not won by conventional superiority alone.[68] In response, the emergent "microdynamics" of civil war literature[69] has come to operationalize power through the lens of territorial control.[70] This approach suffers from two serious limitations. First, territorial size may be irrelevant. Control over an urban neighborhood, a bridge, or even a road can be far more strategically consequential—and, thus, a source of power—than control over many villages or even multiple cities. Moreover, unlike states, rebel groups do not necessarily need to control territory to operate. They may be dispersed among the civilian population,[71] as was Narodnaya Volya in tsarist Russia,[72] or reside on foreign soil, as did the Afghan Taliban following the 2001 US invasion of Afghanistan.[73]

Second, it is not territorial control per se that drives collaboration and defection, which are key to success in insurgency[74] and counterinsurgency.[75] It is *perceptions* about which side is most capable of punishing defection or rewarding collaboration.[76]

War may be policy by other means. But, it is still war. It involves the application of physical force. Consequently, in times of war, power is only as good as it fares on the battlefield. Each side's efficacy in force employment, or the tactics by which actors use their materiel in the field,[77] determines military outcomes. The military outcomes, in turn, shape the new strategic calculus in the theater of war. As Mao put it, "War is a contest of strength, but the original state of strength changes in the course of war."[78] More accurately capturing the local power balance would, thus, incorporate the efficacy of force employment and change over time. In this book, "local balance of power" refers to a highly contextualized understanding of relative power within a geographically limited theater of war. It is local in that it is specific to the contested region and is relative to the force-employment capabilities of the opposing sides.[79]

SCOPE CONDITIONS

The proposed framework is applicable to cases that satisfy the following conditions. First, it applies only to cases in which states are capable of enlisting proxies, that is, offering administrative or operational support to nonstate allies. Such states need not have high infrastructural power, or the capacity "to penetrate civil society, and to implement logistically political decisions throughout the realm."[80] They do, however, require high despotic power, or the capacity to take action "without routine, institutionalized negotiation with civil society groups."[81]

Second, the balance-of-interests framework applies only to cases in which the insurgents are actually capable of tipping the local power balance in their favor. The term "robust insurgency" has been used to label such cases, but, as Shivaji Mukherjee has shown, even weak insurgencies may gain territorial control simply because the state does not consider them worth the resources necessary for their defeat.[82] The number of robust insurgencies spiked during the Cold War due to the competing superpowers' "abundant provision of material support to rebel forces across the world" and declined with the post–Cold War decline in superpower competition.[83] However, as the Syrian civil war shows, superpowers are not the only ones capable of providing extensive support to warring parties. So can neighboring states and secondary powers.

Finally, a caveat is in order. States cannot enlist proxies when the latter are not strategically viable. For example, when the Kashmir conflict was largely limited to the Valley, the Kashmiri Pandits were the closest India had there to activists (those who might be willing, for ideological or identity reasons, to assume the immense risks of collaboration). But, because of the significant oppression they faced from the local population, and their ensuing flight from the Valley, the Pandits were not strategically viable. It may be hypothesized that activists are generally harder to come by than opportunists because the state can use coercion to compel the latter into an alliance, but not the former. The cases investigated in this book indeed suggest this. Yet, the cases cannot offer conclusive evidence, as that would require a different research design.

The above scope conditions and caveat render Pakistan's and India's civil wars an ideal set of cases to study. First, both countries have strong armed forces. Pakistan's despotic power may be proportionally higher to its infrastructural power than that of India, but the Indian state has sufficient capacity to act autonomously from society. Second, all the insurgencies examined in this book may be classified either as robust (due to the substantial external support they received from neighboring states or powerful groups, such as al-Qaeda) or ones the state was willing to let live for some time, at least until they became robust. Third, in most of the South Asian cases there was a supply of strategically viable opportunists and activists, as well as variation in states' socio-ideological links with them. This was largely due to Pakistan and India's shared historical background and parallel characteristics. The latter includes marked ethnic heterogeneity and divisions, as well as postcolonial state-building practices that at times mirrored their colonial precursors'. Moreover, there is significant variation in state-nonstate alliances across these states.

CASES, DATA, AND RESEARCH METHODS

The burgeoning quantitative civil war literature needs more systematic qualitative research if it is to "move beyond statistical association toward causal inference about why (and how) outcomes are produced in civil war settings."[84] Making comparative qualitative work especially scarce are the "poor (or no) data, security concerns, and fluid events" characterizing civil war settings.[85] Even more difficult is studying secretive behaviors of powerful states in times of civil unrest. Yet, by failing to subject states' covert and clandestine practices to systematic and detailed analyses, we are left with partial and, at times, even inaccurate images of civil war processes. The goal of this book is to illuminate one controversial and nontransparent civil-wartime practice: state outsourcing of violence to nonstate actors. Doing so not only provides a fuller and more accurate account of counterinsurgency, but it also raises new questions about the relationship between states and violence, what it means to be a "state," and what constitutes "security."

Research Design and Case Selection

This book develops a theory of state-nonstate alliances in civil war by tracing the variation in outcomes across time in important cases drawn from South Asia. The primary method of analysis is process tracing—the "systematic examination of diagnostic evidence selected and analyzed in light of research questions and hypotheses."[86] Process tracing pays close attention to temporality and sequencing and is particularly useful for boosting an argument's internal validity. In addition to pursuing strong internal validity, the argument also builds robust external validity with a comparison of findings across different cases—first within and then outside South Asia. If the same drivers and mechanisms are observed in contexts as diverse as Pakistan, India, Russia, and Turkey—and the explanation based on them outperforms the existing alternatives—then the new theory may be considered empirically well grounded.

The first two cases comprise Pakistan's counterinsurgency campaign in East Pakistan/Bangladesh (chapter 3) and that of India in Kashmir (chapter 4). Each chapter traces the processes through which the counterinsurgency campaigns unfolded, describing in rich detail the making, maintenance, and breaking of state-nonstate alliances. What emerges is a story after story of a state seeking to reassert its sovereignty over a rebellious territory, a diverse cast of nonstate actors pursuing their varied goals, and fluctuating local power configurations. The varied local power configurations structure the agents' choices and are respectively restructured by the choices the agents make. In what is one of the original contributions of this book, the militias are brought out of the shadows and placed center stage.

The second pair of cases are also drawn from Pakistan and India. They focus on the less known counterinsurgency campaigns in each of the country's respective tribal belts. Chapter 5 begins by detailing the growth of the "Pakistan Taliban" insurgency in the northwestern tribal areas of Pakistan, the rise of local militias, and the role of the Pakistani state in the conflict. It then examines the development of the Naxalite insurgency in India, and how the state came to involve militias in its counterinsurgency operations.

The value of examining the cases of the tribal "awakenings" in Pakistan and India is twofold. First, they offer variation in state interests. In many civil wars, states unshakably seek to reassert their sovereignty as quickly as possible over the rebellious region. But, there are cases in which "medium capacity" states like Pakistan and India sometimes actually choose to "live with" an insurgency rather than waste the scarce resources necessary to suppress it.[87] Including these cases in the analysis thus provides a more complete account of South Asian states' civil-wartime strategy.

Chapter 5 shows that, when a state is uninterested in asserting monopolistic territorial control, robust state-nonstate alliances cannot form—no matter how much the nonstate actors may desire them.[88] But, once state interests change so that the main goal becomes the elimination of the insurgency, proxies can emerge—provided there are nonstate actors willing and able to join the counterinsurgency in pursuit of their own interests.

Second, while the cases presented in chapters 3 and 4 involve high-profile self-determination movements, the underlying objective of the insurgencies presented in chapter 5 is to overthrow the entire country's political and social system. The stakes seem higher, but, at the same time, the rebel areas are virtually invisible to the metropolitan gaze. Far less scholarly attention has been paid to the cases examined in this chapter, and very limited (especially comparative) scholarly attention has been given to the phenomenon of violence outsourcing there. Just as the state saw little value in these "peripheral" regions populated by ethnic minorities with little political power, so did the scholarship.

In chapter 6, the book explores the theory's implications beyond South Asia with two "out of sample" cases: Turkey and Russia. Both Turkey and Russia confronted robust insurgencies during the 1990s and mobilized nonstate proxies to help in their war efforts in Kurdistan and Chechnya, respectively. These two cases are drawn from regions with distinct political and social histories that set them apart from the South Asian cases analyzed earlier. That the balance-of-interests theory explains the varied state-nonstate alliances in such different contexts suggests that the theory has wide applicability beyond South Asia.

Data Collection

Studying states' covert and clandestine practices is notoriously complicated by the dearth and poor quality of public information. The research for this book is based on voluminous data collected during field research trips to Pakistan, India (including Kashmir), Bangladesh, Turkey, and Russia, as well as London and Washington, DC, between 2011 and 2018. The uniquely detailed material comes from extensive archival research and over 200 interviews. Interviewees included army and police personnel, intelligence officials, diplomats, government bureaucrats, local journalists and experts, victims and witnesses of the conflicts, human rights activists, and former militants. Due to the highly sensitive nature of the subject, some of the interviewees are anonymous. The findings from the archives and interviews are supplemented with reports from nongovernmental organizations, newspaper accounts, and memoirs of the key players.

Engaging a wide range of individuals who participated in political violence was both extraordinarily worthwhile and challenging. It required what Diana Kapiszewski, Lauren MacLean, and Benjamin Read call "flexible discipline" in adapting to sometimes unpredictable and even dangerous field conditions, and "triangulation," or bringing in sources with diverse perspectives and agendas.[89] Risks were unavoidable, and the challenge was to make the right call about which of them were worth taking. For example, on many occasions I was invited to travel to a seemingly dubious location in order to obtain some tempting archival document or meet an important interviewee. While I was typically cautious, accepting some of these invitations proved highly productive and allowed me to bring in valuable material.

In addition to exercising judgment, which I had previously honed as a journalist in Russia, I mitigated risk by building what Romain Malejacq and Dipali Mukhopadhyay call "tribes," or local networks.[90] These comprised individuals of varied backgrounds. Many of them became friends. They deepened my grasp of the contexts in which I operated, and this emboldened and enabled me to take greater risks in reaching out to individuals and institutions beyond my networks.

Reflexivity, or critical consideration of my role in the research process, was also an integral part of my approach.[91] Every social interaction required considering how my background, ascriptive characteristics, relative power, and moral inclinations may be shaping the outcome.[92] I found most interviewees to be highly receptive, if not initially, then after repeated meetings. I also found that, as an outsider, I was sometimes able to gain access to individuals who were less inclined to meet with local researchers. Some of them, especially the victims of conflict, wanted to share their story with a "Western" audience. Others perhaps thought they could more easily convince me of their perspective. This is why triangulating interview-based evidence with evidence derived from archival material, government documents, NGO reports, media accounts, memoirs, and other sources was imperative. Claims about events that could not be confirmed were discarded. Claims about unique personal experiences were carefully cited and contextualized with surrounding events and other personal accounts.

SAVING THE HOUSE OF ISLAM
Pakistan's "Volunteers" in the War of 1971

It is not the difference in opportunities which in itself is dangerous but the mental attitude created through it, the attitude of exultation on the one side recklessly pushes its triumph with immediate impunity to ungenerous extremes, and on the other side, the resentment ranking deep seeking to find outlets often in a wrong manner and unreasonable excuses.

—Rabindranath Tagore, "The Communal Award," 1936[1]

It would be an understatement to describe what transpired in the eastern wing of Pakistan in 1971, in what is now Bangladesh, as emotionally and politically charged. Of the most scandalous and persistent problems beleaguering Bangladeshi society is that of the collaborators—civilians who wielded violence on behalf of the Pakistani state. The Bangladeshi government set up a war crimes tribunal in 2010 to try these individuals. Several powerful politicians were convicted and put to death by hanging. Among them was Motiur Rahman Nizami, leader of one of Bangladesh's major political parties, Jamaat-e-Islami.

I met with Nizami's defense attorney, Mohammad Shishir Manir, in 2015, before his client's execution. Shishir's home had not yet been raided by the police,[2] but many Jamaat associates were already in hiding. Shishir had held a leadership position in the party's youth wing, which was linked to numerous wartime atrocities. He did not deny that Jamaat collaborated with the Pakistani government against the rebels. But, according to him, it did not commit the crimes for which it was blamed. Jamaat "took [a] stance for united Pakistan" not because of greed or desire to commit criminal offenses, but because "a united force is stronger for Islamism . . . a united Pakistan is better for Muslims."[3] The interests of two hitherto opponents—the Pakistan army and Jamaat—overlapped. The former needed the latter's help breaking the back of the triumphing insurgent movement. The latter needed the former to maintain "the house of Islam."[4]

This chapter charts the origins of the controversial alliances between the Pakistani state and nonstate actors during the counterinsurgency campaign in the country's eastern wing. The campaign took place between March 25, 1971, when the Pakistani government initiated a military crackdown, and December 16, 1971, when the Pakistani army surrendered to the joint command of the Indian and rebel forces. Given the army's humiliating lack of local knowledge, Pakistan would have benefited tremendously from proxy assistance as it sought to reestablish control of the province in March. But, neither opportunists nor activists were available at first. The opportunists were unwilling to take the risk; the activists were unconvinced the state made a compatible and credible partner. While the Pakistani army worked on building socio-ideological links with the Islamists by publicly committing to the Islamist agenda and offering them concrete political power, it recruited mostly opportunists (and some activists) from among the ranks of ordinary civilians. It did this as soon as it became clear that the rebels were reclaiming the province. In September, although Pakistan was now clearly losing the war to the insurgents (and India), the state-activist alliance became formalized. The Islamists became active, and often brutal, counterinsurgents.

None of the alternative explanations suggested in the existing literature adequately accounts for the state-nonstate alliance patterns in East Pakistan in 1971. Pakistan was a military dictatorship and highly reliant on the United States for aid. The Richard Nixon administration, however, turned a blind eye to the State Department's accounts of atrocities, including "selective genocide" committed in East Pakistan.[5] The US "policy of restraint" was a result of Nixon's reliance on Pakistan for his rapprochement with China and belief that the army would soon "learn the futility of its course."[6]

Some see the Pakistani army's alliance with the Islamists as a natural product of a shared ideological orientation regarding the role of Islam in politics.[7] Accordingly, the Pakistani army "closely colluded with Islamist militants" because "[t]hey were ideologically compatible."[8] However, this view mistakes the past for the present. The Pakistani army of 1971 was far from Islamist in ideological orientation. As a leading Pakistan army expert, Stephen P. Cohen, explains, Pakistan's army prior to the Muhammad Zia-ul-Haq's Islamization period (1977–1988) was "a largely secular army with an occasional nod in the direction of Islam."[9] It used religion instrumentally,[10] constructing a narrative of Islam in danger to attract activists to its cause, with little regard for the eastern wing's sizable Hindu minority population. Islam was not alien to Pakistan's main political arena. But, prior to 1971, Islamism was.

Pakistan's first constitution (of 1956) declared the state simultaneously an Islamic republic and a parliamentary democracy. The former meant that the head of state was to be a Muslim, and no law could contradict Islamic sources of jurisprudence. However, just two years later, Mohammad Ayub Khan established the country's first military regime that pursued a greater separation of religion and state. The word "Islamic" was removed from Pakistan's official name in the new constitution. Ayub used religion "to legitimize selective reforms," but it was not until after the 1971 war that Islam started to occupy "an increasingly prominent position in the political discourse."[11] Pakistan's Islamist parties performed very poorly in the country's elections, including in the elections of 1970.[12] The outcome of the 1971 war generated "a crisis in Pakistan that resulted in a renewed concern with national identity."[13]

Neorealist expectations do not hold either. Observers find particularly disturbing that Pakistan's Islamist proxies were most violent precisely when a united Pakistan had become the war's least likely outcome—when, with India's support, the rebellion was on the cusp of victory.[14] Pakistan was losing. It was the time of Bangladesh's birth.

This chapter shows how the appallingly bloody birth of Bangladesh was the outcome of strategic calculations based on a "balance of interests"—actors pursuing their priorities within the constraints of what they, and those around them, had the power to do. Strategic behavior can sometimes produce outcomes more terrifying than those of mere malevolence. Some of the actors in question, like the civilian "volunteers" who joined Pakistan's irregular ranks when it was faring fairly well, were driven by practical short-term considerations: money, loot, protection, and impunity to commit criminal offenses. Others were willing to take drastic measures for their cause, even while facing the prospect of paying the ultimate price, sooner or later.

Understanding why Pakistan incorporated nonstate actors into its military campaign in the country's eastern wing requires paying special attention to the temporality and sequencing of actions and events, as well as studying the actors themselves. Disentangling actions and events is complicated by the fact that, unlike in most other civil wars, events unfolded very quickly in East Pakistan. The conflict lasted less than nine months.[15] Moreover, collecting data about a politically charged topic in the volatile social climate of post-2010 Bangladesh is fraught with a distinct set of challenges. Much of the war was "largely undocumented."[16] Many of its participants had died or were silenced by extreme poverty. Those with the power to speak typically found themselves mired in the country's bitter ideological disputes. Which memory of the war is the "correct" one matters for which political party can legitimately rule the country. The competition is so contentious that the party in power in 2016, the Awami League, proposed legislation to outlaw denying "historically established facts" or questioning the war crimes tribunal.[17] Among the "historically established facts" is that the Awami League is "the party of liberation, and therefore of government," which means those who oppose it are "'pro-Pakistan,' and therefore dangerous and disloyal."[18]

However, the war crimes tribunal also offers researchers a unique opportunity to glean new information. As opposing sides compete to promote their version of history, the mechanism of outbidding leads each to share more information than it would have otherwise.

What follows is based on evidence drawn from the author's interviews with military and government officials, former militants, victims, civil society activists, and experts in Dhaka, Islamabad, London, and Washington, DC, conducted between 2012 and 2015; rare archival documents; memoirs representing diverse backgrounds and perspectives; and secondary sources. This chapter is not meant to provide an exhaustive account of the conflict, but rather an in-depth analysis of the conflict's little-studied,[19] but highly contentious, phenomenon: Pakistan's relationship with nonstate actors. Its academic goal is to probe the plausibility of the theoretical foundation developed in chapter 2.

PAKISTAN REGAINS CONTROL IN EAST PAKISTAN, MARCH–MAY 1971

Pakistan's 1970 general elections were the country's first ever to be held nationwide, based on universal adult suffrage, which included all women, and on a one-person, one-vote basis. The widespread enthusiasm about the astounding democratic achievement—a military ruler voluntarily relinquishing power to elected civilian authority—was, however, short-lived. An unexpected electoral outcome quickly triggered a political crisis, soon to be followed by mob violence, lynchings, a military crackdown, state terror, genocidal violence, ethnic cleansing, reciprocal extermination, an interstate war, and, finally, secession.

This section describes how the Pakistani army came to dominate the province in six weeks. By early May, in addition to the urban centers, it had regained control over the vast bulk of the strategically important areas bordering India.[20] The hastily trained rebels were no battlefield match for Pakistan's professional troops. However, the latter's highly visible successes and excesses triggered tens of thousands of locals to cross the border into neighboring India to join the rebel ranks. They formed a guerrilla force that eventually reached some 100,000 fighters.

The objective of Pakistan's initial plan, code-named Operation Searchlight, was to suppress a "rebellion" in the country's eastern wing.[21] The uprising was led by a political party, the Awami League, which had three months earlier won the national elections. The Awami League was "a vast umbrella sheltering many disparate elements— poor peasants, militant students, workers, middle class professionals, and wealthy businessmen and industrialists" bound by "Bengali nationalism, or, put another way, anti-West Pakistan feelings."[22] Sheikh Mujibur Rahman (Mujib) headed the Awami League. The party achieved an absolute majority in the national assembly by winning 160 out of 300 seats. The electoral victory offered the Awami League an opportunity to redress the political and economic disparity between the two wings. It also evoked fears within the West Pakistani political establishment that Mujib would now pursue his "true" secessionist intentions.[23] Mujib had since 1966 campaigned for extensive provincial autonomy and had called for a constitution based on a six-point program that would leave the central government with responsibility only for defense and foreign affairs.

East Pakistan's population of 73–75 million occupied a land roughly the size of the state of Mississippi. About 20 percent of it floods during a normal monsoon, and one-third of the land is typically under water by the end of the monsoon season. The average population density in 1971 was roughly 1,300 persons per square mile and rapidly rising.[24] The annual per capita income was about US$60, which in real terms was not much higher than in 1948, and far below that in West Pakistan.[25] The population was 90 percent rural and only about 20 percent literate.[26] East Pakistan was allocated less than 20 percent of the foreign aid received by Pakistan, while purchasing about 40 percent of West Pakistan's industrial products at artificially high prices protected by tariffs.[27] In early March, observers described East Pakistan as gradually slipping into "a virtual semicolonial political status."[28]

A West Pakistani army officer was struck by the scenes of poverty he encountered in Dhaka in 1970:

The women had hardly a patch of dirty linen to preserve their modesty. The men were short and starved. Their ribs, under a thin layer of dark skin, could be counted even from a moving car. The children were worse. Their bones and bellies were protruding. Some of them toyed with a bell dangling from their waist. It was their only plaything. Whenever I stopped, beggars swarmed round me like flies. I concluded that the poor of Bengal are poorer than the poorest of West Pakistan. I started finding a meaning in the allegations of the economic exploitation of East Pakistan. I felt guilty.[29]

The idea of Mujib leading the entire country as the new prime minister was vehemently opposed by Zulfikar Ali Bhutto, head of the major political party in West Pakistan, the Pakistan People's Party (PPP). Bhutto threatened to boycott the national assembly sessions. He sought a formula that would allow him at least to share power with Mujib. What followed was a counterintuitive scenario: a military dictator, General Yahya Khan, making "strenuous efforts to bring the politicians, Mujib and Bhutto, to the negotiating table to arrive at a means of transferring power to the new assembly and an elected government."[30]

The negotiations were failing, and, on March 1, Yahya announced the postponement of the national assembly. The Awami League called for a *hartal*, a mass protest. Between March 1 and 25, "violence including lynching of non-Bengalis, especially Biharis, became a daily occurrence," while the army was ordered to stay in the cantonment and refrain from any action.[31] Yahya arrived in Dhaka on March 15 for negotiations, but, ten days later, he abruptly departed. A military crackdown followed.

The basic plan of Operation Searchlight was drafted on March 18 with an ordinary school pencil, then revised slightly before it was approved on March 20.[32] Unlike the earlier contingency plan, code-named Operation Blitz,[33] Operation Searchlight called for achieving objectives with maximum force.

The Awami League enjoyed high levels of support across the province, where it received 75 percent share of the vote in the 1970 elections.[34] By the time of the crackdown, Mujib was the de facto leader of East

Pakistan. His popularity and agenda soared since the 1968–69 "Agartala conspiracy" trial, when the government of Pakistan accused him of fomenting a secessionist movement with India's support.[35] An ensuing massive popular uprising in East Pakistan forced the government to withdraw the case. It even compelled Pakistan's first military dictator, Field Marshal Ayub Khan, to resign.

Twenty-two thousand West Pakistani troops were flown in to supplement the 12,000 non-Bengali soldiers from the 14th Infantry Division already stationed in the eastern wing.[36] The military planners presumed that all of the 18,000 Bengali troops of the Pakistani military would revolt in reaction to the operation. Consequently, in addition to arresting the Awami League leaders and supporters, the Pakistani troops were to disarm those of Bengali ethnic origin within the Pakistani military establishment.

The operation was carried out with limited success. Mujib was arrested on the night of the army crackdown and flown to West Pakistan. However, most of the Awami League leaders and their sympathizers, which included thousands of youths, escaped the offensive to neighboring India. The West Pakistani troops were astoundingly clueless about what the Awami League leaders looked like and, even worse, "unable to discriminate differences in the features of their Bengali brethren."[37] Prior to the crackdown, government agents marked houses with chalk to help the army find and arrest its targets.[38] Out of the 465 Awami League members of the national and provincial assemblies, all but nine escaped to India.[39]

At Dhaka University, soldiers confused faculty members who had similar names and consequently executed the wrong target.[40] The transcript of the tape recordings of conversations between Pakistani army units operating in Dhaka shows that, on the night of March 25, the army encountered "Lot of [.]303 fire" at Dhaka University.[41] Much of the Bangladeshi literature argues that the Pakistani army carried out a massacre of innocent and unarmed civilians, most notably students and faculty members, at Dhaka University. As a retired lieutenant-general of the Bangladeshi army describes:

The sleeping Bengalees were attacked at night by the soldiers of Pakistan Army . . . The intellectual group or brains of the nation including the students and teachers of Dhaka University had to pay very heavily. About 300 Professors and students of Dhaka University were killed in the first night. The peace loving Bengalees rose up in mass to save their prestige, honour, dignity and culture as well as the brutality of the occupation army was resisted on all fronts in whatever capacity they could.[42]

This claim is challenged by the argument that many of those the Pakistani army encountered at Dhaka University were not students, but outsiders who had come to the university for military training.[43] The brutality of the crackdown is, however, widely acknowledged in the literature.[44] The transcript of the tape recording reveals that the Pakistani soldiers were ordered to issue a public warning: "Any person seen putting up road blocks will be shot on the spot, number one; number two, road blocks put up in any locality, people from that locality will be prosecuted and will houses left and right, left and right of that block be demolished."[45]

Those who carried out Operation Searchlight would have undoubtedly benefited from proxy assistance. The irregulars would have provided the Pakistani army the local knowledge, intelligence, and additional manpower it desperately needed. However, few were willing to step up to the plate. The Pakistani army was a weak force in the region. It had a small military presence there prior to the operation because it deemed the best defense against India was offensive capability in West Pakistan. The military buildup took an unusually long time. Most of the Bengali troops did indeed revolt, and the army was limited in the number of troops it could bring from West Pakistan due to India's ban on all Pakistani flights over its territory.[46]

The Pakistani army's weakness in the region made opportunists hard to come by, but neither were the activists available. Those who were primarily driven by ideology, the Islamists, had opposed Yahya's approach to the conflict. Jamaat leaders wanted the military dictator to allow Mujib to form a government despite Bhutto's objections. When Yahya refused, the Islamists "broke with him" and accused him of "unfair partiality toward the People's Party," which they feared "would have dis-astrous consequences for Pakistan."[47] It was not until April, after meeting General Tikka Khan, the head of the army in East Pakistan, that Jamaat gave "full support to the army's actions against 'enemies of Islam.'"[48] Even then, the support was limited to making diplomatic trips to Europe and Arab countries to explain Pakistan's right to defend its sovereignty. It was not until September 1971 that "the alliance between the Jama'at and the army was made official," at which time the East Pakistan branch "was thoroughly radicalized, and acted with increasing independence in doing the bidding of the military regime."[49]

Islamist proxies were not an option in March 1971, but there was another activist group that might have supported the Pakistan army against Bengali nationalists for reasons of identity—the Biharis. The term "Bihari" was collectively used by the Bengalis to refer to the Urdu-speaking non-Bengali Muslims from the northern Indian states of Uttar Pradesh and Bihar who had migrated to East Pakistan (East Bengal) after the partition of India in 1947. The Biharis made up much of the East Pakistan's managerial class. Their population in East Pakistan in 1971 was over 700,000.[50]

The Bengali-speaking majority of East Pakistan viewed the Biharis "as a foreign element" and discriminated against them, perhaps in part due to resentment of "the fact that these non-Bengali Muslims have succeeded in dominating such a large portion of the business community."[51] However, like the Pandits in Kashmir (discussed in chapter 4), the Biharis in East Pakistan were not strategically viable because of their tactical weakness at the time. Between March 1 and 25, they were constantly attacked and even lynched.[52] The launching of Operation Searchlight triggered "an-other wave of mob violence, in which Bengali mobs slaughtered Biharis or West Pakistanis wherever they held the upper hand, until army units arrived and secured the area."[53] It would not be until the Pakistan army could manage the violence against the Biharis that the latter could join the anti-rebel campaign.

After the military action in March, the center of decision-making in Pakistan shifted from the Office of the President and the headquarters of the chief martial law administrator to the general headquarters of the army. The change reflected Yahya's "perception that the central government's problems in the east were primarily military ones and his greater ease among the officers with whom he had spent his career."[54] The move was followed by the augmentation of Pakistan's military presence to roughly 70,000 regular troops (from the initial 34,000). Three institutions—the East Pakistan Civil Armed Force, Internal Security Force, and a new East Pakistani police force—were swiftly assembled for the maintenance of law and order.

The East Pakistan Civil Armed Force replaced the East Pakistan Rifles, a border security and anti-smuggling force. The Internal Security Force was set up to defend against attacks on strategic communication centers, railroad bridges, transportation networks, and power installations. Its roughly 3,000 recruits came mainly from West Pakistan. The new East Pakistani police force was to supplement and, ultimately, replace its predecessor. About 7,000 policemen came from West Pakistan in May for a six-month tour of duty.[55] The presence of the security forces across the province made visible the reestablishment of the writ of state.

FROM STATE CONTROL TO PARITY, MAY–JUNE 1971

This section details how India's augmented support of the increasingly better prepared rebels and the tactical challenges of operating during the monsoon season foiled the Pakistani army's force employment. The distribution of power in the province shifted from one favoring the army to that which was roughly balanced between the opposing forces. This was when the Pakistani army began enlisting tens of thousands of civilians as proxies through a combination of select material incentives and identity-based appeals. When the power balance began tipping in the rebels' favor, the state stepped up identity-based mobilization, thus bringing in and unleashing the most audacious and odious of its proxies.

The story of the rebel comeback begins with the Battle of the Belonia Bulge. The bulge of Belonia, roughly ninety-five-square miles of East Pakistani land protruding into India like an enclave, was of high strategic value. A railway track connected Belonia to Feni, and a semipaved road ran through Belonia to the border outpost. It was a small corridor linked with India and under the administrative district of Feni. Feni was situated on the Dhaka-Chittagong highway and railway line and was the lifeline between the port city Chittagong and the rest of the country.

The bulge of Belonia was also the last piece of territory still held by the Mukti Bahini (Freedom Fighters) in late May. The 150 fighters allocated to its defense were separated by the Muhuri River and split into small detachments. On June 6, two Pakistani companies (each made up of 120–150 soldiers) suddenly attacked. But they were the ones caught off-guard by what happened next. The rebels unexpectedly struck back with mortar and machine-gun fire, which was shockingly accurate. Local civilians supplied information about where the Pakistani army was concentrated. Ammunition, previously scarce, was suddenly abundant, thanks to India's secret supply. The Pakistani troops were in trouble. It was not a viable option to bomb rebel defenses by aircraft because, in an area as narrow as Belonia, it risked violating Indian airspace and invited retaliation from the Indian air force. Thus the Pakistani soldiers began to retreat, and some of the rebels abandoned their trenches and chased them through the fields.[56]

The Pakistani army returned ten days later but suffered the same fate. It tried again and again, on June 17 and 18, but was beaten back. Finally, on June 19, it launched a combined operation. Five helicopters landed Pakistani troops behind rebel defenses, while an infantry battalion launched a coordinated attack under artillery cover. The foot soldiers suffered heavy casualties, until their heliborne counterparts began converging on the rebel defenses from the rear. The rebels withdrew to avoid being trapped. They abandoned the last patch of territory that had been under their control.

The Belonia battle became "the turning point in the civil war."[57] Rather than congealing Pakistan's sovereignty over the province, it revealed the shifting balance of power from one favoring the Pakistani state to that of rough parity with the rebels. The power shift reflected the significant and visible improvements in the rebels' force employment prowess. The Mukti Bahini had demonstrated "great professionalism" on the battlefield and, in doing so, signaled that they could stage overwhelming attacks "at a time and place of their choice . . . They are not only a volunteer force having short training but also have the capability to confront the enemy face to face and give them the taste of defeat."[58] As one Pakistani officer put it, the Belonia battle was "the first significant demonstration of the new tactics adopted by the Muktis [rebels]. They had been able to pin down a much bigger professional force with a smaller one."[59] It took some serious maneuvering for the Pakistani troops to win the battle. Easy victories were now behind them.

The aftermath of the Belonia battle illustrates why measuring actors' power based on how much territory they control is highly problematic. The loss of Belonia marked an increase, rather than decrease, in the rebels' share of power in the region. No longer did they waste time and resources clinging to land. They were now free to focus wholly on weakening the Pakistani army through guerrilla tactics across the province while, with India's help and on Indian ground, preparing for a conventional showdown. They maintained tremendous popular support in areas under ostensible Pakistani army dominance.[60] So popular were the rebel "heroes" that the Awami League leadership worried that they might become emboldened to take over the entire movement.[61] Territorial control was to come from power, not the other way around.

India's covert sponsorship enabled the rebels' post-Belonia turn to the Maoist doctrine of using guerrilla tactics to make war everywhere, to disperse and weaken the opponent, while building regular forces to strike the decisive blow. Since the onset of the conflict, the Mukti Bahini had the limited support "without specific orders from on high" of India's Border Security Force (BSF),[62] a policing, rather than military, organization. New Delhi expected the Pakistani government to reach a negotiated resolution to the conflict with the rebel leaders who were, after all, fairly elected and enjoyed widespread support in the province. The Indian officials' main objective was to keep a close eye on the Mukti Bahini. They monitored the training camps to ensure they were "under the control of reliable, moderate Awami league leaders or officers from the East Pakistan Rifles or police rather than the more radical political elements in the resistance."[63] The conflict threatened to destabilize the already volatile Indian states of West Bengal, Assam, Nagaland, Manipur, and Mizoram. Some of these states had been experiencing terrorism, while others faced an insurgency. New Delhi's priority was to maintain order within the Indian territories bordering East Pakistan while putting some pressure on the Pakistani government to come up with a political resolution. There was also fear that Pakistani agents were entering the country along with the millions of refugees.[64] As figure 3.1 shows, the average *daily* number of refugees in May surpassed 100,000.

As the Pakistani army consolidated control over the most strategic sites across the province, it became clear that it would unlikely agree to a political solution to the conflict. So, on May 15, the Eastern Command of the Indian Army took over the responsibilities of arming and training the rebels and coordinating all of their operations.[65] A major general of the Indian army was appointed the chief liaison officer with the Bangladeshi government-in-exile.[66]

The force comprising the Mukti Bahini included personnel from five battalions of the East Bengal regiment (a regular Pakistani army unit in East Pakistan); elements of the East Pakistan Rifles (a paramilitary force

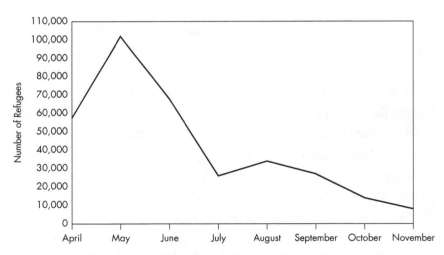

Figure 3.1 Daily Average Number of East Pakistani Refugees Entering India
Source: Data provided by Sheelendra Kumar Singh, Sisir Gupta, Harish Chandra Shukla, Dilip Kumar Basu, Satish Kumar, and Vasant Vishnu Nevrekar, *Bangladesh Documents*, vol. 2 (Dhaka: University Press Limited, 1999), 82.

charged with border patrol, policing, and anti-smuggling functions); and police, ex-servicemen, and students.[67] The Indian army began directly preparing them for an autumn showdown, after the water receded, to create more favorable conditions for the regulars. In the meantime, the rebels took advantage of the monsoons and carried out ambushes, raids, and small lightening attacks. Indian troops assisted them in some of the pitched battles.

The monsoons significantly reduced the Pakistan army's mobility and firepower. As one Pakistani officer recalled, "Except in the north where hard ground was still available for the use of artillery and light armour, the rest of the province was a huge swamp. Artillery shells fell in flooded fields and swamps without damaging a stalk."[68] The rebels celebrated their growing tactical prowess with a jingle:

The day belongs to the army and the night to us.
The sunshine belongs to the army and the rain to us.
The cities belong to the army and the countryside to us.[69]

The shift in the balance of power away from the Pakistani state prompted a dramatic shift in Pakistani strategy. The army began actively reaching out to the local population for assistance in tilting the balance of power back in its favor. It employed a combination of select material incentives and religious appeals. It offered compensation (and immunity for criminal acts) to those who enrolled in the irregular forces while also beginning to recast the conflict in religious terms in order to attract loyal fanatics.

Alliance between Pakistan and Razakar Opportunists

On June 1, the East Pakistan governor, General Tikka Khan, issued the "East Pakistan Razakar Ordinance," thereby officially instituting a force of irregular "volunteers," or *Razakars*.[70] The Razakars were to be men between eighteen and forty-five years of age, though preference was given to the young.[71] Some 35,000 of them were to be raised, but as many as

40,000–50,000 ultimately enlisted.[72] Though called "volunteers," they were typically compensated.

Razakar names were to be suggested by special bodies called Peace (or *Shanti*) Committees. A secret Pakistani government document instructed: "The recruitment will be carried out mainly through the org [*sic*] of loyal political leaders and prominent members of Peace Committees. The political leaders and members of Peace Committees will stand surety for the Razakars who are enrolled and will be answarabled [*sic*] for conduct of Razakars."[73]

The Peace Committees served as the link between the army and the local population. They performed some governmental functions and operated on multiple levels[74]—district, subdivision, *thana*, and village— across the province. Their members were civilians whose responsibilities included recommending reliable Razakar recruits to the Pakistani government, as well as gathering local intelligence and providing local assistance to the Pakistani army.[75] Peace Committee members were the elderly and prominent among the "patriotic elements."[76]

The main criteria for the Peace Committees' selection of the Razakars consisted of young men who had"[l]oyalty to Pakistan and physical fitness."[77] The scheduled length of Razakar training was only ten days. It was conducted by noncommissioned officers, with each officer taking on a group of about fifty volunteers. Fifty (out of a total of eighty) periods of training were devoted to rifle handling and firing practices. Twenty periods were for learning guard duties, patrolling procedures, and field-craft. The remaining ten periods were reserved for political indoctrination.[78] The goal was to transform those driven primarily by the lure of short-term rewards into steadfast fighters.

The irregulars wore ordinary civilian clothes, to which a blue armband with the word "Razakar" written in red in the Bengali language and an accompanying identity pass were later added.[79] They had a simple command system up to the platoon level, with each platoon comprising 15– 20 volunteers, and were typically armed with .303 rifles and allotted fifty bullets.[80] To take advantage of the Razakars' local knowledge, the secret memo outlining the Razakar Ordinance instructed to keep the civilian recruits as much as possible "in their own areas near their home."[81]

The Razakars were to collect intelligence and apprehend rebels.[82] Their responsibilities also included guarding roads, bridges, railway lines, and vital installations. They patrolled areas as well as reinforced posts, border outposts, and isolated regular army detachments.[83]

While there were some among the Razakars who were ideologically motivated, most were opportunists who were far from fanatical about their job. They appear to have been more concerned about their own livelihood and the well-being of their family members than the larger goal of a united Pakistan. Some pursued immediate rewards: an income or the impunity to plunder or abuse their neighbors. Others joined because of intimidation and the need for protection. In an interview, a former rebel recalled the responses he received when questioning Razakars about why they had sided with Pakistan:

> They said, "Sir, they took away my father. And we are three brothers. They [Pakistani officials] said if we don't join, I will shoot you down. They took away my sisters and molested them if you don't join." Then, some people said, "We are hungry, there is no money. The economy is bad, we cannot work. The factories are closed. What will we eat?"[84]

Many of the Razakars seemed to lack "fanaticism and commitment to the Pakistan cause."[85] There were also those among the proxies who defected and joined the rebel ranks.[86] A former rebel concluded from his encounters with the Razakars: "They [the Razakars] may have a rifle and loot. They can have two girls. But, they were the have-nots, the underdogs of the society."[87]

While most of the Razakars were driven primarily by material or security interests, there were those who had a sincere desire "to protect the name of Islam."[88] A former rebel observed: "Many of the poor and illiterate soldiers that fought for the West Pakistani army believed the religious motive and believed they were fighting for the integrity of Islam."[89]

After decades of discrimination against Bengali Muslims and Hindus alike,[90] the Pakistani state tried to appeal to East Pakistanis' sense of Muslim identity. India and, by extension, Hindus were blamed for tearing the country apart. East Pakistani Hindus became "the enemy."[91] The conflict became "characterized as a war for Pakistan's Islamic identity."[92] That most of the opposition comprised Muslims was conveniently ignored.[93]

FROM PARITY TO INSURGENT DOMINANCE, JUNE–DECEMBER 1971

The rebels liquidated collaborators, destroyed communication lines, and engaged in hit-and-run operations against isolated army posts throughout the monsoon season. Their regular counterparts were enlarged, divided into sector troops, and positioned in different areas to provide cover to the guerrillas. The operations undermined the image of the army's success and created perpetual tension for the Pakistani troops and their supporters.[94]

Joining the rebellion was a romantic affair for the tens of thousands of youths swelling the rebel ranks.[95] At one camp, some 3,000 young men waited two months to receive military training, despite its "pitiable" hygienic conditions and "almost non-existent" food and water supplies.[96] Pakistan's favored targets were educated young men, which propelled a large number of school and university students, especially those living in the border areas, to cross into India. Most of them were from lower-middle- and middle-class families.[97] Peasants comprised another large group of recruits.[98] The students formed "the most politically conscious group," but their divergent views "often led to the sharpening of the political rivalry amongst different groups."[99] The peasants "turned out to be the best material for guerrilla warfare, as they did not have any vanity or false pride . . . They never grumbled for the lack of jungle boots, or a blanket or even food."[100]

Figure 3.2 shows the organization of the Mukti Bahini, which had transformed from "a spontaneously-formed, ill-assorted disorganised rabble" into "a very large, complex organization of armed and trained

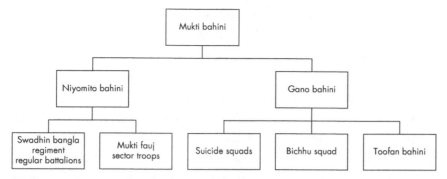

Figure 3.2 Mukti Bahini Organization
Source: S. N. Prasad, *Official History of the 1971 India Pakistan War* (New Delhi: History Division, Ministry of Defense, Government of India, 1992), 153.

men owing allegiance to the provisional government of Bangladesh, and operating under its own officers with their own chain of command."[101] Training was extended from two to five weeks and involved light automatic weapons, mortars, and explosives.[102] By September, the Indian army processed as many as 20,000 new guerrillas each month.[103]

The Niyomito Bahini (Regular Forces) were the official Bangladeshi army, while the Gano Bahini (People's Forces) were the guerrillas. The Suicide Squads' primary task was to kill prominent workers of the Jamaat, as well as Razakars and Pakistani government officials. Their orders were "to commit suicide, if necessary, to avoid arrest."[104] The Bichhu (Scorpion) Squad had a female wing of young girls who carried out sabotage, subversion, and espionage in the urban centers, including Dhaka and Chittagong. The Toofan Bahini (Storm Troops) were the commandos. In addition, grassroot organizations called Sangram Parishads (War Councils) stoked resistance from the underground. They had been organized by the Awami League in nearly every village and town.[105]

Several other rebel outfits operated across the province. Among them was the Mujib Bahini, a force loyal to Mujib and his ideology of nationalism, secularism, socialism, and democracy (i.e., "Mujibism"). It comprised some 8,000 university students from the Awami League's student wing who received special forty-five-day training in guerrilla warfare and ideology. It had its own wireless system and special code of communication outside the control of the commander-in-chief of the Mukti Bahini and even the Bangladesh government-in-exile. Some of its members wore Indian uniforms and carried sophisticated weapons. This elite force may have served as "extra insurance lest the control of the Mukti Bahini fell into the hands of the ultra-leftists."[106]

Some 1,800 commandos of another resistance group, the Uban Force, harassed the Pakistan army and destroyed its lines of communication in the Chittagong Hill Tracts. Its leader may have operated under the supervision of the Research and Analysis Wing (RAW), India's foreign intelligence agency.[107] Eleven other independent guerrilla groups operated inside the province with weapons snatched from Pakistani troops.

One of the most prominent groups was the Kader Bahini. Abdul Kader Siddiqui, popularly known as Tiger Siddiqui, was a noncommissioned officer in the Pakistani army as well as a former Awami League student leader. He organized a force of roughly 17,000 school and college students, between the ages of fourteen and twenty-four, mostly of peasant background. He also formed an auxiliary force of over 70,000 rural school students. Following some successes, which built people's confidence in the force and swelled its ranks, Kader established contact with the Bangladeshi government-in-exile and the Indian army.[108] The latter provided arms, ammunition, wireless sets, and some training. Kader claims to have captured 7,000 Pakistani soldiers and 14,500 Razakars.[109]

Alliance between Pakistan and al-Badr Activists

The summer was drawing to a close, and the rebels were dominating. This brought the Pakistani army closer to its most fervent allies—those who were "very much more motivated by the religious fanaticism."[110] They were young Islamists who were told by their spiritual leader that they "don't justify living if Pakistan disintegrated."[111]

In August, the Pakistani army organized the Islamist volunteers and separated them into two groups. Members of the first, which was named al-Badr (the moon, in Arabic), undertook "specialized operations"; those of the second, the lesser known al-Shams (the sun, in Arabic), were mainly "responsible for the protection of bridges, vital points and other areas."[112] US officials noted that the Pakistani government deliberately sought out "the most deeply orthodox Muslims in the rural villages . . . with fierce loyalty to Islam and equally fierce anti-Hindu feelings."[113]

The al-Badr Brigade acted as a death squad by identifying and killing high-profile supporters and sympathizers of the secessionist movement. Its victims included professors, journalists, writers, and doctors.[114] The goal was "to create a vacuum of 'intellectual leadership' "[115] in East Pakistan. Al-Badr members have also been accused of manning camps in which the rebels were interrogated, tortured, and killed.[116]

The Pakistani military armed the Islamists but did not provide much training.[117] They were "more determined, more skilled, more educated" than the Razakars.[118] Most of the al-Badr comprised members of the student wing of the Jamaat, the Islami Jamiat-e Tulabah. The young Islamists also "galvanized support" from the Bihari population,[119] which had by then restored much of its strength with the help of the Pakistani army.

That it took nearly six months for Pakistan to enlist the Islamists into the fight underscores the challenge of building socio-ideological linkages with activists. It required the then-secular Pakistani army to make a credible commitment to the Islamist agenda—a commitment that has since profoundly shaped Pakistani politics.

By August 1971, the Islamists came to see that there were "gains to be made from their alliance" with the Pakistani state.[120] How did this happen? This was accomplished by the Pakistani leadership publicly declaring its allegiance to Islamism while also actually giving political power to the Islamists. The commander-in-chief of the East Pakistan army, Amir Abdullah Khan Niazi, began to cast himself in the role of a religious zealot. He started quoting "copiously from the Quran, the Sunnah [traditions of Prophet Muhammad] and the history of Islam."[121] Islamists, including Jamaat party members, had been given power over the recruitment of Razakars and entrusted with local intelligence gathering, which allowed them to go after their own enemies or those they deemed insufficiently pious. Four Jamaat members were invited to join the military government of the province.[122]

The al-Badr and al-Shams Brigades were under the administrative control of the civil affairs adviser to East Pakistan's governor,[123] but they never became part of Pakistan's formal military structure. The Pakistani army used the Razakars in tens of thousands all over the province, especially in the countryside. But the al-Badr activists operated mainly in towns and cities. Their mission was to silence the voices of dissent, and these voices were loudest in the urban centers. With the army's "operational blessing,"[124] the al-Badr activists enjoyed significant on-the-ground autonomy and impunity. The exact number of the activist proxies is unknown. It has been estimated that 2,000 Jamaat and Islami Jamiat-e Tulabah members and sympathizers were killed and some 12,000 were held in prison camps during the war.[125]

The al-Badr was a clandestine organization. Its details are particularly scarce because of a lack of a paper trail.[126] The guerrillas operating in Dhaka did not even know about its existence,[127] despite the Mukti Bahini's robust intelligence networks. The foreign correspondent of the *New York Times* observed in late autumn that, at the Intercontinental Hotel, in government offices, and at all the foreign consulates in Dhaka, "roughly half of the local staffs are either friendly toward or active agents of the Mukti Bahini guerrillas."[128]

The death squad gained visibility when it became highly active in December, just as the rebels were on the cusp of victory. The official charge against Motiur Rahman Nizami included this description:

[W]hen defeat of Pakistani occupation and auxiliary forces was imminent, his [Nizami's] organizations IslamiChhatraSangha [another name for Jamaat's youth wing] and Al-BadrBahini mounted Gestapo like attacks to devoid Bangladesh professionals and intellectuals, amongst others, and launched mortal blow to free and independent Bangladesh, by selective elimination of respected professionals and intellectuals, found their homes, dragged out, often blind-folded, tortured, murdered and their bodies then dumped in mass-graves and other places. Such attacks were largely carried out on or around 14th December 1971.[129]

In mid-October, India began using its artillery much more extensively to support the rebel operations in East Pakistan. Indian forces, including tanks and air power on several occasions, were also brought in to back up the Mukti Bahini. Still, the Indian units would usually hit their objective in East Pakistan and then withdraw to Indian territory. On the night of November 21, the Indian forces did not withdraw. Several of their army divisions, which were divided into smaller tactical units, occupied Pakistani territory as part of the preliminary phase to the offensive directed at capturing Dhaka. The Indian government characterized these de facto preparatory tactics as a "defensive" response to Pakistani shelling of Indian territory. But, its plan was to initiate a formal war with Pakistan on December 6, with the launching of an all-out offensive to capture Dhaka. The Indian strategists must have been pleasantly surprised and relieved when, on December 3, the Pakistani air force in West Pakistan suddenly struck at major Indian air installations in northwestern India.[130] It was Pakistan, not India, that could now be blamed for officially starting the conflict. The war ended less than two weeks later with Pakistan's unconditional surrender to the joint Indian and rebel forces.

CONCLUSION

The alliances that materialized between the Pakistani state and non-state actors during the 1971 war were a gamble for both parties. The principal-agent problem was especially acute for Pakistan when it came to the poorly disciplined Razakars. Some of them defected and became insurgents; many acted against the state while in proxy service. In an interview, a former rebel offered a case in point.

The rebel had just received training in India and was crossing the border to begin his operations in East Pakistan. Suddenly, he encountered about ten Razakars guarding the road which he, along with fifteen of his comrades, sought to cross. The Razakars agreed to allow the young men to cross but refused to let them carry over their bags. When asked why, the Razakars explained that the previous night a rebel had killed a Razakar's wife and children, and so extra precautions had to be taken.

As the conversation was unfolding, a voice suddenly shouted that a Pakistani army convoy was approaching. The rebels panicked. Luckily, they were accompanied by an experienced soldier, a *jawan* who had previously served in the East Pakistan Rifles. He gave them instructions to divide and hide: half inside a nearby Chinese-made bunker, and the other half were to cross and hide on the other side of the road. The convoy approached. The Razakars stood visibly nervous, perhaps thinking that what they just observed was a tactical maneuver on the part of the rebels. A major at the front of the car shouted in Urdu to inquire if everything was okay. "Thik hai" [All is fine], the Razakars hurriedly replied. After the convoy left, the rebels regrouped. The Razakars addressed them: "Look, we helped you. Now you have to help us. You have to get us justice." The former rebel recounts: "We did just that. One of the first things we did when we arrived at the sector command headquarters was to complain [about the situation]. And that particular individual [who had killed the Razakar's wife and children] was disarmed."[131]

For the proxies, the gamble was no less stark. The rebels enjoyed widespread popularity across the province, and so collaborators risked serious retribution. As a Dhaka-based *New York Times* correspondent observed, one should not even joke about supporting Pakistan, as there were "roughly a dozen assassinations and as many bomb incidents every day . . . and no one has a sense of humor."[132] Those among the proxies who managed to survive the war but could not flee Bangladesh faced public wrath and prosecution. The deadly consequences for Jamaat activists like Motiur Rahman Nizami came late, but they came nonetheless.

The war of 1971 shows that, when it comes to state-nonstate alliances, power matters—but so do interests. The Pakistani army enlisted proxies only when it was able to satisfy their interests, and when they were able to satisfy its interests. Ideology matters, for some. It mattered to the Islamist activists who joined the fight. But, their participation materialized only after the Pakistani army built robust links with the Jamaat and other Islamist organizations, as well as made (or at least appeared to make) a credible commitment to the Islamist agenda. For many others, it is not ideology but short-term gains that matter most. Thousands of Razakars joined forces with the Pakistani army in the late spring because of the patronage and protection the former was able to offer once it regained some footing in the region.

The balance-of-interests framework also outperforms the plausible deniability hypothesis, which deems dependence on aid from a democracy a major deterrent of violence outsourcing. In 1971, Pakistan was not gambling with US aid. Nixon and his national security advisor, Henry Kissinger, needed Pakistan for their rapprochement with China and had a strong personal dislike of India and its leader Indira Gandhi.[133] The East Pakistan crisis occurred at the time the United States was busy winding down the war in Vietnam and building diplomatic relations with China. The Sino-Soviet ideological conflict of the 1950s and 1960s, and the ensuing 1969 border clashes between the two countries, made South Asia an important zone militarily for both Moscow and Beijing.[134] The former turned to India and the latter to Pakistan as a regional ally. The Sino-Soviet discord also facilitated the late 1960s to early 1970s US efforts to establish a diplomatic link to China, at a time when the US war in Vietnam was clearly going nowhere and the United States could not afford China "entering the Vietnam war or . . . attacking any other vital American interest."[135] Pakistan played a critical intermediary role in the US effort to establish high-level contact with China. It was not the only channel considered by US President Richard Nixon,[136] but it was the one that proved most effective.

By the time of Pakistan's military crackdown in East Pakistan, the United States had come to think of Pakistan as the "sole channel to China; once it was closed off it would take months to make alternative arrangements."[137] Nixon had directly approached Yahya about China on October 25, 1970. He told the Pakistani leader, who was scheduled soon to visit Beijing, that the United States wanted to establish "secret links" with China to enable the two countries to communicate "what was really on their minds and yet have absolute discretion."[138] By December 1970, the Pakistani channel produced an important positive response from Chinese Premier Zhou Enlai. Yahya was quick to point out that it was "significant" that Zhou neither accepted nor rejected the proposal as soon as it was made, but first consulted with the top Communist Party leaders, Mao Tse-tung and Lin Piao. "This in itself reflects a trend which holds out some possibility," Yahya observed, optimistically adding that at no point during his conversation with the Chinese leaders "did they indulge in vehement criticism of the United States."[139] By April 1971, the United States and China were engaged in signaling—the Chinese via "ping-pong diplomacy," and Nixon via public statements of interest in visiting China.

On July 8, 1971, Yahya facilitated Kissinger's first secret trip to China to lay the groundwork for Nixon's official visit. In preparation, Kissinger had scheduled a tour of Asia that was intentionally "as boring as it was possible . . . to shake press attention."[140] His plan worked, and, by the time he arrived in Islamabad, only one American journalist was around to cover the event. Then, Yahya's scheme—code-named Operation Marco Polo—went into effect. During a dinner hosted by the Pakistani president, Kissinger faked feeling ill, and Yahya pretended to urge him to go and spend a few days in the mountains to recuperate. Yahya even sent a decoy motorcade from Kissinger's residence to the mountains. The following morning, Kissinger headed for a military airfield, and a Pakistan International Airlines plane took him to Beijing.[141]

During Pakistan's military campaign, the US relationship with Pakistan became complicated by the unprecedented rebellion within the US State Department ranks against Nixon's approach to Pakistan.[142] Few outside Nixon and Kissinger's inner circle knew anything about the China initiative, and the State Department was among the organizations kept in the dark.[143] Confronted with evidence of genocide against the Hindu population of East Pakistan,[144] and unaware of the China initiative, the State Department began to act autonomously. In April, without clearance from the White House, it began limiting Pakistan's economic aid and initiated a new arms embargo. Some $35 million in arms to Pakistan was cut off, leaving roughly $5 million "trickling through the pipeline."[145]

India's relationship with the United States, meanwhile, was in "a state of exasperatedly strained cordiality, like a couple that can neither separate nor get along."[146] India consequently drew closer to the Soviet Union. In

August 1971, Moscow signed a treaty with Delhi specifying mutual strategic cooperation between the two countries. When India finally attacked Pakistan, the Soviet Union moved its troops to the Chinese border "in an unsubtle attempt to tie up Chinese forces and prevent them from going to the aid of Pakistan."[147] In hindsight, Kissinger reflected: "What prompted Yahya to his reckless step on March 25 [the day of the crackdown] is not fully known."[148]

The East Pakistan case shows that pursuit of plausible deniability does not necessarily lead states to ally with nonstate actors in times of civil war. If it was plausible deniability Pakistan was after, then it would have incorporated proxies during Operation Searchlight. But, it could not because (1) it was too militarily weak to attract opportunists, and (2) it had not yet built the socio-ideological links needed to attract activists. The Pakistan army's brutal methods during the crackdown immediately attracted negative publicity and condemnation. By the time Pakistan began using proxies, there was little left to plausibly deny.

"GUNS PLUS INTEREST"
Renegades and Villagers
in India's Kashmir War

Amidst the roar of gun[s], you have to behave ... You have to put up a face today but bow tomorrow. It all depends on the situation ... It was not only the gun which mattered. It was perhaps interest as well. The interest of boys wielding guns. So, guns plus interest.

—Abdul Gani Bhat, Kashmiri politician[1]

Khurshid Ahmad's windowless office brimmed with books and binders.[2] The senior Kashmiri separatist leader was no doubt "under scanner," that is, surveilled by Indian authorities. Over tea and *nadru monje* (lotus stem fritters), he reminisced about his experiences with various militant groups fighting for Kashmiri independence. One topic he did not want to talk about: his work for the Indian army. What led him to help his erstwhile enemy, India, to end the very movement he had worked so hard to create? Ahmad's response, as was typical of others in his position, was that it was all very complicated. It would require understanding the conflict's "real history" pulsing beneath the official covers.

In the late 1980s, India faced a crisis in Kashmir. Strikes, public protests, and occasional acts of terrorist violence erupted in massive demonstrations and systematic attacks on state officials and institutions. A rigged election and subsequent crackdown on those who worked for the defeated opposition party[3] "brought to a boil latent anger over corruption and discrimination against Kashmiri Muslims"[4] and roused the onset of an uprising. Hundreds of Kashmiris crossed the Line of Control into neighboring Pakistan to receive arms and training. A militant nationalist organization, the Jammu and Kashmir Liberation Front (JKLF), emerged as the vanguard of the insurgency. The long decade that followed witnessed the stunning eclipse of the JKLF and the rise of jihadist outfits.

The face of the insurgency underwent dramatic changes, but so did that of the counterinsurgency. When the local police proved ineffective against the rebels, the army and the paramilitary forces (most notably, the Border Security Force and the Central Reserve Police Force) stepped in. Over time, they incorporated into their robust counterinsurgency apparatus some unexpected allies. In the Valley, they partnered with the very insurgents they had been fighting and, in the Jammu region, ordinary villagers with minimal combat experience. The ex-rebels and villagers were not mere informants. They were expected to combat the insurgents.

The existing literature fails to account for why the "world's largest democracy" engaged in the outsourcing of violence. In the 1990s, India's press was "vigorous and free" and "unafraid to challenge the government," the judiciary was institutionally autonomous, and election turnout exceeded those typical in some advanced Western democracies.[5] A Human Rights Watch report exposed India's "secret army" in 1996.[6] Plausible deniability may have been important for some Indian officials but not for others.[7] Moreover, the use of proxies did not preclude the regular armed forces from simultaneously committing human rights abuses that were as brutal as – or, in some cases, even more brutal than – the irregulars'.[8]

Ideology, or rather identity, helps account for the Indian army's relationship with Hindu villagers in the Jammu region of Kashmir, but it does not explain the alliance with pro-independence and pro-Pakistan ex-rebels in the Kashmir Valley. Finally, as this chapter shows, it was not preoccupation with postwar spoils that turned many of the rebels and villagers into proxies. For many of the rebels and some villagers, it was the immediate payoffs of collaboration: survival, patronage, and impunity from prosecution for criminal offenses. Some were coerced, while others were genuinely disillusioned with the rebel movement. There were also those, mostly among the Hindu villagers, who felt that it was their patriotic duty to defend India.

As in East Pakistan in 1971, the principal factors driving the state-nonstate civil wartime alliances in Kashmir were "guns," or the local balance of power, and "interest"—the key actors' goals. The alliances followed a "balance-of-interests" logic: they materialized when the local power balance incentivized and made it possible for each side to use the other to pursue its primary objectives. Each side did not have to share the same goals. It had to be willing and able to satisfy those of the other side.

When the power balance in the Kashmir Valley favored the insurgents, India would have benefited tremendously from a local partner, especially because the local police were unreliable. Kashmiri Pandits were the closest India had in the region to *activists*—those who might be willing, for ideological or identity reasons, to assume the immense risks of collaboration. This group was, however, far from strategically viable because of its tactical weakness and ensuing flight from the zone of conflict.[9] It was not until the Indian army demonstrated force employment prowess through significant military expansion and a subsequent string of military victories that it was able to attract *opportunists*. These were rebels who were willing to ally with India in pursuit of their more immediate goals: local power, profit, and security.

The ex-rebel proxies—most notably the Ikhwan-ul-Muslimoon in the north, as well as the Jammu and Kashmir Ikhwan and Muslim Mujahideen in the south of the Kashmir Valley—were "instrumental to decisively shifting the balance of power" in India's favor.[10] The new local power balance triggered "piling-on bandwagoning": an abundance of collaborators hastening to join the winning side.[11] Most of them were incorporated into the security apparatus as auxiliaries. India's victory in the Valley

prompted the insurgency to move to the mountainous and sparsely populated Jammu region. There, the security forces turned to those select
villagers who were particularly committed to Kashmir staying with India.
Mostly Hindus, they were handpicked by Indian army officers and India
loyalists.

This chapter presents an in-depth study of India's policy of outsourcing violence to nonstate actors against the Kashmiri insurgents.
It exposes the main drivers of the Indian army's use of nonstate actors,
and the nonstate actors' use of the Indian army. The evidence is drawn
from the author's interviews with military and government officials,
former militants, victims, civil society activists, local and national journalists, and experts in Srinagar, New Delhi, Islamabad, London, and
Washington, DC, in 2012, 2014, and 2015; interviews conducted by
local Kashmiri researchers; accounts by reputable journalists with firsthand experience covering the conflict; and secondary sources. No account can do justice to the full complexity and tragedy underlying the
conflict. By carefully tracing the experiences of key actors and groups,
this chapter demonstrates the power of the main argument while also
uncovering the emotions, contradictions, and unintended consequences
accompanying their decisions.

FROM INSURGENT CONTROL TO PARITY IN KASHMIR VALLEY, 1989–1993

In 1993, Sopore was a "liberated zone": the militants' *rajdhani* (capital). Some 1,500 armed men regularly prowled the streets of this
northern Kashmiri apple town of roughly 70,000 residents. A company
of insurgents openly played badminton in the park. Flapping in the
Himalayan breeze was the crescent moon of the Pakistani flag hoisted
atop a water tank. Makeshift barricades greeted visitors. Local youths
stopped and questioned passengers of each vehicle entering the town.
Military and security trucks stayed away, instead taking the circuitous
route from Baramulla to Bandipora. Whenever the Indian army or the
Border Security Force (BSF) tried to penetrate the *rajdhani*, they were

forced to retreat. Only two BSF bunkers remained since, back in January, the BSF set fire to over 200 shops and residential buildings and killed more than forty people in retaliation for two of its troops killed by militants.[12] Of the remaining bunkers, the one housed in the J&K Bank building was attacked almost on a daily basis.

Then, on November 27 at 2:30 a.m., the tide turned. Twelve Indian army columns marched into Sopore. The surprise move caught the rebels off guard. Thinking that the military was there to cleanse the entire town, the rebels set houses and shops on fire in a residential area close to the main *chawk* (square). Their makeshift plan was to pin the arson on the army. But, this time, the army was better prepared with a new approach to force employment. It intentionally did not cross the Sopore-Bandipora Road into the residential areas. After a fourteen-hour battle, Indian soldiers pushed the rebels out of their hideouts bordering the important road and installed five BSF bunkers there. The road was now open. Most of the rebels fled to the countryside, and the remaining 200–300 headed to the town's residential areas. They hid in specialized bunkers inside houses. Stairs hidden behind cupboards led to underground rooms. In one case, a fake Indian-style toilet seat opened up to a tunnel that descended into the basement of a nearby shop.[13]

The year 1993 was a momentous one for the Indian army. It had successfully dealt with a major police revolt back in April,[14] and, in October, it effectively extracted insurgents from Srinagar's famous Hazratbal mosque. The army's performance in Sopore and opening of the Sopore-Bandipora Road in November signaled a clear turning point in the balance of power between the rebels and the Indian armed forces. No longer did the latter seem, in the words of an Indian army officer who served in Kashmir at that time, "clueless." To be sure, the Indian military was still "struggling to understand how the militants operated," but "it no longer seemed that Kashmir might go away."[15]

It took over three years, but the Indian army had finally learned how to outmaneuver the Kashmiri insurgents on a sparsely peopled urban battlefield in a way that did not inadvertently boost the rebels' popularity. Where it still floundered—and what kept the balance of power from decisively tilting in its favor—was in thickly populated residential and thinly populated rural areas. This was precisely where the insurgency headed.

This section focuses on how the balance of power in the Kashmir Valley tilted in India's favor, and the origins of the state-nonstate alliance that made the tilt possible. Activists were markedly scarce in the Valley, and so the Indian army partnered with opportunists, but only after it was able to signal its credibility as their partner. Collaborators became abundant after the local power balance unequivocally tilted in India's favor. Most of these former rebels were incorporated as auxiliaries into the Indian security forces. They acted as force multipliers, but no less important an objective of their incorporation was demobilization.[16] India's success in the Valley prompted the insurgency to relocate to the thinly populated and poorly policed Jammu region.

India's first prime minister, Jawaharlal Nehru, a descendent of Kashmiri Pandits, famously described Kashmiris as "soft and addicted to easy living." He would have been mightily surprised by the scenes of audacious Kashmiris pouring into Pakistan for arms and training to fight for self-determination, or *azadi* (freedom). In 1988, violence in the Valley turned from "spasmodic" to "orchestrated and deliberate."[17] The Indian government's December 1989 release of five militants in exchange for the daughter of India's home minister, who had been held hostage, convinced many Kashmiris that "independence was achievable."[18]

The year 1990 witnessed a mass exodus of the Valley's Hindu minority—Kashmiri Pandits—who comprised roughly 4 percent of the Valley's population.[19] The Kashmiri Hindus were widely viewed in Kashmir as having had "close connections with the Indian establishment" and as having been "always targeted and cultivated by Indian intelligence machinery."[20] Yet, they were far too weak to serve as India's *activist* proxies. Those who could afford it headed to Delhi.[21] Most of the over 200,000[22] fleeing the "intimidation and violence" settled in "squalid camps" in Jammu.[23]

The year 1990 also witnessed the imposition of governor's rule in Kashmir. Under the leadership of Governor Girish Chandra "Gary"

Saxena (a former head of India's premier foreign intelligence agency Research and Analysis Wing, RAW), the government passed the Jammu and Kashmir Disturbed Areas Act. It authorized police personnel (of the rank of sub-inspector and above) operating in "disturbed areas" to use force "even to the causing of death, against any person who is indulging in any act which may result in serious breach of public order."[24] The parallel Armed Forces (Jammu and Kashmir) Special Powers Act gave the governor (in addition to the central government) the power to declare an area "disturbed," and authorized army officers to use lethal force if they were "of opinion that it is necessary so to do for the maintenance of public order."[25]

By 1993, the Indian army had broken the back of the JKLF-led militancy in Srinagar, " 'the nerve center' of the revolt in 1989–92."[26] This feat was largely accomplished through the so-called cordon-and-search operations. A typical operation started between 3:00 a.m. and 4:00 a.m. BSF troops cordoned off an area. At about 6:00 a.m., they assembled the area's male population in a large space, such as a sports ground or a mosque compound, and separated the males by age. The rest of the morning and afternoon involved identification parades: men were paraded one after another before a hooded informant, who was usually a captured militant. Those whom the informants identified were subsequently taken in for interrogation.[27]

The JKLF's decline was also precipitated by the marginalization the Kashmiri nationalists encountered from the Pakistani Inter-Services Intelligence (ISI), which now favored the pro-Pakistan groups. A new organization, Hizbul Mujahideen (a.k.a. the Hizb), was beginning to emerge as the leading insurgent outfit. While the JKLF's slogan was *Kashmir banega khudmukhtar* (Kashmir will be sovereign), the Hizbul Mujahideen's was *Kashmir banega Pakistan* (Kashmir will be part of Pakistan). The Hizb characterized the JKLF's position as "childish and highly irresponsible" and accused the Kashmiri nationalists of indirectly helping India.[28] By 1993, the Hizb controlled several "liberated zones" in the Baramulla, Srinagar, and Anantnag districts.[29]

Enter the Rashtriya Rifles, an elite counterinsurgency force created specifically to offset the Valley's weak local police in tackling the increasingly well-armed pro-Pakistan insurgents. The Rashtriya Rifles signaled a marked expansion of the army's role in the Valley. A new "unified command" was also set up in 1993 to coordinate the armed forces in the region. This too marked a major boost to force employment.[30]

Along with the increased military capacity in the region came serious efforts to improve intelligence gathering. According to an army officer who served in Kashmir, the army had "very little" information in 1993–94 about the insurgency. The newly expanded forces began actively reaching out to the growing number of splinter groups.[31] According to another army officer who had been stationed in Kashmir, the Indian army "did not know how these militants operated. In the sense you know broadly how the militants operated. But, you did not have any inside information on how things were happening . . . we were struggling to know who is a militant and who is not."[32]

The Indian strategists recognized the importance of the local balance of power. As an Indian officer who was stationed in Kashmir during the conflict put it:

> People are constantly trying to process what the balance of forces is, who has the upper hand. The real story of "hearts and minds" is how you are faring. If are doing better [than the insurgents], it's safer for us [locals] to be with the army. Hearts and minds are fundamentally about shaping people's perceptions. You have to get an upper hand on the insurgency.[33]

Indian army officers who served in Kashmir reported a deep sense of desperation gripping local military commanders in 1993–94. The expectations for them were rising with the increasing resources allocated to the counterinsurgency efforts, but few could deliver. Most were hopelessly detached from the hostile local population and, consequently, had little reliable intelligence. A former army commander explained why his counterparts embraced the idea of ex-rebel allies: "Let's say you are a post commander. You know you want to kill the militants operating in your area. You damn well don't care for anything [else] at that point in time. It's easy to sit back and reflect now. But, at that point in time, the question is—How do I get rid of this nonsense?"[34]

The Indian army desperately needed to improve its selective targeting of the militants to gain the upper hand over the insurgency.[35] Meanwhile, the rise of the ruthlessly hegemonic Hizbul Mujahideen and the corresponding decline of its competitors generated a group of rebels disillusioned with the entire movement. They presented the Indian army with an opportunity. Manoj Joshi, a prominent Indian journalist who covered the conflict, describes the process whereby the prospective proxies were cultivated:

A lot of what happened was intelligence officers. Their job is to try to break these guys away. So, they lay out divisions, and they say: "You can come over, we will amnesty you." And so they are able to divide the groups. This is part of the intelligence craft. The initial Kashmiri militancy and uprising—many of them [militants] thought that India would simply walk away. They didn't realize that India would respond as it had. Then, the pressures increased. They [the militants] felt the pressure, and the underground army [Hizbul Mujahideen] is chasing you. So, at some point, you don't have the motivation to carry on. And you say, "Why don't I surrender?" As far as the police and the army are concerned, they are on the lookout. Their intelligence people and others are looking for people like that. And so when one signals to them that they want to surrender, they say, okay . . . So, if you come with a weapon, and you surrender, some packages would be given. You will be given some amount of money for some period of time.[36]

FROM PARITY TO INDIA'S CONTROL IN KASHMIR VALLEY, 1993–1996

This section details the process whereby anti-India rebels turned into India's proxies. Focusing on the rebels' perspectives, it offers a uniquely in-depth account of the Valley's largest and most powerful proxy groups: the Ikhwan-ul-Muslimoon (an umbrella group which included the Jammu and Kashmir Ikhwan) and the Muslim Mujahideen. The investigation reveals the main drivers of the rebels' switch. For the leadership cadre, it was a refusal to surrender their local power to the rising hegemon, Hizbul Mujahideen, and conviction that India was willing and able to provide the security and patronage needed to maintain their local influence. For the rank-and-file, the main drivers were profit, security, and belief that the Indian side would provide them with both. The rebels' opportunism was not always a mark of duplicity. Many turned to practical goals after being genuinely disillusioned with the movement and its jihadist direction.

Alliance between India and Ikhwan-ul-Muslimoon Opportunists

Few wedding singers become fierce rebel commanders. Even fewer lead notorious counterinsurgency outfits. Kuka Parrey did both. "He was very un-terrorist-like; sort of a fat, portly guy," journalist Praveen Swami describes his first impression of Parrey, noting that the militant "declined the invitation to sing a little."[37] Code-named "Koel" (which is a large, long-tailed cuckoo bird) by his Indian handlers, Parrey was the first and the leading Kashmiri insurgent to fight on behalf of the Indian state. In the summer of 1994, radio-frequency waves began containing a cryptic message: "Ask the Koel what song it will sing tonight." It would be a mid-ranking military intelligence officer working with the Rashtriya Rifles asking about Parrey's operations in the "hard-hit" Bandipora belt in northern Kashmir.[38]

Parrey was an unlikely hero of India's counterinsurgency campaign. Few could have imagined that the man who composed and so beautifully performed a song celebrating young Kashmiris crossing the Line of Control for arms and training, called "Shahzaad Lukh Draayih Azad Kashmir!" ("The Princes Are Marching to Free Kashmir!"),[39] would be instrumental in bringing the Valley under India's control. Parrey came from a family of *zamindars* (landowners). His father owned some 500 square miles of land and apple orchards in Hajin village in north

Kashmir. "Kuka" was what he was called by his two-year-old niece, and the name stuck.[40]

Parrey's prosperous family had been harassed in the late 1980s by Jamaat-e-Islami thugs who demanded jihad money. The JKLF offered protection in exchange for Parrey joining the organization. The folk singer began cooking and washing for JKLF commanders. By 1991, the thirty-five-year-old had risen to the rank of an area commander of the JKLF's Students Liberation Front (SLF). That year, JKLF leader Hilal Ahmed Baig proposed opening a JKLF branch in every village. Some senior commanders objected for fear of diluting their influence, which led to a split within the SLF ranks.[41] Pakistan was also shifting its support from groups favoring independence, most notably the JKLF, to those favoring Kashmir becoming a part of Pakistan. The ISI stopped supplying weapons to the SLF. Parrey and several of his colleagues abandoned the SLF in April 1991 and launched the Ikhwan-ul-Muslimeen. The new organization worked "directly at the behest of the Pakistani authorities."[42]

The Ikhwan-ul-Muslimeen was especially notorious for targeting Indian army informants. Its militants even kidnapped and tortured a nineteen-year-old girl because they suspected she sought assistance from the BSF in identifying her younger brother's kidnappers.[43] Ikhwan-ul-Muslimeen also played "a prominent role" in the "systematic campaign of intimidation and assassination, launched against all non-militant political activists" and did not spare "even retired and reclusive politicians for past sins."[44]

Among the leading commanders within the Ikhwan-ul-Muslimeen ranks was Liyaqat Ali Khan. Liyaqat had gone for training to Pakistan with the Hizb in 1990 and had even spent six months training in Afghanistan. Some 150 militant outfits were then operating in Kashmir, and Liyaqat was struck by the torrent of groups he observed training in Pakistan. He became friendly with the ISI official in charge of his camp, who reportedly revealed to Liyaqat that the ISI "created confusion so that one leadership doesn't rise," which would allow Pakistan "to dictate terms."[45] The strategy of playing multiple groups may be linked to the ISI's experience in the 1980s in Afghanistan. Joshi explains: "They [ISI officials] wanted multiple groups so that they could manipulate easier . . . When you have multiple groups, you can use one group to undermine the other."[46]

Liyaqat returned to the Valley in 1991 and began operating in Anantnag (which the locals called Islamabad) as a division commander of the Ikhwan-ul-Muslimeen in South Kashmir. "Security forces dreaded moving in these [Anantnag] villages and forest areas, as encounters with Hilal Haider, as I was called, left them depleted in numbers," Liyaqat boasted.[47] "I ran the insurgency movement unrivalled until the day I realized that infiltrators under the aegis of Hizbul Mujahideen and Harkat-ul-Ansar had been sent to the area with full logistical and financial support by their Pakistani mentors." Like Parrey, Liyaqat did not want to give up his land to the Hizb.

Among Liyaqat's gaudier comrades in Anantnag was Basir Ahmad Wagay, alias "the Tiger." A builder by trade, the Tiger sported a flamboyant moustache that curled around his cheeks. He enlisted in the Ikhwan-ul-Muslimeen in 1991 after his father was arrested and tortured by Indian soldiers. He was proud of the organization's initial successes against, as he put it, the "*suor ka bacha*" (sons of pigs). "But things changed in 1994," the Tiger lamented.[48] "Our discipline eroded, and the true militancy became no more noble than mugging. We were *gandu* [assholes] and badly outgunned by the Indian dogs." The Tiger's disillusionment with the movement led him, and hundreds of others like him, to prioritize more immediate goals: power, patronage, and protection.

Parrey and his associate were traveling on a rickshaw to a market one day when, suddenly, the latter spotted an intelligence official. He sprang and ran. Parrey followed and managed to escape. But he could not help but wonder how his companion recognized an intelligence agent wearing civilian clothes. After finally admitting that he had been spying for the Indian authorities, the companion offered to connect Parrey with his handlers.

Parrey said he would meet only with top officials. He told his family that he was going to treat a boil, but instead he headed to New Delhi for an initial introduction. The most important meeting took place at

Lodhi Gardens. The BSF officers did not realize they were meeting Sonawari's top militant and were pleasantly surprised when "the dreadest terrorist" revealed his identity.[49] They told Parrey that, henceforth, he would be protected and to contact a local unit in Kashmir for further instructions.

When Parrey returned to his village, he found the Hizbul Mujahideen pressing even harder to take over his territory. So he mobilized his "boys" and raided the same houses that the Hizb had raided earlier in order to send "a message that his group was strong and aggressive."[50] Parrey then reached out to the local army unit. He proudly recalls: "On the day I reached the Army camp, I found the entire camp abuzz with the news that a top militant was expected. I got a very warm reception. Colonel Gaur told me that if I helped the Army in the operations against the HM, the Army would help me in all respects."[51] Parrey then stood at Hajin Chawk and publicly declared his war against the Hizb. He said nothing of his alliance with the Indian army.

Parrey's interest in maintaining control over his territory powered his alliance with India. As Swami notes:

He [Parrey] did not really come across as a very political person. It was a bunch of guys in this area who were operating here, and then you have the HM coming in and saying "No you can't have your little empire of twelve people in this little area." And that's where the feuding and the squabbling really began. Who's going to run this village, or who's going to run these four villages? A lot of guys did get killed . . . and the Indian army capitalized on this. But, the fishers came out really because of local factors and local fights for control.[52]

Parrey renamed his organization the Ikhwan-ul-Muslimoon and became the leader of the roughly 6,000 "Ikhwans" or, as the Indian government called them, "renegades" operating in the Valley.[53] Parrey came to dominate the north of the Kashmir Valley, particularly the Hajin Sonawari area. Liyaqat emerged as the leading commander in the south of the Valley.

In 1994, Liyaqat, like Parrey, was losing control of his territory. He was surrounded by the Hizbul Mujahideen on the one side and the Indian army on the other: "In town [Anantnag] there was fear of army and outside of the town in the villages was the problem with HM [Hizbul Mujahideen]. By 1994 the Ikhwan [Ikhwan-ul-Muslimeen] had become very weak. People had left etc. and we were stuck in just town. The army was in the town in the daytime. We were therefore stuck inside the house. Outside of town we had to contend with HM."[54] Liyaqat also found that the local people who "earlier looked upon mujahideen as heroes and saviors no longer exuded the same warmth."[55] After fleeing to Srinagar, he considered abandoning militancy altogether but feared that the insurgents would slaughter his family. He also figured that surrendering to the security forces would result in torture.[56] Then, an unexpected opportunity arose:

> Kuka Parrey's name came forward. A new thought emerged. This was to keep one safe, and to keep the family safe. There was clearly only one option. There were 20-25 of us. We got organized and we contacted the army. This was probably end 1994. By then I was back from Srinagar. For the connection with army there was no option in Srinagar, and I had to come back to Islamabad [Anantnag]. . . The army had already sent us feelers to meet. Feelers came when news of Kuka Parrey was coming in – this was around 1994. By the time the feelers came the Ikhwan as a militant group was breaking. Some of the boys who did not agree with the direction of the new Ikhwan ran away from Ikhwan. We had no terms and conditions with the army. The only thing was that we would work together. M.P. Singh [a Rashtriya Rifles brigadier] was the initial contact. Initial six or eight months we had contact with him. But then the Ikhwan spread like fire.[57]

The Indian army made credible its commitment to the Ikhwanis by offering various perks and significant autonomy, and by turning a blind eye to their abuses. For example, the Tiger was issued a laminated identity card with his photo. The card described him as a "Battalion Commander" and was stamped by the 36th Battalion of the Rashtriya Rifles. It also contained the serial number of his rifle, which had been previously issued to him by Pakistan. Working under the Tiger were thirty-five renegades spread across six or seven large villages and several hamlets. "I am the fucking law now," the ex-rebel taunted the police.[58] Liyaqat also noted that, at that time, the police was basically "defunct," and the army was "the only functional thing—and their functional link [to the local Kashmiris] was Ikhwan."[59]

Liyaqat and Parrey met on multiple occasions, but they usually did not coordinate their actions. By 1995, proxies had become all the rage within the Valley's military and security establishments. Administered primarily by the army, Parrey's and Liyaqat's groups were the largest and most robust proxy outfits. The Central Reserve Police Force and the BSF also organized and administered their own Ikhwan units in Pulwama and Budgam. "Even local army camps started small groups," observed Liyaqat.[60] The other groups included the Muslim Liberation Army, which operated around Kupwara, the Al-Ikhwan, the Indian Al Baraq, and the Taliban. The Taliban was a Gujjar militant group which operated in the Kangan area in Srinagar, where Gujjars predominated. The name was deliberately chosen to create confusion with the militant Islamist Afghan group with the same name.[61] Other groups included the Kashmir Liberation Jehad, which was created by the BSF to lead the security forces in operations against militants in Srinagar.[62] Behind the proliferation of the different proxy outfits was not just their handlers' desire to have their own group. Each group's leader sought to control his territory. An Indian army officer who worked with the renegades observed that "every group would want to maintain its own independence in its own area."[63] Each leader became a de facto state-sponsored warlord.

Parrey's move emboldened hundreds of lower ranking militants to surrender to the Indian authorities and join the Ikhwan-ul-Muslimoon. Some of them sought protection, others profit, still others both. As one ex-member of Ikhwan-ul-Muslimoon put it: "Some people joined Ikhwan only because it was a fashion and they were greedy. People joined for money."[64] However, at the foot-soldier level, the proxies "might not have taken as much benefit as Kuka Parrey and others in the top leader-ship did."[65]

How was India able to convince its nonstate allies that it would actu-ally provide for them? A state seeking to signal its alliance commitment has two basic tools: words and deeds. It could issue a public statement about its intention to support an ally, or it could "take actions calculated to demonstrate its commitment."[66] It was mostly through deeds that India signaled its alliance commitment. It did so by allowing the Ikhwanis to operate with impunity. Each illegal and inhumane act—from smuggling timber to taking journalists hostage,[67] to assassinating human rights activists[68]—served simultaneously as the Ikhwanis' test and as India's testament of the strength of the alliance.

Much of the cost of the "costly signaling" was borne by civilians. One Baramulla resident recounted numerous experiences of being randomly stopped on the street and assaulted by the proxy warriors. He described one experience while traveling on a bus from Baramulla to Sopore. A group of Ikhwanis had stopped his bus and told the passengers to step out. It was raining. The Ikhwanis ordered the passengers to remove their shoes and sit on the muddy ground. They then collected their valuables. Some of the passengers were forced to crawl in the mud for the militants' amusement. When they saw another bus approaching, the Ikhwanis moved on to their next group of victims.[69]

"The Ikhwanis would put [a] check post, stop the buses. They will frisk you, they will collect money from you. Everything you still have," ad-mitted an Indian army officer who was stationed in Kashmir at that time. "You think the army didn't know. Of course, the army knew the Ikhwanis were doing it. That's the only way they [the Ikhwanis] make money."[70]

The armed proxies typically operated independently "within broadly defined limits to their discretionary powers and the full expectation on the part of the security forces that they will use their discretion to take initiatives within the overall counterinsurgency strategy."[71] For ex-ample, the Tiger's group was administered by the Rashtriya Rifles, but it usually hunted rebels on its own. It had its own network of unofficial informers—villagers who received small amounts of cash for reporting on the rebels' activities and whereabouts. Journalists Adrian Levy and Cathy Scott-Clark describe how the Tiger's team operated: "Whenever the Tiger's men got a call from one of these sources, they commanded a fleet of taxis to get to the fight, since they had no cars of their own. And in a remote and under-resourced region riddled with poverty and petty village disputes, this DIY government hit squad also used their newly-gifted power to settle a lifetime's worth of grudges."[72]

Select proxies operated with the army. They would, for example, visit the houses of their informants to collect information or be contacted by their informants about the militancy in a given area. The Ikhwanis would then cordon the area and look for the rebels together with the army or the Special Operations Group (SOG).[73] The proxies might even be witnessed arresting and beating their sources in front of the locals "just to avert any disclosure of their identity as informers."[74]

Liyaqat describes his responsibilities as a proxy:

The main things I did for militancy were: fought and contained militancy, ensured a sense of safety and security amongst general masses, and political workers who had migrated from Kashmir came back and started a political process. It took us only a few months to spread outside the town. HM people also surrendered before us quietly. Even today people do not know that they had surrendered. The encounters used to be fake as well. Or they used to give us guns and run. One HM battalion commander came to us and said that they had left weapons somewhere and sent off the boys. They would ask to be saved. Then we would collect the weapons in fake operation to save their faces as well. We did not kill people as much as [the] people [who] surrendered before us.[75]

The proxies had considerable operational autonomy, but the army exercised significant administrative influence over them. Some were even housed in military compounds.[76] The extent of this influence is illustrated by the experience of Zafar Salati. Salati was a businessman residing in Anantnag. Liyaqat had once come to his office and asked to borrow his Maruti Zen car. When he ran into Liyaqat a few days later, it became clear to the local businessman that the Ikhwan had no intention of returning the car. When Salati demanded to have his car back, Liyaqat stepped out of the vehicle, pulled out a gun, and began shouting at Salati. He demanded money in return for the car. The enraged businessman threatened to report Liyaqat to the police but instead turned to a local army official whom he knew personally. The officer said that he had seen Liyaqat that very morning with the car. He told Salati to go home; the car would be there by 4:00 p.m. The officer explained: "whenever we want we can end these people's lives . . . they [Ikhwanis] were living a lease life."[77] It was 3:00 p.m., and Liyaqat was already in front of Salati's residence, presenting the car keys and returning the car.

The Ikhwanis enjoyed a high degree of autonomy and impunity but, as the remark made by Salati's friend suggests, their life was difficult. One Indian army officer explains:

> There was a lot of pressure on Ikhwanis also. If [an] Ikhwan came to camp, there is a lot of pressure on him to deliver. Somebody would say, "Get me militants." It is not that [the] Ikhwanis' life was easy. He has to go for every operation; he has to get people. If he does not get people, then we will say "What nonsense. Why are we feeding you?" It was a very chaotic, very complex scene. It was not as simple as it was made out to be. We had to go out to get information. If he [Ikhwan] goes out, does he go out alone? Does he go out with two guys? Is his family under pressure? What his family is telling him? [If] he gets killed, then what happens? So it was a huge mess.[78]

Performance anxiety generated countless abuses. In one case reported by Human Rights Watch, members of the Ikhwan-ul-Muslimoon detained a hospital worker they suspected of militant sympathies. They then "ordered his colleagues to buy him a pistol so that they could confiscate it and pretend to the security forces that they had succeeded in getting a militant to surrender."[79] Similarly, India's policy of rewards for officers who arrested or killed suspected militants "deepened corruption in the police and the army."[80] A top counterinsurgency officer serving in Kashmir was discovered "encouraging men to join rebel groups before turning them in or killing them to receive rewards."[81]

Alliance between India and Muslim Mujahideen Opportunists

It was embarrassment that prompted Mohammad Ahsan Dar to join the militancy. The year was 1984, and Dar was visiting Bombay with a cousin who was undergoing medical treatment. A stranger approached Dar and, correctly guessing that he was a Kashmiri, asked something about Maqbool Bhat. Maqbool Bhat was a separatist leader and co-founder of the JKLF. He had just been hanged by the Indian government, but the name did not sound familiar to Dar. When he later discovered who Maqbool Bhat was, Dar felt deeply embarrassed. And, after returning to Kashmir a few months later, he reached out to a member of the separatist movement. The new acquaintance instructed him for a year, and Dar excitedly shared his lessons with friends.

In 1986, Dar headed to Pakistan on a passport. The Pakistani authorities said that they were not prepared for him, but he would be informed when they were. Dar was given a letter, which he destroyed and rewrote from memory after returning to Kashmir. He and his friends then began staging attacks. They called their group Ansur-ul-Islam, though they considered themselves an unofficial branch of the JKLF.

Dar spent eight months in prison after the Indian authorities finally caught up with him in 1988. He escaped after eight months of incarceration, but few comrades were around to greet him. Some were arrested; most were in Pakistan. So, Dar headed to Pakistan. He stayed there for about a month. No camps were set up yet. Aspiring insurgents rented houses. Dar shared space with twenty others. When he returned to Kashmir in the summer of 1989, he met Syed Ali Shah Geelani, an influential member of Jamaat-e-Islami. Dar tried to pursue a partnership with Jamaat, but he was told that Jamaat could not support the militancy because its constitution barred it from carrying out underground activities. Geelani was with Dar, but not as Jamaat.[82]

In the fall of 1989, Dar co-founded a new organization called the Hizbul Mujahideen, and Geelani wrote its first constitution. The idea for the Hizb originated during Dar's meeting with a colleague, Hilal Ahmad Mir, who had just been released from prison. Mir (alias Nasir-ul-Islam) told Dar that he should take more credit for his work. The propaganda for his activities was solely benefiting the JKLF. Dar suggested continuing as Ansar-ul-Islam, but Mir said that he needed to distance himself from that name in case he got caught again and suggested the name Hizbul Mujahideen.

Pakistan accepted the Hizb in 1990 and began training and arming its members. As the chief of operations, Dar again reached out to Jamaat.[83] Dar's insistence that the Hizbul Mujahideen partner with Jamaat led to the Hizb's first major rift. Mir left the group and founded Jamiat-ul-Mujahideen, which distinctively drew recruits across sectarian lines.

Dar played an active role in establishing the Hizb's partnership with Jamaat. But, by 1991, he came to regret it. Fissures started to develop over the extent of the party's influence. The main split was between Dar and the Hizb's newly appointed head Mohammad Yousuf Shah alias Syed Salahuddin. Salahuddin was a former Jamaat *amir* (leader) for the Srinagar district, and his appointment "signaled the formalization of the links" between the Hizb and Jamaat.[84] Dar felt that the two organizations were now too close, not least because Jamaat had replaced him with Salahuddin. Jamaat enjoyed strong social ties to local communities and was actively involved in resolving local disputes. Dar felt that Jamaat's involvement of Hizb personnel in the local conflicts would ultimately lead to the organization's loss of local support. He reasoned: "we are deciding local civil disputes and by this many people are getting angry. Even if the decision is right, the person gets angry."[85]

In June 1992, Dar left Hizbul Mujahideen and, with the support of an erstwhile JKLF commander named Bilal Ahmad Siddiqui, formed a new militant outfit, initially called Mujahideen-e-Islam. Its goal was "a limited militancy."[86] Roughly 350 of Dar's supporters also disaffiliated themselves from the Hizb and joined the new organization. Before heading to Pakistan formally to launch his group, Dar secured support from Professor Abdul Gani Bhat of the Muslim Conference, a constituent of All Parties Hurriyat Conference. Hurriyat was a Kashmiri separatist conglomerate comprising some twenty-six religious and political groups committed to Kashmiri self-determination. Partnering with Dar was an offer Bhat could not refuse. Bhat explained: "we could not exercise choice—at least not in a democratic manner. Everyone wanted a group."[87] Militant groups had to have political parties "as their associates for registration and legitimacy on Pakistani side."[88] Dar announced the establishment of Muslim Mujahideen, which was the new name he gave his organization, from Pakistan in January 1993. He then returned to Kashmir and spent several months in command.

Fayaz Ahmad Bhat alias Tanveer was one of the Hizbul Mujahideen militants who cast their lot with Dar. He had crossed the Line of Control in 1989 for arms training and, a year later, returned to Kashmir as a JKLF member. Tanveer experienced firsthand the increasing competency of the Indian armed forces and the devastating rivalry between the JKLF and the Hizb. In 1991, he was arrested with his Pakistan-provided AK-47 rifle in hand. He then officially surrendered. Tanveer was released from prison six months later and severed his ties to the JKLF. However, a few weeks following his release, Hizbul Mujahideen militants raided Tanveer's residence and forced him to join their organization.

According to Tanveer, he joined Dar's new group because he was "fed up with the disorder and fuss among the militant groups particularly from HM."[89] But, by the time Siddique returned from Pakistan in the spring of 1994, "things had changed. No one knew who was where."[90] Bhat allegedly informed Siddique that "a senior operations army officer had told him that the army could assist the MM against the HM onslaught."[91] Both Dar and Siddique refused to collaborate with the Indian authorities. But, Tanveer, and several hundred other Muslim Mujahideen militants, accepted the offer. They tipped the police about Dar's whereabouts and surrendered "at a secret ceremony on a parade ground, watched by Kashmir's Inspector General of Police."[92] The police registered their names and weapons.

The group was initially sent to North Kashmir to fight the Hizbul Mujahideen there. But, after logging two hundred kills, it was redirected to Anantnag, with Shelipora as its base.[93] "Shortly, we became operatives in counter insurgency operations with police in South Kashmir," Tanveer recounts.[94] "We established our encampment at Shehlipora village [in Anantnag] because MM already had a strong hold in the village. All 350 activists were staying in same village and our chief commander was Ghulam Nabi Azad alias Naba Azad. Police returned our weapons and provided us ammunition for combating militants." Tanveer's team "specialized in operations that the state could deny, also developing a round-the-clock interrogation programme to keep the general population cowed that was renowned for its brutality and indiscrimination."[95] Curiously, Pakistan continued to fund Muslim Mujahideen until as late as 1996,[96] despite it becoming an "open secret" by early 1995 that the organization was working with Indian authorities.[97] This shows the complexity of the proxy game: an enemy's friend is not necessarily an enemy.

Naba Azad, known in the field by his call-sign "Alpha," also used to be part of the Hizbul Mujahideen. He worked as a constable driver with the state police deployed in the Valley until 1989, when he deserted and crossed the Line of Control for training. He enlisted with the Hizbul Mujahideen and became its district commander. In 1994, Indian intelligence officers reached out to him and offered "sanctuary from HM and arms with which to fight his former brothers."[98] As the leader of Muslim Mujahideen, he maintained the group's connection to Hurriyat, with the help of the Indian authorities. Bhat recalls meeting with an army officer after Dar's capture: "On Kashmir I talked to him straight. He was also straight. He said I recognize Kashmir is a dispute but I am from army and I have nothing to do with politics, my business is to tackle militancy. We have captured Ahsan Dar. Ahsan Dar has fallen out with HM boys. He has fallen into our hands and he is in prison."[99]

Another Muslim Conference leader recalls army intelligence and other officers visiting the Muslim Conference office in 1995 and 1996: "I was always against these meetings. But he [Bhat] used to say it was just to balance things."[100] Bhat insists that his organization did not support any counterinsurgency group. However, the larger Hurriyat "did not publicly distance itself from or denounce the violent acts of these [Muslim Mujahideen and other Ikhwan] groups."[101] It justified its position by reasoning that "probably the cause of the existence of Ikhwan and MM was only their opposition to HM and Jammat-e-Islami . . . a natural response to the domination of HM and Jamaat-e-Islami."[102] It was acting opportunistically, not out of ideological considerations.

In 1995, at the insistence of Jamaat-e-Islami (which was then a Hurriyat member), the organization conducted a fact-finding mission to probe the allegations against the Muslim Mujahideen and other Ikhwan groups. It concluded that the Muslim Mujahideen's alliance with the Indian authorities did not indicate ideological alignment. It did not mean that the militant group was no longer committed to Kashmiri self-determination.[103]

Hurriyat had hoped to reconcile and reunite the Hizbul Mujahideen and the Muslim Mujahideen.[104] In addition to maintaining the cash flow from Pakistan, what the Muslim Mujahideen accomplished by affiliating with the Muslim Conference was maintaining a degree of local legitimacy by keeping politically influential Kashmiri voices from openly denouncing it. The Muslim Mujahideen's ability to maintain some of its local connections and influence despite working for the Indian state made it a more valuable ally for India.

The Muslim Mujahideen operated in South Kashmir, specifically the Anantnag district.[105] The proxy group collaborated with the army. But, it most frequently worked with the police, tackling suspected insurgents in thickly popsulated urban and thinly populated rural areas. While in the early 1990s the police were "virtually defunct," it still managed to "mobilize and direct the MM, albeit under army supervision."[106] The police paid MM commanders INR 4,500 per month, and INR 1,500 per month to the rank-and-file. Naba Azad collected and distributed the cash. Muslim Mujahideen activists assisted the police by collecting information from their paid local sources. They carried out most of the operations alone. For the larger operations, they worked "with the assistance of police and SOG and sometimes other military or paramilitary agencies."[107]

Reyaz Ahmad Khan's story shows how the different actors—proxies, the police, and the army—operated together:

> Pin Jinn, who was with MM, was my next door neighbor . . . This incident happened on 8 July 1995. I was sleeping in my house. It was early in the morning around 5:30 or 6:00 am, and I was in my night clothes. My mother had woken early and was praying . . . There was a knock on the door. Pin Jinn came inside. Though he was our neighbor he was very arrogant with us. You cannot imagine his arrogance! That morning, he entered the house and with no explanation he began physically dragging me out . . . He did not give me a chance to change my clothes, though I managed to put on my jeans. I was barefoot. He took me straight to the DFO [District Forest Officer] office where the MM had a camp. He took me inside and he and others started torturing me. I cannot describe the nature of the torture. I still shiver as I speak of it . . . The only thing they kept telling me was, "You have five pouches and five guns—give them to us." I said I was a student, studying in Degree College Islamabad.[108]

The police suspected Reyaz of hiding weapons in his orchard. After enduring more torture, Reyaz took his tormentors to the orchard. "I was not sure what to do once we had arrived, as there were no hidden weapons," he recounts. At the orchard, an opportunity to flee came about, and Reyaz seized it. He was quickly caught and brought back to the Muslim Mujahideen camp, where he was severely beaten. This was when Reyaz said he had one gun in his house. His hope was that it would allow him to return home and see his family one last time. While being transported back to his home, Reyaz's vehicle stopped at a police station. He saw Naba Azad standing there. "Tiger him!" Naba Azad told Pin Jinn when he saw Reyaz, which meant "Kill him." Once at home, Pin Jinn took Reyaz to his room. This was when Reyaz told him that there was no gun. Reyaz was then taken to an army base. There, an army captain remarked: "You are *chutiyas*—you can't manage to break even small kids. Give him to me." The ensuing interrogations involved sexual and other forms of torture. Meanwhile, Reyaz's uncle, who was an ex-minister, went directly to the governor's house to demand Reyaz's release. Reyaz was released at around 8:00 p.m. He went to Srinagar for treatment and then fled to Bangalore.[109]

The operational autonomy the Muslim Mujahideen enjoyed sparked creative initiatives. Among them was a scheme to infiltrate and destroy Harkat-ul-Ansar. Muslim Mujahideen's main target was the Hizbul Mujahideen, but sometimes militants of other groups, including Harkat, were killed during the operations. Harkat retaliated with a violent campaign against the Muslim Mujahideen. In 1995, Nabi Azad negotiated a ceasefire with Harkat by emphasizing that both groups had the same enemy: the Hizbul Mujahideen. "Despite working with police we discussed with Harkat not to harm each other and jointly combat HM militants," describes Tanveer. "After ceasefire Nabi Azad sent many MM spies to join Harkat who used to work as secret agents. Harkat entertained our cadres and deemed them normal militants who combat security agencies."[110] Muslim Mujahideen spies collected information about "the actions and plans of Harkat minutely," which helped the Muslim Mujahideen "eliminate whole Harkat outfit from the district."[111]

1996 Elections Mark a Turning Point

India's success in Sopore and several other high-profile victories in 1993 sent a strong signal across the Valley that the Indian armed forces were no longer "clueless" and that Kashmir was no longer slipping through their fingers. They were now a force to be reckoned with. This attracted opportunistic allies—some of the very rebels they had been fighting. The proxies made possible a historic event that signaled to local Kashmiris and outsiders alike that the balance of power in Kashmir had decisively tipped in India's favor. It was the 1996 Jammu and Kashmir assembly elections.

The turnout for the Lok Sabha elections in Kashmir in May was modest, though higher than anyone expected. The local authorities tried to entice voters by placing television sets on racks outside voting booths and announcing that the first to cast a vote would receive the prize. Meanwhile, the rebels intimidated voters by placing coffins outside polling stations. The message was clear: those who entered the polling station would exit in a coffin. Rebels put up posters in villages warning locals that their fingers would be cut off for voting.[112]

However, by 1996, the renegades had severely weakened the insurgency. The Hizbul Mujahideen "was at its weakest, literally on the run."[113] And Parrey was not shy about taking credit: "I was one of those who can take credit for holding an election in Jammu and Kashmir in 1996."[114] An Indian army officer stationed in Kashmir in 1996 concurs: "Because of the Ikhwan support, a certain amount of legitimacy, a certain amount of voting took place. And at that point in time, nobody believed that the 1996 elections would be a success. People were surprised that whatever voting actually took place."[115] The modest victory in May encouraged the Indian government, for the first time since 1987, to hold full-scale state assembly elections in September.

The robustness of India's alliances with the renegades in the mid-1990s is demonstrated by the fact that the latter were allowed to field their candidates. Parrey formed his own political party, the Jammu and Kashmir Awami League (JKAL), with members mostly comprising former rebels. The JKAL represented the political wing of "the largest, best-financed and most heavily armed Kashmiri faction"—the Ikhwan-ul-Muslimoon.[116] Figures 4.1 and 4.2 show the areas where the JKAL contested and won seats. Parrey contested elections from the Sonawari constituency of North Kashmir and won, though many attributed his victory to manipulation. Renegades were said to "force people to come out and vote at gunpoint; they would man the election booths and mark the ballots of persons as they wished to."[117]

The assembly elections were widely hailed as a success and made possible the state's return to local control. Half the voters turned out to cast their ballot. The country's two largest parties, Indian National Congress and the Bharatiya Janata Party (BJP), even fielded candidates in some districts. After the National Conference had boycotted the parliamentary elections, India's home minister instructed Liyaqat's Ikhwan to meet with the party's leader, Farooq Abdullah, "to make him strong"[118]—i.e., to convince him

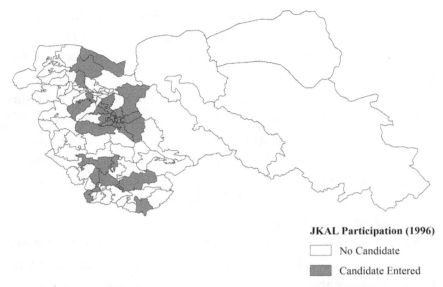

JKAL Participation (1996)

☐ No Candidate

■ Candidate Entered

Figure 4.1 Jammu and Kashmir Awami League Participation in the 1996 Kashmir
Assembly Elections
Source: GIS map created using data from the Election Commission of India, *Statistical Report
on General Election, 1996, to the Legislative Assembly of Jammu & Kashmir* (New Delhi: Election
Commission of India, 1997).

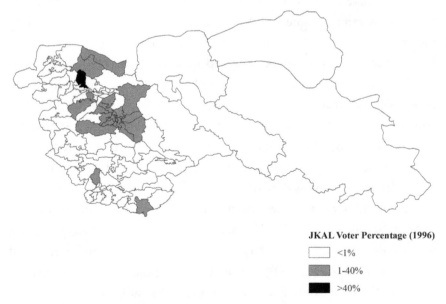

JKAL Voter Percentage (1996)

☐ <1%

■ 1-40%

■ >40%

Figure 4.2 Jammu and Kashmir Awami League Vote Share in the 1996 Kashmir
Assembly Elections
Source: GIS map created using data from the Election Commission of India, *Statistical Report
on General Election, 1996, to the Legislative Assembly of Jammu & Kashmir* (New Delhi: Election
Commission of India, 1997).

to participate in the next election. Abdullah's participation in the state assembly elections marked a clear victory for the Indian establishment and for the National Congress. The party won a two-thirds majority. Farooq Abdullah, who together with Congress Party leaders had been responsible for rigging state elections in 1987,[119] became the chief minister of the first civilian government since 1990.

Despite the reported rigging, the Jammu and Kashmir Awami League fared quite poorly. Only Parrey won a seat. Praveen Swami sums up the irony: "the people who supposed to have done the rigging ended up losing quite badly."[120] Among those who lost was Javaid Hussain Shah, a former militant commander and, subsequently, deputy leader of the Ikhwan and head of Kashmir's Taekwondo Association. He abandoned the JKAL and joined the National Conference.

After the 1996 elections, the Ikhwan hit hard times. The Indian army no longer had interest in them, and so provided neither patronage nor protection. "The Indian state never had a long-term plan for the Ikhwanis. It was a short-term strategy, to use for a limited period," explains an Indian army officer.[121] "Maybe I should have just stayed on with the Hizbul Mujahideen. I would have been dead, but my family would have been richer than it is now, and we would have been living on our land. And I wouldn't have had the welfare of a wife and a daughter to worry about," reflects a former Ikhwan.[122]

The 1996 elections were a key battle for legitimacy between the separatists and the Indian state. The Indian state won. The success triggered a torrent of surrenders. The governor had announced a formal policy of welcoming surrenders on August 15, 1995, and offered Rs 1,500 per month for six to eight months and additional sums for surrendered weapons.[123] It was after the elections that the policy began bearing substantial fruit. Unlike Parrey and his colleagues, the new surrenders were incorporated as auxiliaries into the local security apparatus. They were officially called Special Police Officers (SPOs), armed with Lathis or canes, but not required to wear regular police uniforms.[124] One Indian official described them as "the wild arm of the JK police."[125]

The SPO scheme was not unique to Kashmir. Under Section 18 of the Police Act No. II of 1983, "due to sudden emergency or due to breaches of peace being threatened volunteers . . . shall be enrolled out of respectable and law abiding residents of the area to assist the police in the discharge of their legitimate duty of preserving public peace."[126] Multiple Indian states have used at least 70,000 domestic nonstate actors in this manner to fight insurgents.[127] In 2011, the Supreme Court of India condemned the central Indian state of Chhattisgarh for arming over 6,000 young men in the tribal tracts to confront the Naxalite-Maoist insurgents.[128]

NEW THEATER OF WAR IN JAMMU

The rebel proxies helped the Indian state reassert control over the Kashmir Valley. The success, however, bred an unintended consequence: the insurgency moved to the Jammu region. Jammu's mountains and dense forests provided easy cover for the insurgents. Jammu's three districts were operationally "crucial": Rajouri and Poonch provided easier access to the Valley than the border district of Kupwara; Doda commanded the heights along the only all-weather road to Kashmir— National Highway 1.[129]

Alliance between India and Village Defense Committee Activists

In Jammu, the armed forces turned to those who were "fiercely loyal to the Indian state."[130] Recruitment required carefully identifying the activists—those who were, for identity or ideological reasons, particularly loyal to the Indian state. Indian army officers would approach a village notable and ask him to prepare a list of his friends.[131] These individuals would then be enlisted in the counterinsurgency efforts "in their areas until security forces could be deployed."[132]

Over 90 percent of the villagers who were recruited into the so-called Village Defense Committees (VDCs) were ethnic Hindus.[133] Some were ethnic Sikhs. Muslims were generally treated as unreliable by the Indian military due to their potential sympathy for the insurgency, or, in other words, their insufficient motivation to fight the insurgents. "The Hindu (and Sikh) minorities of Rajouri and Poonch naturally feel deeply threatened by the upsurge of guerrilla activity in their immediate neighbourhood . . . Muslims, obviously, do not wish to join or are regarded as unreliable by the organisers," observed Sumantra Bose during his visit to the region.[134] An Indian army officer explained: "You were only forming VDCs in areas where you felt there was considerable resistance towards the militancy."[135] Another Indian army officer elaborated: "If they [insurgents] come to a Hindu village or Sikh village, they would kill people at random. The threat against the Hindu village would be much greater [than against a Muslim one]."[136]

The villagers were armed and trained to fight the insurgents. "We gave these guys some old rifle kind of weapons, gave them some basic training," explains an Indian army officer who had been stationed in the region.[137] Swami sums up the logic of outsourcing violence to villagers: "Giant mountains. Very dispersed populations. No question of ever saturating them with force. So, why don't you subcontract?"[138]

Bose describes an encounter with a Village Defense Committee:

> The patrol we encountered consisted of some twenty villagers, all Hindu, dressed in tattered clothes and scuffed shoes and clutching antiquated .303 rifles. They had a litany of complaints: they are paid a pittance, given bolt-action rifles and a rationed supply of bullets to confront the guerrillas' AK47s and grenade launchers, and denied wireless sets needed to communicate news of guerrilla movements and attacks to the nearest army base. However, they were determined to defend their village to the best of their ability.[139]

According to an official statement released by the Jammu and Kashmir Legislative Assembly on March 30, 2012, the number of villager proxies was roughly 6,000,[140] while a reputable Kashmiri NGO puts the number in the Jammu province at over 15,000.[141] A prominent Kashmiri journalist estimated the number to be as high as 23,000.[142]

The Village Defense Committees system was not without drawbacks. Misuse of weapons has been well documented.[143] The village proxies also became the favored targets of the insurgents. They were poorly armed and trained and, thus, easy prey. Several villages were attacked by insurgents because of the presence of the Village Defense Committees there.[144]

In 1996, members of the Hindu nationalist party, the Bharatiya Janata Party (BJP), and the right-wing Hindu nationalist militant organization, the Rashtriya Swayamsevak Sangh (RSS), volunteered for the Village Defense Committee system, and successfully used it to score "political mileage" for the BJP in the 1996 general election.[145]

The empowering of selected ethnic groups aggravated the existing communal tensions. The administration of the Doda community, where the measure was first introduced, initially opposed the Village Defense Committee system specifically for fear of communal violence. In one reported incident that took place in Doda after the system was introduced, an intoxicated Village Defense Committee member tried to rape a Muslim girl. The girl resisted and pushed him. The attacker fell from a hill, became seriously injured, and died in a Jammu hospital. The incident sparked a series of clashes between Hindus and Muslims. As a result, four Muslims were stoned, beaten, and thrown into the river.[146] One Indian army officer admitted: "If I have any surprise, it is that things did not get more out of hand."[147]

CONCLUSION

"Get them by their balls—hearts and minds will follow," the Indian state instructed its proxies in a sign adorning the courtyard of a Kadi Pora renegade camp.[148] The message summarized India's proxy policy in Kashmir: use whatever means necessary to establish New Delhi's domination of the region; the Kashmiris will eventually come around.

It may be tempting to infer from the military success of the "get them by their balls" approach that India was not taking serious risks when it outsourced violence. But, bringing into the fold and arming former enemies was inherently a gamble. For example, a former Indian army officer who worked with the proxies witnessed a rise in the number of attacks on Indian army camps: "The rise in attacks on the Indian army camps was due to the fact that a lot of these Ikhwanis went back to militancy. And, because they had stayed with us, they had seen our processes, they knew our weaknesses."[149]

For the proxies, an alliance with the Indian state was no less a gamble. There was never a guarantee that the Indian military would not abandon or, worse, eliminate its proxies once they had served their function. Many were killed in retaliation. Of those who survived, many were shattered by what they had experienced and done.

Bashir Colonel was among the rebels who, in 1994, handed over their weapons to the police. The police registered the weapons and handed them back to the newly minted counterinsurgents. According to Bashir Colonel, he and his colleagues joined the Ikhwan-ul-Muslimoon in pursuit of security and a better future. Few achieved either. Bashir Colonel reflects on the price he paid for joining the counterinsurgency:

> Our life was completely ruined. Future of our children is in dark. We are not able to work because we are hated in the society everywhere. Due to insecurity and impending threat to life from more than 75% locals we cannot live in our houses. I have hired a small room near to the army camp where I stay for night along with my family. Even I am not able to arrange Rs. 600 [less than $10], which is my room rent. This time I visit army camp and talk to officials about the miseries, which I face but no help is given except some alcohol bottles are given. I drink to avert depression because we achieved nothing and lost everything. Sometimes, I think to commit suicide.[150]

Even for the proxy commanders, working for the Indian army did not automatically guarantee security. In fact, it made them the insurgents' prime targets, which served further to reinforce their dependence on the army. Liyaqat recalls: "In the beginning no one was sure we would survive."[151] Parrey was gunned down by militants in 2003 while on his way to inaugurate a cricket match in his native Hajin village.[152]

Around the time of Harkat's ceasefire with Muslim Mujahideen, Harkat commissioned Sameer Darzi alias Babloo, an ex-Ikhwan, to assassinate Ikhwan-ul-Muslimoon's commanders, including Liyaqat. Babloo agreed and enlisted two other ex-Ikhwanis for the job. Their plan was to stop their targets' green Maruti Gypsy vehicle on the road and execute the passengers. Unexpectedly, on the morning of the operation, Babloo received a phone call from Liyaqat. He told Babloo that he knew about the plan. One of Babloo's partners was Liyaqat's spy. "But I handled the situation that day by talking myself out of it," recalls Babloo. "10-15 days later I took 30 boys and ran. We took guns." The band looked for another militant group to join. Babloo then fled to Srinagar and hid in a shop near a minibus stand. He was alive but could not shake feelings of shame. So, in 1997, he wrote letters of apology and dropped them off at different mosques. "[I]f I have harmed anyone and if anyone has a problem with me, please pardon me," he wrote. "The first day that I worked with Ikhwan I felt I did wrong. Even today I thought I did wrong. If I had not remained for a few days with Ikhwan I would not have been alive. I was also young then."

Babloo regretted "beating people," but not killing Hizbul Mujahideen militants "because when my brother was arrested [and] my sister was divorced and the HM people came and did raids etc. . . . I was also vulnerable with no one at home."[153] The stories of Babloo and countless others left baffled and devastated by having done things they could have hardly imagined doing reflects how the tangled web of interests spun by shifting power dynamics during war can lead to extraordinary measures, not least unexpected alliances.

TRIBAL "AWAKENINGS" IN PAKISTAN AND INDIA

Then our Mussalman brothers, the Pathans, would come out as a swarm of
locusts from their mountain valleys, and make rivers of blood to flow from their
frontier in the north to the extreme end of Bengal.

—Sir Syed Ahmad Khan, 1888[1]

To pursue policies whereby guns are distributed amongst barely literate youth
amongst the poor to control the disaffection in such segments of the population
would be tantamount to sowing of suicide pills that could divide and destroy
society.

—Supreme Court of India, 2011[2]

In 2008, anti-Pakistan insurgents established a base around Adezai, a
small village about fifteen miles south of Pakistan's provincial capital
city of Peshawar. It was their first settlement near the city, and it was
necessary in order to establish Tehrik-e Taliban Pakistan (TTP) control
of Peshawar. Some of the roughly 7,000 village inhabitants were initially
sympathetic to the rebels. The mayor, Abdul Malik, even enrolled as a
TTP commander.[3]

But, Malik was unlucky. The local police captured and arrested him.
This began a new career for Malik. The former insurgent commander

became the leader of a civilian-manned counterinsurgency organization called Adezai Aman Lashkar. Under his command were some 400 to 500 "volunteer" counterinsurgents.[4]

Adezai Aman Lashkar was among the numerous proxy forces in Pakistan's larger effort to encourage the rise of tribal armies, locally referred to as *lashkars,* across the rebel-ridden territories neighboring Afghanistan. Malik became "a linchpin in resisting the spread of Taliban in the [Peshawar] area."[5] But, it did not take long for his luck to run out once again. He was killed in a suicide attack at a cattle market in 2009. Such attacks were the TTP's signature style of assassinating local rivals, with ordinary civilians usually bearing the brunt of the blast.

The rise of the lashkars in Pakistan's tribal belt has been compared to the "Anbar Awakening"[6]—when the local tribes of Iraq's Anbar Province turned against al-Qaeda and allied with US forces to take back control of the region. Yet, one need not look as far as war-torn Iraq for an apt comparison. A strikingly similar dynamic of state-nonstate collusion was simultaneously unfolding in central India.

This chapter compares the drivers of the alliances Pakistan and India formed with their respective tribal partners in an effort to combat their respective insurgencies. It demonstrates how actors' varying interests and shifts in the local balance of power drove the striking variation in the state-nonstate alliances in both cases. The balance-of-interests framework outperforms the leading factors identified in the literature: regime type, dependence on aid from a democracy, ideology, and concern with postwar spoils. The existing explanations do not elucidate the puzzling variation in each case across time, and, in some cases, they actually predict the opposite outcome.

Why did the Pakistani state ignore the tribal "awakening" from the time it began in 2003 until 2008? Why was the ensuing alliance so weak? The existing explanations are insufficient for addressing these questions. The role of ideology is not borne out by the evidence. This chapter shows that Pakistan's policy toward the northwestern tribal region was driven primarily by material concerns: political influence in Afghanistan, a desire to avoid a larger tribal uprising that could envelope the rest of the country and make Pakistan vulnerable to India, and US aid. And it was not ideology that primarily drove the Sunni and Shia tribes to form lashkars but rather a desire to preserve their local power and wealth. Those who expect democracies not to outsource violence would be surprised to learn that it was a democratically elected civilian government that turned to proxies. If it was fear of losing aid from the United States that held Pakistan back from supporting the lashkars in 2003, why then did the outsourcing begin in 2008—during a time when the United States was particularly vigilant about Pakistan's activities in the tribal areas? In fact, it was partly US pressure to do something about the militancy problem in the region that encouraged Pakistan to turn to the lashkars.[7] Was Pakistan awaiting a balance of power between the insurgents and anti-insurgents that would maximize its share of postwar spoils, as the neorealist model would predict? When we look closely at the Pakistani state's interests, we see that what motivated the alliance was less concern with postwar spoils than fear of the insurgency spreading to the rest of the country.

The Indian case is no less puzzling, both empirically and given the theoretical expectations of the existing literature. The locals of what is now the state of Chhattisgarh had mobilized against the insurgents in 1991, 1992–93, and 1998. Why did the state not join them until the early 2000s? The existing explanations in the literature cannot account for this variation. India had maintained the same regime type (democratic) and was no more dependent on foreign aid from a democracy in the early 2000s than it was in the 1990s. Plausible deniability would thus have been equally valuable in the 1990s and the 2000s. It was also not ideological compatibility between the state and the tribes that drove the state-nonstate alliance formation. It was material interests. In the early 2000s, the insurgency became robust and began threatening the central state. It also challenged India's strategy for the country's economic development. The insurgency was encroaching on the mining corporations that, in the late 1990s and early 2000s, stepped up their operations in the mineral-rich region. The area suddenly became valuable to the central government, corporations, and local officials eager to make business deals. The interests of the nonstate allies were also more material than ideological. There were those who were concerned about their share of postwar spoils, but many were coerced and merely sought to survive.

The focus of this chapter is on the main mechanisms of tribal "awakening" in Pakistan and India: the *lashkar* in the former and the *Salwa Judum* in the latter. Both of the insurgencies are still in progress, and so reliable data on military operations are particularly difficult to come by. Still, there is adequate material for the assessment of the balance-of-interests framework vis-à-vis its alternatives. This chapter draws on and triangulates evidence from interviews, NGO reports, court documents, and media accounts.

ANTI-TALIBAN "AWAKENING" IN PAKISTAN

This section traces the relationship between the Pakistani state and anti-Taliban tribes in northwestern Pakistan.[8] Despite the unprecedented rise of anti-Taliban tribal armies (lashkars) across the region starting in 2003, state-nonstate alliances did not materialize until as late as 2008. Even then, they remained markedly weak. The state offered modest material backing and no real operational support. The Pakistani state was barely present in the region when the militancy started and so would have very much benefited from proxy assistance. Why then did robust state-nonstate alliances fail to materialize?

Answering this question requires paying close attention not only to the local balance of power and nonstate actors' interests (which all strongly favored an alliance) but also to the interests of the state. Multiple local tribes sought to drive the militants out of their lands and actively sought Pakistani state assistance.[9] But, the latter was unwilling to devote the resources necessary to end the militancy. In the eyes of influential Pakistani military and intelligence officials, the conflict did not pose a serious threat to the rest of the country and was not as important as the threat coming from India.[10] Some within the Pakistani military-intelligence establishment even believed that allowing the Taliban to operate on Pakistani soil benefited the Pakistani state by enabling it to influence Afghan politics after US withdrawal.[11] The state became more involved in the conflict in 2008, after the rise of the "bad" (or anti-Pakistan) Taliban, which threatened national security beyond the northwest. A combination of pressure from the United States, which in 2007 finally began to notice the ties between the Pakistani intelligence agency and the Taliban, and Islamabad's desire to counter the threat of the anti-Pakistan Taliban, convinced the Pakistani state to aid the tribal forces. But, the state's commitment to its partners was weak. It remained reluctant to abandon the British colonial model[12] and formalize the writ of state over the region—until as late as 2016.[13]

Pakistan's Interests in Context

In the wake of the September 11, 2001, attacks, then Pakistani President Pervez Musharraf (an army commander who seized power in the 1999 coup d'état) had a difficult decision to make: collaborate with Washington or collaborate with the militants operating in Afghanistan. Allying with the Americans meant overthrowing and destroying the very group Pakistan had so painstakingly supported for nearly a decade. A friendly Taliban regime in Kabul offered Islamabad "strategic depth" against India, a country long regarded as an existential threat by Pakistan's powerful military-intelligence establishment. The prospect of Afghanistan becoming a client state of New Delhi, thereby leading to India's strategic encirclement of Pakistan, also struck a powerful chord.[14]

The questions of whether India actually poses an existential threat to Pakistan and whether Pakistani officials really believe that it does have been hotly debated. Some see the Pakistani strategists' judgment as clouded by irrational and self-serving ideological biases.[15] Others point to the historical and structural conditions underlying the preoccupation with Delhi—be it Britain's "failed management of the partition,"[16] India subsequently antagonizing Pakistan "without compromise or compassion,"[17] a "geostrategic curse,"[18] or the basic security dilemma.[19] A secret British document prepared after the Partition describes India's threat to Pakistan at that time as real:

Even if the present bitterness between India and Pakistan lessens somewhat, it can hardly be doubted that for some years to come, at all events, it will be the policy of the Indian Government (or most of its members), whether by obstruction or more positive methods, to make it as difficult as possible for Pakistan to exist as a separate Dominion, in the hope that it will collapse within a measurable period of time.[20]

There are also those who believe the military-intelligence establishment is pushing the anti-India narrative mainly to justify its unrivaled position in politics and society.[21] Curiously, a classified 2000 report commissioned by the Pakistani army had concluded that the country's security threat was primarily internal and related to Islamist extremism.[22] Conversations with members of the Pakistani political establishment after the 2014 Peshawar school massacre suggested acknowledgment, at least in some circles, that the gravest security threat to Pakistan no longer came from India but from the armed nonstate groups operating inside the country's borders.[23]

Allying with the Taliban at the time of the US invasion of Afghanistan meant forgoing substantial economic assistance and incurring the wrath of the world's leading military power. Then US President George W. Bush put it starkly in his September 20, 2001, address to a joint session of Congress: "Every nation, in every region, now has a decision to make. Either you are with us, or you are with the terrorists." The message marked "a line in the sands of time . . . Henceforth, nations and subnational groups who acted as sponsors of terrorism would be held to account."[24]

However, by 2002, the United States "quickly lost interest in the Taliban, who fled to Pakistan."[25] The CIA station chief in Islamabad at the time, Robert Grenier, explained the strategic calculus behind this puzzling development:

I refused to allow Pakistani hedging regarding the Taliban to become an issue between us. We were focused as a laser beam on al-Qa'ida. Countries will not act in ways which they believe detrimental to their interests.

Knowing that I would get no traction on the Taliban, I wasn't about to let a moot issue complicate or undermine the success we were enjoying against al-Qa'ida . . . I believed the Taliban were spent . . . If they [the Afghans] succeeded in governing themselves, there would be no need of, or political space for, a Taliban.[26]

It was not until 2007 that the CIA began actively monitoring the links between the Inter-Services Intelligence (ISI) and the Taliban.[27] Washington continued to provide substantial assistance to Pakistan "even as individuals in the ISI, the Frontier Corps, and other organizations provided support to militant groups . . . who were attacking U.S. forces in Afghanistan."[28] *New York Times* reporter Carlotta Gall tells a curious story of a former Taliban commander who fled Afghanistan after the police detained him there. "But far from opposing his connection to the Taliban," she reports, "the ISI agents threatened him with prison unless he returned to Afghanistan to fight U.S. forces."[29]

Further fueling Islamabad's support of the Afghan Taliban was a strong public sentiment in Pakistan that the organization was engaging in a legitimate war of resistance against foreign occupation, as did the *mujahedeen* against the Soviets in the 1980s.[30] There was also the belief that the United States was going to fail in Afghanistan and, upon withdrawal, leave anarchy and civil war behind, just as the Soviet Union did.[31] Daniel Markey sums it up: the Pakistani strategists' calculations "may have been more cynical than altruistic. But they were not, in the main, implacably hostile or irrational."[32]

In 2003, the ISI helped the Taliban restart their insurgency in Afghanistan. It provided them with supplies, training camps, and infrastructure, while, at the same time, collaborating with the United States on capturing and killing leading members of al-Qaeda. Ahmed Rashid details the ISI's support for the Afghan Taliban:

The ISI helped the Taliban raise funds in the Arabian Gulf states and facilitated their acquisition of guns and ammunition. It set up training camps manned by its own officers in Baluchistan province, where many Taliban leaders had settled. It set up a secret organization to run the Taliban, even as it was cooperating with the CIA in apprehending Al Qaeda. Retired army and ISI officers, operating outside the traditional military structures, manned the secret organization . . . The main Taliban under Mullah Omar set up offices in Quetta and Peshawar; its leaders in Quetta directed the insurgency in southern Afghanistan . . . From their bases in Pakistan, the Taliban launched attacks into Afghanistan while recruiting Pakistani Pashtuns to provide them with base security and additional manpower, even as they radicalized them for their cause.[33]

Rashid connects Pakistan's support of the Afghan Taliban to the inception of the Pakistani Taliban (Tehrik-e Taliban Pakistan, or TTP; "Taliban Movement of Pakistan"). The ranks of the groups that united under the TTP banner in 2007 swelled with "local Pakistani Pashtun tribesmen who became radicalized after spending years in the company of either Al Qaeda or the Afghan Taliban and receiving generous payments for services rendered."[34] When Musharraf attempted to crack down on them, they became convinced that "the Pakistan Army was the lackey of the Americans and an enemy of Islam, so now God ordained them to overthrow Pakistan's state through an Islamic revolution."[35]

The Pakistani Taliban represents blowback from the country's attempt to collaborate simultaneously with the United States and anti-US militants in the so-called war on terror. It was formed in December 2007 by tribal leaders with the support of al-Qaeda. The organization began coalescing "when many small militant groups operating independently in the area started networking with one another."[36] It became the most powerful and lethal insurgent outfit operating in Pakistan.[37]

Many Pakistani experts see the TTP primarily as a criminal outfit that regularly engages in bank robberies, kidnappings for ransom, and smuggling.[38] However, drawing on her interviews with TTP insurgents and analysis of their material, Mona Kanwal Sheikh offers a unique glimpse of the militants' perspectives. The Pakistani Taliban, she concludes, are powered mainly by religious and political concerns and consider themselves to be the ones under attack.[39] The invasion of Afghanistan and

Pakistan's deployment of some 70,000 troops in the frontier area in 2002–2004 were the primary drivers of their movement. The Pakistani army's intrusion into the tribal areas threatened tribal autonomy and right to self-determination.[40]

The main objective of the Pakistani Taliban is to establish *sharia* in Pakistan—first locally and then nationally. This is to be done by waging a "defensive jihad" against the Pakistani army, which is seen as a US ally against the Afghan Taliban.

Starting in 2002, the war zone spread from Afghanistan to Pakistan's tribal territories, namely the Federally Administered Tribal Areas (FATA) and parts of Khyber Pakhtunkhwa. Still, the Pakistani army remained "extremely selective" about whom it targeted: it pursued only those who opposed the Pakistani state but allowed the Afghan Taliban (including the notorious Jalaluddin Haqqani network) to operate in North Waziristan.[41] Washington pressured Islamabad to go after the Afghan Taliban and the Haqqani network, but it was reluctant to push too hard given Pakistan's crucial role in the US efforts in Afghanistan.

The United States strongly insisted that Pakistan pursue al-Qaeda deep into the northwestern tribal areas. But, Pakistan's military officials hesitated for fear of backlash and a bigger conflict on their hands. Their fear was of what ultimately came to pass: the rise of an insurgency targeting Pakistan and spilling into the rest of the country, especially major cities like Islamabad and Karachi. Grenier observed firsthand the reluctance while working with General Ashfaq Pervaiz Kayani, a high-ranking ISI officer who was soon to become the agency's director general and then chief of army staff. Grenier asked Kayani whether his special forces could go after al-Qaeda's hidden sites if the CIA provided precise information, including satellite imagery. Kayani said that they could but also warned: "If we operate as you suggest, within a short period of time, we will have a major tribal uprising on our hands."[42]

What followed became a chief trigger of tribal Talibanization. It was Operation al-Mizan, a 2002 military campaign carried out by 70,000–80,000 Pakistani troops in South Waziristan. This was the first time since the creation of Pakistan that its army deployed such a high number of troops to the region.[43] The campaign generated backlash: "militant groups proliferated, and several groups originally formed to fight in Afghanistan instead became engaged in the fight against the Pakistani security forces. In the tribal areas, the Pakistani army's intrusion was perceived to be a violation of their autonomy."[44] Musharraf's banning of religious-political organizations suspected of militant activities further increased the popularity of the Taliban, "bringing it new recruits and fostering alliances with other Islamist organizations."[45] So did the 2004 intensification of US drone attacks in the tribal areas and Musharraf's 2007 strike against the Red Mosque in Islamabad.

The United States deemed Operation al-Mizan and the Pakistani army's subsequent occupation of South Waziristan a success. But, it also led to al-Qaeda militants fleeing to North Waziristan. The CIA then asked the ISI to take charge in North Waziristan. Grenier notes Kayani's reaction:

> Kayani didn't need to say a word. I could tell in an instant what he was thinking. ISI, in my view, had few capabilities in the Tribal Areas. It had always been primarily a security service, not an intelligence organization in our sense of the term. Its officers could operate well in areas they controlled, but the tribal agencies were like foreign ground to them. To put pressure on al-Qa'ida in North Waziristan, the Pakistan Army would have to move in. Circumstances may have forced him to occupy South Waziristan, but it seemed to me that Kayani was not spoiling for another fight, especially in an area where the tribal structure had been thoroughly degraded and the influence of radical mullahs was far greater than in South Waziristan.[46]

Misalignment of Interests and Weak Alliance between Pakistan and Lashkars

A *lashkar* is a tribal militia assembled on an ad hoc basis to resolve a particular issue and then disband.[47] A law enforcement mechanism of *jirgas* (tribal councils), it has traditionally been used for catching criminals and resolving major family disputes. *Jirgas* often address disputes peacefully but can also form lashkars (comprising members of one or multiple tribes) when force is necessary. Lashkars do not typically receive state backing, and their members traditionally use personal weapons and supplies. "Most people in FATA have small weapons like pistols, Kalashnikovs etc. for personal security because the Pakistani state does not provide security to the tribesmen," observes Farhat Taj, a researcher (and native of Khyber Pakhtunkhwa) who interviewed hundreds of residents of FATA and Khyber Pakhtunkhwa, including lashkar members.[48] When heavy weapons like machine guns are necessary, the tribesmen donate a certain amount of money per household for their purchase.[49]

Lashkars are not part of the Pakistani state's security forces. Their members do not wear a distinctive uniform. Neither do they receive any formal or informal training in the use of weapons nor in the law of armed conflict.[50]

Since achieving independence in 1947, Pakistan has followed the British colonial tradition of maintaining a largely hands-off policy toward the tribal belt. FATA is constitutionally part of the Pakistani state, but it is governed by the federal government through a special set of British-era laws—the Frontier Crimes Regulations of 1901. FATA's administrative head (and representative of the president) is still the political agent, whose support staff still includes Khassadars, the tribal police force.

The high degree of autonomy the predominantly Pashtun tribes enjoyed from Britain and then Pakistan began to erode with the arrival of al-Qaeda and Taliban militants from across the Afghan border, and the subsequent introduction of an unprecedented number of Pakistani troops. Local resistance against al-Qaeda and the Afghan Taliban ensued, but it was too poorly armed and coordinated to tackle the well-armed and highly motivated insurgents.

In 2003 and 2007, thousands mobilized in lashkars to expel al-Qaeda fighters from South Waziristan. The scale of tribal mobilization was unprecedented. "Never in the Pakhtun [Pashtun] history have there been so many lashkars in a given time as have emerged in the context of the war on terror," observes Taj.[51] But, they ultimately failed and became a major target for the militants.[52] The Pakistani state provided the tribes with no assistance up until 2008. One observer summed up the difference between before and after 2008: "Initially, the Lashkars . . . were organized as indigenous resistance groups without help from local government administrations, but now both the military and the provincial government support them."[53]

In 2008, the Pakistani government began actively encouraging the formation of new lashkars, which re-emerged in FATA and Khyber Pakhtunkhwa: in Bajaur, Peshawar, Khyber, Swat, Dir, Buner, and Lakki Marwat.[54] This was the first time since 1947[55] that the Pakistani government actively supported the formation of lashkars.[56]

Still, the Pakistani government's support of the lashkars was rather limited. For example, the leader of a lashkar operating in Matani area of Peshawar has "long demanded more money and weapons from the government" but said that his fighters continued to rely on "our own old-fashioned guns."[57]

The aforementioned Adezai lashkar was the brainchild of a local Khyber Pakhtunkhwa politician Khushdil Khan. Khan proposed the idea on the floor of the assembly in 2008, after militants destroyed a local electricity pylon, a telecommunication office, and a girls' school. The Peshawar police soon began supplying arms to Adezai "with the hope of raising a local militia to contain the militants' advance."[58] The Adezai lashkar endured numerous attacks by the Taliban and, by 2011, lost almost fifty members. Despite this, it continued to press on and managed to clear most of the area of Taliban militants. In collaboration with the local police, it forced militants in the area to vacate their houses.

The alliance between the Adezai lashkar and the Pakistani state was, however, thin. The resources the state typically provided its tribal allies were enough to keep the Pakistani Taliban busy fighting the lashkars for some time, but not enough for the lashkars to win. The government kept records of lashkar members and their families,[59] but the proxies received scant material assistance: "a few initial rounds of supplies," but not the "promised ration, arms and ammunition."[60] Taj confirms: "Minus an initial support in terms of Kalashnikov rifles and ammunition, the lashkar hardly received any support from the government."[61] Some lashkar members even sold their property to buy arms.[62]

Why did the Pakistani state ignore the tribal "awakening" prior to 2008? How did the lashkars then become the government's "informal force forming a frontline resistance against militancy"?[63] Why was the alliance weak? After all, many of the local tribes wanted, and actively sought out, Pakistani state support. Plus, over five decades of British-style approach to the region meant that tilting the local balance of power in favor of the state would be virtually impossible without local support.

Addressing these questions requires a focus on the Pakistani state's interests vis-à-vis the tribal northwest. All of the balance-of-interests factors favoring a strong state-nonstate alliance were present, except for the Pakistani state's interest in doing what it took to end the conflict. In the previous cases examined in this book, states' main goal was to reestablish their sovereignty over the rebellious region. This was not the case in the northwestern tribal areas of Pakistan.

But, before turning to the state's interests, it is important to consider the interests of the nonstate actors. The main goal of the tribes that rose up to resist the Taliban insurgency was to maintain their local power and wealth. This required preserving the old tribal order.

There were also those who were appalled by the ruthlessness they witnessed and viewed it as incompatible with their way of life. A former Taliban supporter explains why he switched sides:

> At the beginning, the Taliban closed down CD shops, and we thought they were doing good, so we supported them. Youngsters were attracted to the Taliban because they delivered good sermons. Later on they started killing innocent people, so most of the young boys deserted them.[64]

Initially, some in the Salarzai tribe (one of five main tribes in the Bajaur district, FATA) were sympathetic to the Islamists, who had promised to restore law and order to the loosely governed semiautonomous tribal area. But, many rebelled after the militants tried to impose a harsh system of Islamic rule on the local population.[65]

But, overall, the considerations underlying the anti-Taliban sentiment among the more powerful tribes were more pragmatic than ideological. Christophe Jaffrelot traces the formation of the Salarzai lashkar to tribal leaders' material interests. The Salarzai were the area's dominant tribe, and they owned most of the land. Eliminating the Taliban, comprising "poor ordinary people," and reinstating the old tribal order allowed the Salarzai to maintain their local power and wealth.[66] So the Salarzai tribe mobilized some 4,000 armed men who attacked the TTP's strongholds and destroyed their houses and "command centers" in the Bajaur tribal region.[67]

Between 2001 and 2010, militancy was spreading across the tribal belt. The Pakistani army's counterinsurgency operations were generally unsuccessful in holding territory. Sometimes, to avoid announcing defeat, the army entered into peace deals with the insurgents that "called for the military to withdraw from forward locations, compensated the militants for their losses, and allowed them to retain their small arms."[68] In return, the insurgents typically promised not to harbor foreign fighters or to set up parallel governments. The government's engagement of the insurgents endowed them with political legitimacy. Because the deals did not have adequate verification or enforcement mechanisms, they were usually quickly broken.[69]

Pakistan sought to avoid getting actively involved in the tribal areas. It lacked an official counterinsurgency doctrine. The military's primary focus was on a war with India.[70] Powerful officials like Kayani feared a larger tribal uprising that would spread beyond the tribal region and undermine Pakistan's ability to defend itself against India. Pakistan's reluctance to crack down on the insurgency prior to 2008 was also a product of having little interest, for strategic reasons in Afghanistan, in destroying the Taliban. Even when the "bad," or anti-Pakistan, Taliban rose to prominence, some within the military-intelligence establishment were not fully convinced they were a serious threat.[71]

It was the democratically elected civilian government, which replaced Musharraf in 2008, that actively pursued alliances with the local tribes and made lashkars "the backbone of a Pakistani government effort to take on the Taliban" (i.e., Tehrik-e Taliban Pakistan) in the tribal areas.[72] The party that came to power in 2008, the Pakistan People's Party (PPP), and the secular Pashtun Party (the Awami National Party, or ANP), which won the election and took power in Khyber Pakhtunkhwa in coalition with the PPP, were anti-Taliban. The PPP lost its leader, Benazir Bhutto, and several party workers to the Taliban. The ANP lost many of its legislators and workers. "The key idea was to defeat the Taliban through a popular *jirga*-backed resistance supported by the democratically elected government," explains Taj.[73] "The authorities, therefore, promised money, weapons, ammunitions, and other kinds of state support to the lashkar leaders."

But, the government's promises seldom materialized. Most security decisions remained in the hands of the powerful military-intelligence establishment, and the latter was unwilling to expend the resources necessary to defeat the insurgency. The story of Orakzai shows how much the army was willing to risk by keeping the lashkars weak. Many TTP militants relocated to this strategically important FATA agency after Pakistan's 2009 military offensive in South Waziristan. Orakzai became the TTP's "second home" and served as a base for attacks in Punjab Province not only for the TTP but also other militant groups, such as Lashkar-e-Jhangvi. The Pakistani military was absent in the area, and so was the Frontier Corps. The Khassadars were too poorly trained and equipped to confront the militants. After the Taliban arrived in Orakzai, the area's biggest tribe, the Ali Khel, convened a *jirga* and formed an anti-Taliban lashkar in October 2008. The *jirga* was subsequently attacked by a suicide bomber, which resulted in the death of over eighty tribal leaders. The attack "decimated the tribal leadership of Orakzai and paved the way for the Taliban to take control of the entire agency."[74] The Pakistani military's refusal to provide operational support to the Ali Khel lashkar made it possible for the Taliban to gain control of a strategically important area.

Why did the Pakistani state not assist the lashkars in the strategically important Orakzai or provide adequate support in other crucial areas, such as Adezai? The state's interests were complex. But, most consequentially, the country's military-intelligence establishment, like the British before them, had little interest in establishing the state's sovereignty over the northwestern tribal areas. Pakistan needed to show the United States that it was doing something to combat the militancy, but it also did not consider all Taliban "bad." Pakistan feared that amply arming the lashkars might cause the conflict to spiral out of control and envelope other parts of the country. Not only could it plunge the entire country into chaos but also make the state vulnerable to its "real" enemy—India.

ANTI-NAXALITE "AWAKENING" IN INDIA

This section charts the alliances the Indian state formed with nonstate actors during its counterinsurgency campaign in Chhattisgarh—then the epicenter of the Maoist insurgency. It illuminates the factors that gave rise to the highly controversial civilian-manned counterinsurgency outfit known as the *Salwa Judum*.

The anti-Taliban operations in Pakistan and the anti-Naxalite operations in India took place at roughly the same time. Both involved state-nonstate alliances. But, unlike Pakistan, the alliances the Indian state formed with nonstate actors were robust. This section shows that what made the difference was not regime type, dependence on aid from a democracy, ideology, or concern with postwar spoils. It was the India's stronger desire to establish its sovereignty over the tribal areas. Like Pakistan, India preferred a hands-off approach to its tribal belt. But, in the early 2000s, the insurgents became bolder, more capable, and more violent. They now also stood in the way of India's neoliberal scheme for economic development, which involved corporations exploiting the minerals in the mineral-rich insurgency-affected areas. The region suddenly acquired tremendous value for the central government, corporations, and local officials eager to make business deals. Defeating the insurgents became worth the required investment.

This section begins with the relevant background, as the conflict has received scant scholarly and international attention. The chapter then shows how the balance-of-interests approach outperforms the other explanations for why state-nonstate alliances formed in the 2000s but not in the 1990s.

Background of Naxalite (a.k.a. Maoist) Insurgency

It began as an armed peasant uprising in a West Bengal village called Naxalbari in 1967. In 2006, India's prime minister called it "[t]he single biggest internal security challenge ever faced by our country." His announcement surprised those accustomed to the headlines of the seemingly perpetual Kashmir crisis shaking the foundations of India's sovereignty and national identity.[75] The government was now claiming that the "Naxalite" insurgency was a bigger problem than Kashmir. How did this come to be?

The Naxalites have received little scholarly attention compared with their northeastern counterparts.[76] The geography of their Maoism-inspired movement rendered them virtually invisible to outsiders. The Naxalites wage their "people's war" in some of India's poorest areas, which include forests and jungles, where they enjoy "a large mass following that is not much visible to the outside world."[77] This section traces the trajectory of the Naxalite insurgency from its origins to the establishment of "liberated zones" in the Dantewada district of the central Indian state of Chhattisgarh—the center stage of our case study.

The Naxalite struggle is markedly distinct from India's northeastern self-determination movements. It is an attempt to transform the entire Indian society—to carry out a "new democratic revolution" in order to overthrow "the semi-colonial, semi-feudal system under neo-colonial form of indirect rule, exploitation and control."[78] The plan for "smashing the existing state and building an alternative state" involves "proceeding from remote and neglected rural areas to the more developed rural areas, and the urban areas finally."[79] The Naxalite movement comprises a political and an armed wing, with the latter involving a standing army (the

People's Liberation Guerrilla Army) and guerrilla squads. The latter typically receive support from armed informers (comprising *jan militias*).

Naxalbari-type struggles date back centuries. In his classic work on peasant insurgencies in India between 1783 and 1900, Ranajit Guha describes the phenomenon as "the necessary antithesis of colonialism."[80] To the Marxist-Leninist parties operating in central India since the 1960s and 1970s, colonial-style exploitation did not end with India's independence. Millions comprising the country's "depressed classes" continued to struggle for their livelihood and dignity. Among them were the *adivasis* (indigenous people), or tribals.[81] The crux of their predicament was the state's gradual—and often coercive—appropriation of land and natural resources, which they considered theirs and required for survival, with little "socioeconomic development" in tow.

By 1972, the Naxalite movement had nearly vanished because it was violently suppressed by state and paramilitary forces and subsequently fractured into over forty distinct groups. But these groups began to remobilize, consolidate, and turn more active in the 1980s and 1990s, particularly in the state of Andhra Pradesh.[82] The "remote and forsaken" areas comprising the tribal heartland offered the rebels "a place to breathe, to hone tactics, to plan social experiments."[83]

A Naxalite group called the Communist Party of India (Marxist-Leninist) People's War began operating in present-day Dantewada district around 1980.[84] Among the issues it took on was the locals' lack of *patta* (ownership papers) on the forest lands under cultivation and the practice of forest officials levying fines and demanding illegal payments for the locals' collection of minor forest produce. What followed was mainly a low-intensity conflict involving some 15,000 rebels. The Naxalites chased away forest and revenue officials from villages and attacked rural police outposts. With some exceptions, the government offered little resistance. About two-thirds of the forests became off-limits to government officials, and, in many districts, 40 percent of police posts remained unfilled.[85] The policing of the region (especially areas that are now Dantewada and Bijapur districts) was treated as "punishment posting"—a thankless job meant to be difficult.[86]

Since the 1960s, the Naxalites' focus has shifted from sharecroppers and landless peasantry to tribal rights in states like Chhattisgarh.[87] Three decades later, Naxalite groups spread across large parts of Bijapur, Bhopalpatnam, and Konta *tehsils* (subdistricts) of present-day Dantewada. They established *sangams* (councils) in villages to replace the traditional and state structures of authority. By the time the state of Chhattisgarh was created in 2000, the rebels had formed "substantial bases in the forest areas of [the southern districts of] Bastar, Kanker, and Dantewada."[88] They took over government tasks such as distributing land records to the villagers, settling land disputes, and establishing schools and health-care centers.[89] They even organized street theater performances to spread their ideology. Among the more controversial practices was forcibly recruiting one cadre from each *adivasi* family. Some families gave up female members, which constituted a social taboo.[90]

Chhattisgarh is heavily forested. About a third of its population comprises "Scheduled Tribes," which the Indian government officially recognizes as historically disadvantaged and deserving of "positive discrimination." In Chhattisgarh's southern district of Dantewada, tribals comprise some 79 percent (roughly three-quarters of whom are members of the Gond Scheduled Tribe). The Dantewada district has the lowest population density in the state of Chhattisgarh, which itself has one of the lowest population densities in the country. It is divided into four *tehsils*: Bhopalpatnam, Bijapur, Dantewada, and Konta. The vast majority (93 percent) of Dantewada district residents (719,487 in total, according to India's 2001 census) are rural and only 25 percent are literate.[91] The 2001 census revealed that fewer than 14 percent of Dantewada's 1,220 inhabited villages had a middle school (while 214 villages did not even have a primary school) and only 201 villages had a medical facility.[92]

India's Interests in Context

The hilly and heavily forested tribal territories had historically served as buffer areas in between princely states. The tribes paid tribute to rulers of the plains but were largely ungoverned by states. Following India's independence in 1947, the Congress Party "made informal deals with influential local 'big men' who controlled 'vote banks,' used in its original sense to describe the political influence exerted by notables—often upper caste patrons or tribal headmen—over lower caste and tribal clients."[93]

Unlike the insurgency in Kashmir, the Naxalite struggle has not received significant material support from an outside sponsor—be it Pakistan or China. Most of the Naxalites' weapons were looted from the police and paramilitaries during insurgent raids. The Naxalites' territorial achievements thus did "not come from the support that they receive from outside donors, but from their capacity to generate resources within the areas they control."[94]

In September 2004, the two largest armed factions—the People's War and the Maoist Communist Centre of India—merged to form the Communist Party of India (Maoist). The new organization announced that its aim was to establish a revolutionary zone stretching from Nepal to Bihar to Andhra Pradesh and beyond. The next month witnessed the first-ever "direct" peace talks between state-level Naxalite leadership and the government of Andhra Pradesh. The talks lasted three days. They ultimately failed but produced "a windfall" for intelligence officers who, for the first time, were able to take photographs and videotape the Naxal leaders (prior to the talks, they only had names and aliases, but did not know what these individuals looked like).[95]

The government of Andhra Pradesh conducted effective counterinsurgency operations in 2004–2005 with the help of elite police commando units, called Greyhounds. Many Naxal fighters in search of a safe haven subsequently fled to Chhattisgarh. By May 2005, large parts of Dantewada and Bijapur were under Naxalite control. The rebels used their network of *sangams* to set up *janata sarkar* (people's rule) and declared Dantewada area a "liberated zone." The bold move made the Naxalites "the main target of the Indian state, with thousands of paramilitary forces being poured into the areas where they are strong."[96]

While the bolder and better-organized insurgents began attracting the attention of the central state, local government officials became interested in gaining control of the territory for their own reasons. The liberalization of India's mining sector started in the 1990s but especially picked up in 1999, when the Mines and Minerals (Development & Regulation) Act of 1957 was amended and delegated more powers to state governments. It introduced the concept of reconnaissance operations as a stage distinct from and prior to actual prospecting operations. The policy changes spurred many multinational companies to invest in the exploration of base metals, noble metals, and other scarce minerals. By 2004, 165 reconnaissance permits involving an area of over 75,000 square miles were approved.[97]

The mineral-rich land over which the Naxalite movement sought jurisdiction gained tremendous value for corporations and the state governments eager to make deals with them. The formation of the state of Chhattisgarh in 2000 further energized the efforts to exploit the region's natural resources. The new state government actively pursued agreements with powerful industrial houses such as the Tatas and Essar to set up steel plants on land leased from the state. The prospective profits "made it important to vacate the areas of Maoists,"[98] who, since 2003, "posited themselves as the only bulwark against mining and land acquisition."[99]

From India's Weakness to Parity in Chhattisgarh

The central state's approach to the Naxalite insurgency was largely hands-off during the 1990s. Delhi mostly delegated to the local governments the task of securing their territories, while the insurgents occupied areas where the government had little presence. As the previous section explained, this began to change in the early 2000s. The newly formed Communist Party of India (Maoist) demonstrated grand designs, high capacity, and a strong commitment to violence. It also stood in the way of India's neoliberal scheme for economic development, which required "greater private sector participation in exploration and exploitation of minerals" in the mineral-rich Naxalite-affected areas.[100]

And so Delhi began boosting its military and security presence in Dantewada and the surrounding areas, as well as its support for the local police. The Home Ministry added two battalions of the Central Reserve

Police Force (CRPF) to the one which it had already permanently stationed in Dantewada in 2001.[101] An India Reserve battalion from Nagaland entered the equation.[102] The Home Ministry also significantly increased its commitment to modernizing and strengthening the local police forces through special reimbursement schemes of security-related expenditures. Chhattisgarh experienced the most dramatic increase (by over 300 percent) in law enforcement funding.[103]

In order to "develop local capabilities . . . to effectively undertake anti-naxal operations," the Home Ministry also committed in 2003–2004 to funding 100 percent of the expenditure in Naxalite-affected districts under the scheme of "Modernization of State Police Forces within the overall Central Share." The 2004–2005 focus was on the "fortification/upgradation of Police stations in terms of infrastructure, weaponry, communication equipment and mobility in naxalite affected districts."[104]

So too did the training of the local police forces in counterinsurgency tactics become a priority. Of the fifty-three training slots allocated to Naxalite-affected states to learn "Counter Insurgency and Bomb Disposal, Weapons & Tactics, Un-armed Combat, etc." from the CRPF, Chhattisgarh had the most number of slots.[105] A new training facility, called the Counter Terrorism and Jungle Warfare College, opened in Bastar in 2005. It began taking some 400 trainees every six weeks through a grueling "jungle warfare module" designed to produce commandos for the anti-Naxalite operations. Its motto: "Fight the Guerrilla, Like a Guerrilla." The first class graduated in September 2005.[106]

These measures allowed the government to gain control of the main roads in Dantewada, Bastar, and Kanker. These were previously areas with very little law enforcement presence. Observers witnessed the transformation of these strategically important sites into those "full of CRPF and other security personnel, out on combing operations."[107] The Naxalites, meanwhile, maintained control of the forested areas, secondary roads, and areas over six miles away from the major roads.[108]

The local balance of power, which had previously unequivocally favored the Naxalites, was now shifting toward the state. But it had yet to shift decisively in its favor. A close observer described the condition as a "stalemate."[109] To overcome the stalemate, the government turned to local proxies. The state's prior absence from the insurgency-affected areas made it virtually impossible to build on previous or new socio-ideological links with the local population and thus attract activists to its cause. Luckily for the government, there was a marked supply of opportunists willing to join the counterinsurgency efforts. The timing of the government's interest in receiving local population backing coincided with the self-interested mobilization of a group of local tribals against the Naxalites. What followed was a highly controversial state-nonstate alliance, detailed in the next section.

Alliance between India and Salwa Judum Opportunists

Why did the government of Chhattisgarh bring in proxies to supplement its regular security forces in the anti-Naxalite counterinsurgency operations? What explains its callous proxy choice—"thousands of mostly illiterate or barely literate young men of the tribal tracts"[110]? Why did the central government not put an end to this highly controversial practice? In 2011, the Supreme Court of India declared the government's outsourcing of violence to the Salwa Judum unconstitutional. It ordered Chhattisgarh to "take all appropriate measures to prevent the operation of any group . . . that in any manner or form seek to take law into private hands, act unconstitutionally or otherwise violate the human rights of any person."[111]

The origins of the Salwa Judum bear a striking resemblance to those of the Kashmiri "renegades." The grassroots organizer of local counterinsurgents was a Kuka Parrey-type figure. Mahendra Karma (a.k.a. Bastar Tiger) was a wealthy local politician and leader of a major tribe. His clan owned multiple landed households. (Karma's father was a clan leader and used to collect taxes for the raja.)[112] Karma's scheme of using local tribals against the Naxalites "started as a drive to save his farmland" but then quickly transformed into a major venture when Karma realized that there was "big money" in it: the Naxalites leaving the region would bring in more industries, which would drive up land prices and thereby enrich the landed elite like himself.[113]

Like Parrey, Karma had an unsuccessful prior career. It started with the Communist Party of India (CPI). In 1978, he became a CPI member of the legislative assembly. But, in 1981, he was denied a CPI ticket on the grounds of his poor performance. Karma then turned to the Congress Party, but he then lost the Dantewada seat to the CPI.[114]

Karma did not give up on politics. In 2005, he was an elected legislator from the Congress Party—leader of the opposition in the state assembly. He was also allegedly involved in the illegal business of teak wood and facing arrest. One of his close associates claims that Karma "was told [by representatives of the ruling Bharatiya Janata Party] to work closely with the administration and they will postpone his arrest."[115] Karma was "known to have a comfortable relationship with the Bharatiya Janata Party government in Chhattisgarh."[116]

Karma's anti-Naxalite venture took place at a time the Home Ministry was seriously thinking about raising local proxies and promising local governments lump sums to finance them.[117] The interests of the two actors—Karma with his desire to make money and allegedly avoid jail, and the state with its desire to establish control over the mineral-rich area to bolster the country's economic development—converged in the summer of 2005. As one close observer put it: "In 2005, Mahendra Karma, by now the Congress leader of the opposition in an assembly dominated by the ruling BJP, and facing various criminal charges for his involvement in a timber scam, found common cause with the security establishment, which had decided on a policy of promoting 'local resistance groups.' "[118] The joint state-nonstate counterinsurgency project, called the *Salwa Judum*, was thus born.

The existing explanations in the literature offer few clues for understanding the Salwa Judum phenomenon. The "political regime type" and "dependence on aid from a democracy" hypotheses fail to account for the variation in the outsourcing across time. So does ideology. This was not the first time the state had an opportunity to ally with local tribals against the Naxalites. Karma tried to organize local resistance throughout the 1990s: in 1991, 1992–93, and 1998. But, during that time, the government was not seriously interested in proxies or in the Naxalites for that matter. This was not because India was a democracy, needed foreign aid from a democracy, or because it had ideological compatibilities with the prospective proxies. It was because the region was viewed as having little value. It was not considered economically or strategically important, and the "low-intensity" conflict brewing there did not present a major national security challenge. The state was thus largely absent from and uninterested in the tribal areas. As one expert put it: "[T]he Naxalites do not really *replace* the state: the state is simply not present."[119] Karma's experience led him to conclude: "In 1991, I started the Jan Jagran Abhiyan [People's Awakening Campaign] against the Maoists, but without any support. But, now everyone is serious, because the TATAs could not acquire the land in Lohandiguda [in Bastar district]."[120]

Despite the local balance of power and nonstate actors' interests strongly favoring a state-nonstate alliance, the 1990s anti-Naxalite movements vanished quickly due to a lack of state interest in investing the resources necessary to defeat the insurgency. In contrast, in the early 2000s, the Salwa Judum "quickly spread to hundreds of villages in Bijapur and Dantewada districts in southern Chhattisgarh" with the "active support of government security forces."[121]

The government denied supporting the Salwa Judum and described it as a "spontaneous citizen's anti-Maoist movement."[122] Between 2005 and 2008, the media was "largely quiet, especially in Chhattisgarh" due to "a combination of government censorship and threats against the media; the enactment of the Chhattisgarh Special Public Security Act 2005, which penalized anything that could be construed as support for the Maoists; and a language and reality disconnect between journalists and *adivasis*."[123] However, Indian human rights activists and an intrepid Delhi School of Economics sociology professor (who, along with others, filed public interest litigation against human rights violations in Chhattisgarh and took the case all the way to the Supreme Court) exposed that civilian-manned counterinsurgency project "had the unequivocal backing of the government. Complete backing."[124]

Salwa Judum operations in villages received "the assistance of the CRPF and the Naga IRB [Indian Reserve Battalions]."[125] As a Delhi-based NGO concluded after conducting research in the region: "Without the support of the state government, the Maoists would have violently crushed the Salwa Judum campaign."[126] The central government was also likely to have been heavily involved not only in initiation and funding of the *Salwa Judum* but also in structuring it. According to a prominent Indian journalist with military experience, the very structure of the Salwa Judum was likely masterminded "from top"—a central government organ.[127]

It was a Supreme Court decision in 2011 that ended the Salwa Judum campaign. But the government continued to work with many of the former proxies by incorporating them into its security apparatus. The Special Police Officers (SPOs), as many of the Salwa Judum members were designated, were absorbed into the state police as *sahayak arakshaks* (auxiliary constables). Many of them were "retrained" at the Jungle Warfare College and presented as "Koya Commandos" (some of the SPOs are from the Koya tribe) to be deployed alongside the CRPF.[128]

The major shift in the state's interest in the region explains the alliances it made there in the early 2000s with nonstate actors but not the choice of proxy. Key to understanding why the government allied with opportunists such as Karma was the state's dearth of socio-ideological ties, or really any ties, to the local population. Activists were thus not an option. But, the local power balance was enough in the state's favor to attract opportunists. At the time Karma became the state's first (of many) local allies, the local power balance was shifting in the government's direction. The latter gained control of strategically important sites (e.g., main roads), while the Naxalites maintained control of the jungles.

The Salwa Judum campaign entailed arming and paying some 6,500 local civilians, mostly poor tribal youths, to fight the Naxalites.[129] Those among them appointed SPOs underwent two months of training in skills such as musketry, field craft, and yoga.[130]

Like their Kashmiri counterparts, members of the Salwa Judum became involved in illegally checking vehicles passing through their area and levying an illegal tax on the drivers or occupants. Armed with *lathis* (heavy sticks), as well as bows, arrows, and other traditional weapons, Salwa Judum members have been reported (by researchers who said they had also experienced it) to "stop the vehicles, direct the occupants to get down and thoroughly check the vehicle and luggages [*sic*], seize the contents they find objectionable and subject the occupants to extensive interrogations."[131]

Salwa Judum members did not wear uniforms and carried little or no identification. Observers initially reported seeing them typically on bicycles, in groups of five, carrying assault rifles, two-inch mortars, and Sten guns. By 2007, the groups reportedly grew larger (fifteen to twenty people) and carried more deadly weapons. Table 5.1 details how many villages participated (and did not participate) in the Salwa Judum Campaign across the Dantewada District.

Most of the Salwa Judum proxies are under twenty years old, while "many appear to be no more than 15."[132] Among the illicit practices connected to the Salwa Judum are the recruitment of child soldiers and the government-run "relief," or "Salwa Judum," camps. The International Labor Organization describes forced recruitment of children for military purposes as one of the "worst forms of child labor" and "entirely unacceptable for all children under the age of 18 years."[133]

The Salwa Judum proxies assisted in the relocation of tens of thousands of locals to twenty-three "makeshift government-run Salwa Judum camps set up along main roads [controlled by the state]"[134] and near

Table 5.1 The Salwa Judum Campaign in Dantewada District

Development block	Number of participating villages	Number of nonparticipating villages
Geedem	28	47
Bhairamgarh	324	0
Bijapur	96	0
Usur	56	76
Bhopalpatnam	0	186
Konta	140	200
Total	644	509

Source: Data provided by District Collector K. R. Pisda, in Asian Centre for Human Rights, *The Adivasis of Chhattisgarh: Victims of the Naxalite Movement and Salwa Judum Campaign* (New Delhi, 2016), 18.

police stations[135] in Dantewada and Bijapur districts. Karma summarized the logic of villager displacement: "Unless you cut off the source of disease, the disease will remain. The source is the people, the villagers."[136] By March 2006, some 46,000 tribals from 644 villages in six blocks of Dantewada district came under the Salwa Judum program and relocated to temporary relief camps. The conditions they faced have been described by observers as "deplorable." There were no educational facilities (despite the government's claim to provide business education), houses had tree leaves for roofs, and few provisions were made available.[137] The camps were turned into "centres for military training and anti-Naxalite indoctrination education": by March 2006, 3,200 tribal boys and girls were recruited as SPOs in Dantewada district alone with a promise of an honorarium of INR 1,500 per month (which was not always paid).[138] The recruitment and training of Salwa Judum fighters in the relief camps led some observers to conclude: "When people already are at the margins of poverty and then have their livelihoods hit, this becomes a despicable way the government is inducing people to take up arms in its offensive against the Maoists."[139]

The tribal proxies were "centrally part of the central and state government's anti-Naxalite policy" at a time when the central state sought to tip the local balance of power in its favor.[140] The counterinsurgency strategy also involved bulking up the local police and building their guerrilla expertise; bringing in the armed forces; and propaganda "to sensitise the people about various policies and programmes of the State/Central Governments being implemented for the socio-economic development of the tribal areas, particularly the naxal-affected areas, and the futility of senseless violence resorted to by the naxalites."[141] It also involved internal displacement, which helped to recruit more proxies. These mechanisms were all meant to function in unison and to reinforce one another.[142]

The bulk of the Salwa Judum cadre joined the counterinsurgency for its material and security benefits. Neither ideological considerations nor their identity played an important role in their decision. This was the case for both the rank-and-file and the leadership. As one expert summed up: "They [the government] took these people [locals], armed them, and said you do the fighting. We give you the money and the arms."[143] Another expert confirmed: "Salwa Judum recruits victims of Naxal violence, opportunists who wish to profit from security services, aspiring politicians, criminals, conscripts, and residents of IDP camps who have no other job opportunities."[144]

The Salwa Judum project benefited from "the joint patronage of the state government, the leader of the opposition in the state Assembly [Mahendra Karma], sections of the Congress party, the state police and the Central Reserve Police Force."[145] Based on extensive interviews with Salwa Judum members and their families, researchers of the Asian Centre for Human Rights, a Delhi-based NGO, categorized those who joined the Salwa Judum as (1) victims and relatives of victims of Naxalite violence; (2) those who are induced by free rations and money; (3) those who want security in the form of recruitment as SPOs and police informers; and (4) those who support the Naxalites (e.g., secret agents). These categories are, of course, not mutually exclusive. At a Bangapal "relief camp," nine female minors expressed that they joined the Salwa Judum because of the monthly salary of INR 1,500 and the prospect of being permanently absorbed into the police department.[146] A widow of a Salwa Judum member said that what motivated her husband to join the counterinsurgency campaign was "a monthly salary of Rs. 1,500 plus free ration[s]."[147]

Also prominent among the rank-and-file are contractors, transporters, and traders from small towns of Dantewada district "who have much to gain from industrialization in the region."[148]

Some were coerced into Salwa Judum membership. Those who refused to join the civilian proxy force reportedly risked torture and even death at the hands of Salwa Judum members.[149] Many of the tribals whose family gave up one family member to the Naxalites were "forced to leave their villages, take shelter in temporary relief camps and join the Salwa Judum. Consequently, fathers, brothers, sisters and other relatives now in Salwa Judum are being made to fight with their sons, brothers, sisters and other relatives who are with the Naxalites."[150]

The Salwa Judum leadership comprised those who have been adversely affected by Maoist policies and violence. Among them were those in traditional positions of authority within the village, those whose lands have been redistributed, and traders whose profits have been hit by struggles over *tendu patta* (East Indian ebony leaf) and forest produce. According to a local Salwa Judum leader, Salwa Judum leadership consists primarily of headmen, sarpanches, and panches along with their clans people; as well as nontribal immigrants seeking economic opportunities.[151]

Since the launch of the Salwa Judum, the Dantewada and Bijapur districts became "the center of Naxalite-related violence in Chhattisgarh."[152] Rather than establishing law and order, the Salwa Judum appear to have stoked more chaos. Their operations significantly increased the violence in Dantewada and "increased exponentially" Naxalite recruitment.[153] One observer described the absurd state of affairs in Dantewada: "[T]he police wear plain clothes and the rebels wear uniforms. The jail-superintendent is in jail. The prisoners are free (300 of them escaped from the old town jail two years ago). Women who have been raped are in police custody. The rapists give speeches in the bazaar."[154] Dantewada became "the frontline of the Indian battle against the Naxals, constituting over half of the total casualties of the conflict in India."[155]

In 2009, the state government of Chhattisgarh and the central government launched Operation Green Hunt across Naxalite-affected districts in Chhattisgarh, Jharkhand, Orissa, and West Bengal. Mahendra Karma succumbed to the same fate as Kuka Parrey. He was killed by the rebels in May 2013.

In May 2006, India's Planning Commission set up an expert group focused on "Development Issues to deal with the causes of Discontent, Unrest and Extremism." It concluded that the Salwa Judum campaign "delegitimizes politics, dehumanizes people, degenerates those engaged in their 'security,' and above all represents abdication of the State itself."[156] Historian Ramachandra Guha describes the Salwa Judum as "a model of how not to fight left-wing extremism" and argues that defeating Naxalism requires "prompt and efficient policing" while "providing the tribals a greater share in political power and in the fruits of economic development."[157]

CONCLUSION

This chapter presented two little-known but highly consequential rebellions in Pakistan and India, and the state-nonstate alliances that were forged to combat them. The balance-of-interests framework offers useful insights into the emergence of state-nonstate alliances in both cases. In Pakistan, what led to the alliance was the local tribes' desire to take back their land from the Taliban and the state's willingness to collaborate with tribal forces to prevent the further spread of the "bad" Taliban outside of FATA and parts of Khyber Pakhtunkhwa. Islamabad was not prepared to enforce full sovereignty over the tribal belt, and so its alliance with the lashkars remained half-hearted and unreliable.

In India, the balance-of-interests theory explains the emergence of the Salwa Judum as a proxy. The Naxalite insurgency enjoyed free reign over a region that remained for many decades a backwater to the Indian government. Sporadic repression of the Maoist forces did not end the simmering insurgency in central India. The government's interest in the region peaked when the insurgency gained serious steam and private companies developed plans to exploit its mineral deposits. Increasing military and police presence in Chhattisgarh first leveled the local balance of power between the state and the insurgents. Then, opportunistic local actors, such as Mahendra Karma, attracted government support in establishing civilian-manned counterinsurgent movements. The Salwa Judum was thus born. It was a result of the changing balance of power in the local terrain in favor of government forces, under the conditions of growing government interest in asserting its sovereignty over a region where it was previously absent.

In the opening quote of this chapter, famed nineteenth-century Muslim reformer Sir Syed Ahmad Khan pinned the survival of South Asian Muslims on the northwestern frontier tribes. But, when the tribes sought the assistance of the Pakistani state with their survival at stake in the early 2000s, help did not arrive quickly or amply. The anti-Taliban uprising in northwestern Pakistan was no Anbar Awakening. The Pakistani state's support paled in comparison to what the Iraqi tribes received: millions of dollars and the backing of the Third Infantry Division of the US Army.[158]

If the disastrous 1947 incursion into Kashmir and ensuing war with India taught anything, it was that the tribes were not the secret weapon Sir Syed had imagined. Only a strong military could defend the "Muslim homeland." The weak alliance the Pakistani state formed with anti-Taliban lashkars in 2008 was cruel to those who consequently suffered serious harm, but it may have actually been Pakistan's most "responsible" (i.e., least risky) case of violence outsourcing. Strong lashkars could have intensified the conflict and created new heavily armed militants, undermined Pakistan's hard-earned influence in Afghanistan via the Afghan Taliban (to be filled-in by India), and redirected precious military resources from defense against India. Not supporting the lashkars may have been a viable option in 2003, before the rise of the anti-Pakistan Taliban and while the United States was still turning a blind eye to Pakistan-supported militancy. But the benefits of providing some support to the lashkars started to outweigh the costs with the rise of the "bad" Taliban and US pressure to crack down on the militancy.

In the opening quote of the chapter, India's Supreme Court describes the Indian state's support of the Salwa Judum as "tantamount to sowing of suicide pills that could divide and destroy society." The point is that violence outsourcing is a gamble not just in Clausewitzian terms. It does not just present security risks to the state and existential risks to the nonstate actors. It also degrades the state by corrupting the social contract with its citizens. It turns civilians whom the state exists to protect into cannon fodder.

ALL THE STATE'S PROXIES IN TURKEY AND RUSSIA

This chapter considers how far the balance-of-interests framework travels beyond South Asia with cases drawn from Turkey (1984–1999) and Russia (1994–96 and 1999–2002). These countries' historical and political endowments are very different from those of Pakistan and India. The latter two are former colonies, whereas the former were imperial centers. Each state also pursued very different international alliances and geopolitical strategies. During the Cold War, Russia stood at the rank of a world power. Turkey sided with the United States, as did Pakistan, but not India. The military has played a dominant political role in Turkey and Pakistan, but not in Russia or India. Since the early Kurdish uprisings of the 1920s and 1930s, Turkey had not faced significant rebellion until the rise of Kurdish ethnic separatism in the late 1970s. The Soviet Union experienced multiple revolts (from the Basmachi movement in Central Asia to the Hungarian Uprising), and post-Soviet Russia confronted Chechen resistance within several years of its transition. India has experienced rebellion almost continuously—e.g., in the Northeast, beginning soon after the country gained independence in 1947, and in the Punjab in the 1980s and early 1990s. Unrest in Balochistan has beleaguered Pakistan since the country's founding, and conflict in East Pakistan was frequent until 1971. Since 2004, Pakistan has battled an insurgency in the tribal areas bordering Afghanistan.

Despite their differences, Turkey and Russia behaved very similarly to Pakistan and India during their respective counterinsurgency campaigns. When the local balance of power was in their favor, they worked alone. They turned to proxies when the distribution of local power was roughly equal and when they were weak vis-à-vis the rebels. In the former scenario, opportunists and activists joined their cause; in the latter, only activists took the plunge.

When the local balance of power in the Kurdish countryside unexpectedly tilted in favor of the rebels in the mid-1980s, the Turkish army allied with activists—nationalist (pro-Turkish) clans that were ideologically at odds with the separatists. They helped tilt the local power balance in favor of the state, which facilitated the enrollment of opportunists— those who joined the counterinsurgency for the salary and security it provided. They, and the concurrent village evacuation policy, helped shift the power balance in the Kurdish countryside in favor of the state, thereby triggering piling-on bandwagoning. Unlike the early waves of collaborators, who served mostly as proxies, the new recruits were incorporated into the security apparatus as auxiliaries. They helped keep the rebels from returning to the populated rural areas that had previously supplied them with recruits and logistical support.

Like in Kashmir, Turkey recapturing the rebellious areas resulted in rebel relocation. The separatists moved to the symbolically valuable towns and city neighborhoods where, at the time, the state had little capacity to project military force. The ardently secularist Turkish army then turned to Islamist militants for assistance. So effective were these activist proxies that, by the late 1990s, they were no longer necessary. The balance of power in the region shifted decisively in favor of the Turkish state, and the proxy policy was abandoned.

As a weak democracy heavily dependent on the United States and other NATO members for aid and aspiring to join the European Union,

Turkey in the 1980s and 1990s was a prime candidate for evasion of accountability through outsourcing. And, yet, it actively publicized the collaboration of the villagers in the Kurdish countryside. It did so to signal Kurdish support for its cause.

Why was Turkey not worried about its international reputation? President George H. W. Bush's trip to Turkey in 1991 was the first visit by a US president in over thirty years. "There has been no country as resolute as Turkey and no ally like [Turkish] President Özal," he told his hosts.[1] While Turkey needed US aid, the United States needed Turkey to serve as a "frontline" state in the Middle East.[2] Consequently, as Human Rights Watch observed:

> Despite reported behind-the-scenes efforts to persuade the Turkish government to make changes, and public criticism of Turkey's human rights practices by the State Department and the U.S. Embassy, the [George H. W.] Bush Administration has had no visible impact on the human rights situation in Turkey. This inability to promote an end to serious human rights violations was due in large part to the Administration's unwillingness to link aid and human rights, as required by U.S. law.[3]

The Turkish army kept secret its alliance with the Islamist militants. But, it did so not just to avoid accountability for the human rights abuses they committed. It sought to maintain the collaboration of the rank and file. Their commanders deliberately kept them in the dark about their partnership with the state.

Ideology played a role in inspiring the collaboration of the nationalist clans but not the opportunistic joiners in the Kurdish countryside. The ideology hypothesis predicts "deep collusion" with the former. But, the state treated them no differently than the nonideological proxies once both of the groups' operational functions had been exhausted.[4] The then-secular Turkish state used a shared religion to build an alliance with Islamist militants. It was not concern with postwar spoils that primarily motivated the proxies. The Islamists formed a strategic, religion-based alliance with the state in pursuit of long-term ideological goals in opposing what they perceived as an atheist threat from the PKK. The Kurdish clans' driving interests ranged from ideological (unity of the Turkish state) to immediate (enrichment and security).

The existing explanations also fare poorly in the Russia cases. The ideology-centered approach to state outsourcing of violence would have envisaged "thin collusion" between Moscow and the Chechen separatists. It would have predicted "a lowest-common-denominator form of collusion that does not involve extensive coordination or institutionalization."[5] Yet, the relationship between Russia's President Vladimir Putin and his proxy, Ramzan Kadyrov, could not be deeper. Putin made Kadyrov president of Chechnya, a post he has held for over a decade. Kadyrov, in turn, has seized every opportunity to showcase his loyalty to Putin—be it by delivering a miraculous number of Chechen votes to Putin and his party[6] or through not-so-subtle Instagram messages. When Zaur Dadayev was accused of killing one of the country's leading Putin critics, Kadyrov wrote on his Instagram page: "I knew Zaur as a genuine Russian patriot."[7]

Neither can avoidance of accountability adequately explain why Russia outsourced violence in Chechnya. The country was, at the time, a weak democracy[8] receiving aid from democracies, including the United States. But, this was when its brutal campaign received the most support from both the domestic and international audiences (during the second war)—when it enjoyed so much impunity that it did not need proxies for plausible deniability[9]—that it engaged in violence outsourcing most prevalently and most publically. Moreover, many of its proxies operated and engaged in human rights violations alongside, not instead of, the regular forces.[10]

Concern with postwar spoils played an important role in motivating the alliances between Moscow and proxy leaders. Both Bislan Gantamirov and Mufti Akhmad Kadyrov (Ramzan Kadyrov's father) were concerned with postwar spoils, and the former joined the Russian side when the local balance of power was roughly equal between the state and the rebels. However, when Kadyrov went with Moscow, he was joining the demonstratively stronger side that had the capacity to exploit him. In doing so, he was following "a lifelong pattern of serving whomever the dominant authorities were at any particular time."[11] This is exactly what made him attractive to Putin, and why Putin handed Chechnya over to him, rather than to Gantamirov, once the latter had served his purpose. The case of Gantamirov shows that it is virtually impossible for proxies to accurately predict whether their partner will share the postwar spoils, especially if that partner is a state.

The next section provides an in-depth study of the Turkish case; the subsequent section details the Russian cases. The empirical evidence is drawn from fieldwork in Diyarbakır, Ankara, and Istanbul, Turkey, and Moscow, Russia. Interviews were conducted during summer and winter research trips between 2012 and 2016 at these locations, as well as in Washington, DC and London. Interviewees included security officials, politicians, journalists, local experts, and victims and witnesses of the conflict. The interviews are supplemented with reports from nongovernmental organizations, newspapers, and scholarly works.

TURKEY'S WAR AGAINST KURDISH REBELS

In the 1970s, Turkey's major cities were on fire. Right- and left-wing political organizations violently clashed on the streets of Ankara and Istanbul. The 1970s were also a time when a wave of Kurdish youth from predominantly rural, southeastern Turkey arrived in the major cities to study and work. Among them were the founders of a militant organization that combined Marxism-Leninism with Kurdish separatist nationalism—the Kurdistan Workers' Party (PKK). The goal, as articulated by PKK leader Abdullah Öcalan, was to liberate "Kurdistan" from Turkish colonialism. Its attainment required not only attacking the institutions and agents of Turkish repression, along with their foreign supporters, but also the reorganization of the feudal power structure of Kurdish society. The PKK inaugurated its violent campaign on August 15, 1984, with attacks on two gendarmerie (rural military police) stations in Siirt and Hakkari.

The rebels based their logistics network on local production and relied heavily on the local population for recruits, intelligence, and shelter. The region where the PKK flourished was predominantly rural, characterized by low population density.[12] The difficulty of policing dispersed population settlements, combined with rural norms of solidarity and an economy based on subsistence farming, made rural areas especially conducive to insurgent influence.[13] The rugged terrain provided the PKK with concealment, while proximity to the Syrian and Iraqi borders offered "strategic depth"—the space to withdraw, regroup, and respond to state offensives.

Ankara was unprepared for the PKK's rapid advances in southeastern Turkey. Prime Minister Turgut Özal described the PKK as a "group of marauders," no more worthy of comment than the old bandits of the Anatolian mountains. Turkish officials had been fixated on Greece. But, as the increasing confrontations between the rebels and the security forces made it clear that the Kurdish separatists constituted a well-organized guerrilla force, the army began to increase its presence in the region.

The Turkish army was a conscription-based NATO military designed predominantly for interstate warfare under the conditions of the Cold War. Its tactical weaknesses in the context of guerrilla warfare quickly became apparent. The PKK was far more skilled at navigating the mountainous terrain. The army overshadowed the guerrillas in terms of sheer numbers and firepower but found it difficult to isolate and engage them to its advantage. The PKK dictated the terms of military engagement. It was able to avoid detection, gain materiel and intelligence support from the local population, and attack military targets of its choosing.

With the balance of power in rural Kurdistan having tilted in the rebels' favor, Turkey turned to proxies. The latter were not merely to provide intelligence or share their local knowledge. They were to fight the PKK. The rough road ahead was not for the fainthearted. The first ones to sign up were the ideologically emboldened—the activists. They were Kurds associated with the right-wing, Turkish-nationalist, political parties and deeply hostile to Kurdish separatism. As the state increasingly regained power, the ranks of the irregulars began to swell with opportunists. Many of these individuals joined the state for the material benefits of collaboration, but most did so in response to the state's coercive tactics, in pursuit of survival and basic well-being.

Alliance between Turkey and Kurdish Clans

In April 1985, when the rebels enjoyed significant advantages in force employment over the Turkish army, the Turkish government amended the Village Law of 1924 authorizing the provincial governors to appoint "temporary" (paid) and "voluntary" (unpaid) village guards in the rebellious provinces.[14] The new legislation allowed the Turkish army to train and arm select villagers to serve as irregular counterinsurgents. Some 80,000 village guards were recruited, armed, and "given privileges to roam in the area like security forces and take the law into their own hands."[15]

The first to be recruited and to step up to the plate were those with whom the state had already enjoyed socio-ideological ties. They were members of clans that identified with the right and far-right (ultra-nationalist) political parties. The state had at its disposal detailed information about the ideological leanings of each clan in the Kurdish-majority regions of the country. Ankara had long been suspicious of Kurdish political mobilization since the Sheikh Said uprisings shook the republic shortly after its founding. The state's intelligence agencies closely monitored the local power struggles between the Kurdish clans and noted their ideological sentiments.[16] Army conscripts provided a continuous flow of valuable intelligence about clan politics in the region.[17] This intelligence enabled the armed forces to identify the clans most ideologically inclined to support the central government in its struggle against the separatists. They made informal deals with influential leaders (*aghas*) from the sympathetic clans. The *aghas* facilitated speedy recruitment of thousands of activist proxies.

The early proxies mostly comprised ethnic Kurds who were ideologically committed to the state. Some of them did not shy away from collecting selective benefits for their collaboration. The most notorious was the Jirki clan in Hakkari, whose chief was still wanted for the killing of six gendarmes in 1975. The tribal chief struck a deal with state officials and, after a token court appearance, raised a force of Jirkis as village guards around the Beytussebap region. Another Hakkari chief demanded the release of his son from prison before supplying any village guards.[18] The *aghas* usually collected and were responsible for distributing the monthly salaries of their clan's village guards, which reinforced their local influence. It would be erroneous, however, to conclude that most of the early clan leaders joined the counterinsurgency primarily for patronage and power. Many of them had already been "in conflict either with the PKK directly, or with local clans which enjoyed PKK support."[19] The PKK had become a powerful force in the region. Patronage and power were not enough to convince those who were not ideologically committed and vehemently against the PKK to risk their lives without adequate cover by the armed forces.

The Turkish state made no effort to keep its violence outsourcing a secret. The village guards signaled local support and threatened the rebels' legitimacy. Consequently, the PKK issued a decree in 1987 that called for the village guards' "mass destruction." The majority of the civilian casualties between the years 1986 and 1988 comprised individuals living in the villages whose members participated in the village guard system.[20] The rebels carried out numerous violent raids and attacks specifically on the villages whose members had volunteered to become part of the village guard system. Turkish soldiers taken prisoner were often exchanged, while captive village guards faced summary execution.[21]

In addition to the activist proxies, several policy measures helped the Turkish state achieve rough parity with the rebels in rural Kurdistan by 1991. On July 19, 1987, the Turkish parliament granted a state of emergency rule (Olağanüstü Hal, OHAL) in eleven provinces that faced substantial PKK activities and violence. An OHAL governor was appointed to synchronize and coordinate the security forces (military, gendarmerie, and police) while exercising certain quasi-martial law powers, such as restricting press and freedom of expression and association, over roughly 6 million people.[22] On December 16, 1990, the OHAL governor was also granted the authority to evacuate residential areas and transfer the local population.

An official from the Diyarbakır branch of the Human Rights Association estimates that about 4,000 villages were forcefully evacuated in the 1990s.[23] OHAL officials report 905 villages and 2,523 hamlets (a total of 378,335 forced migrants) evacuated in and around the provinces under emergency rule by 1997, while some NGOs estimate the number of the internally displaced persons in the region as between 1 and 4 million in 2005.[24] Population resettlement is a classic tool of counterinsurgency. As chapter 5 shows, India used it to combat the Naxalite insurgency. The logic is that "since the government does not have the capability of dispersing and projecting its military strength to cover these important remote settlements . . . it must bring the inhabitants of these villages to areas which it can directly control."[25] At the time, the Turkish government projected military strength in the cities and large towns of southeastern Turkey better than the surrounding rural areas, and, consequently, the Kurdish villagers were moved to the urban areas.

The period between 1990 and 1993 was crucial for changing the balance of power between the state and the PKK in the region. The Turkish military made significant inroads in the Kurdish countryside not only through the village evacuation policy but also by transforming its force employment. The Turkish forces had previously been stationary. They remained at their bases until the PKK initiated contact. The reactive strategy enabled the rebels to dictate the timing and location of engagement. But, in 1992, the government labeled separatist activities a threat to national security[26] and adopted a "regional defense strategy." The military divided southeastern Turkey into a grid and established zones of responsibility for each division. Individual units began patrolling their assigned area against rebel incursion. The armed forces also became mobile, laying ambushes and observing remote areas. This increased contact with the rebels reduced their freedom of movement. "No-go zones" were created in the mountainous regions. A former Turkish military officer described force employment there: "We fired artillery at anything that moved in those areas, civilian or guerrilla, it didn't matter. Anyone who goes in there is shot at."[27]

By 1993, the Turkish military apparatus was reoriented toward internal war-making (rather than against Greece). One-third of the armed forces were permanently deployed in the region.[28] Then Chief of Staff General Doğan Güreş summarized this change: "As far as strategic concepts are concerned, I have changed the priorities of the Turkish armed forces vis-à-vis possible threats. From now on internal threat is the first priority for the Turkish Army."[29]

The changing balance of local power between 1990 and 1993 in rural Kurdistan made it possible for the state to make more credible offers to local collaborators. The carrots in these offers were the material rewards: village guard salaries, unlike earlier, were backed by military protection. The proposed salaries were significantly higher than the average per capita income in the region, which was plagued by high unemployment and underemployment. The monthly stipend of a village guard was approximately US$250 in areas where the annual per capita income was about US$400.[30] The sticks comprised credible threats of forced displacement. Military commanders threatened civilians with village evacuation[31] or made village guard service "an informal requirement for return" after the evacuation had taken place.[32] There were also cases of villagers being tortured for refusing to collaborate with the state.[33]

The village guards received two weeks of training[34] at military bases.[35] Their syllabi covered the use of weapons, wireless communication technology, and basic tactics, such as keeping one's heels down while exchanging fire with the enemy, as the PKK snipers notoriously targeted the heels of the foot. Some of the village guards also served as auxiliaries alongside the regular soldiers when the military sent troops near their villages.

The village guards earned "a reputation for being the least disciplined of the Government's security forces."[36] Hundreds of them were involved in crimes, including drug trafficking, corruption, theft, rape, and murder of rivals falsely identified as terrorists. Some, willingly or unwillingly, collaborated with the PKK.[37] The state turned a blind eye to many of these offenses so long as its proxies facilitated its primary objective of wrestling power from the PKK. Immunity from criminal offenses served as a reward for loyalty and facilitated the outsourcing process.

The village guard system was first launched in nine provinces and expanded to twenty-two provinces in 1993—from the southeastern border region (adjoining Iraq and Syria) to the rest of the southeast. Figure 6.1 shows the expansion of the village guards between 1988 and 1995.[38] Whereas the 1988 data capture mainly the activist proxies, the 1990 statistics capture some of the growth stemming from opportunists joining. The village guards who joined in 1995, by the time the state had gained the upper hand over the rebels, mostly reflected piling-on bandwagoning. They hastened to join the winning side and were typically incorporated into the security apparatus as auxiliaries.

The auxiliary forces worked with the army and gendarmerie.[39] As a Turkish ministry of interior official explained: "The civilian authority often did not even know when, where, and how they [the village guards] were used."[40] Unlike their proxy counterparts, the auxiliaries were operationally managed. They typically walked in front of the regulars during operations, carrying automatic rifles and radios.[41] Most of them did not wear uniforms, though some preferred the uniform because they were otherwise the first ones to be targeted by the PKK.[42]

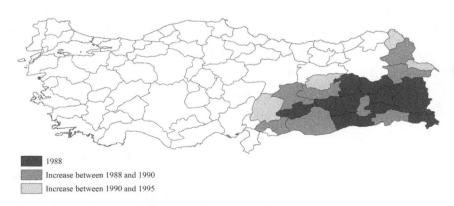

1988

Increase between 1988 and 1990

Increase between 1990 and 1995

Figure 6.1 Expansion of Village Guards in 1988, 1990, and 1995
Source: GIS map created using data provided by Şemsa Özar, Nesrin Uçarlar, and Osman Aytar, *From Past to Present, a Paramilitary Organization in Turkey: Village Guard System* (Diyarbakır, Turkey: Institute for Political and Social Research, 2013).

Alliance between Turkey and Kurdish Hizbullah

Kurdish villagers were not the only ones comprising Turkey's irregular ranks. The village evacuation policy accelerated the urbanization of the Kurdistan region.[43] Along with the heavy inflow of Kurdish villagers into the cities of southeastern Turkey was a corresponding inflow of PKK followers and sympathizers. In 1990, the balance of power in several of the strategically important cities began tilting away from the state and toward the PKK.[44] A former subprovincial governor observed: "The migrants from the villages formed the support bases of the PKK in the cities. They [PKK rebels and sympathizers] took over areas where the government previously had full control."[45] The towns of Cizre and Bismil (Diyarbakır Province) had several PKK-occupied "liberated zones."[46] In Cizre, the Nur and Cudi neighborhoods were under PKK control.[47] Multiple armed confrontations involving the PKK took place in the Bağlar and Suriçi districts of the city of Diyarbakır.[48] The Petrol district of the city of Batman had a strong PKK presence.[49] The PKK was highly active in the Hakkari Province, especially in the towns of Yüksekova and Şırnak.[50]

The army began facing serious limitations to its force employment in these urban areas. It took increasingly more time and resources for it to confront the rebels there. For example, Şırnak had to be transformed from a subprovincial town to a province as the army built up its capabilities there against the PKK via a large military installation. About 950 houses in Şırnak became unusable after the military assaulted them while targeting PKK supporters.[51]

The spread of the PKK into the cities caught the state off guard and ill-prepared. The government did not possess information about the ideological loyalties of urban residents as it did with the clans in the countryside. The last census that asked about ethnic identity was taken in 1965. This made it difficult to recruit sympathizers along straightforward ideological lines, as Pakistan did in East Pakistan and Turkey did in the Kurdish countryside, and along ethnic lines, as India did in Jammu. While the military bombarded Kurdish citizens with Turkish nationalist propaganda, the PKK appealed to the local population with a more posi-tive message celebrating their Kurdish identity.

The state's nationalist message was not resonating with the urban Kurds the way it did with some of the Kurdish clans. So, the state turned to a common identity: Islam. Mobilizing along the religious lines followed Kautilya's legendary "enemy of my enemy" logic. The PKK's socialist roots distanced the group from organized religion. Turkey's ardently secular military thus turned to the enemy of its enemy—the Kurdish Hizbullah.[52] The Turkish state did not need to (nor did it) share its proxies' commitment to Islamism, and the proxies did not need to (nor did they) share the state's commitment to secularism. But, each side satisfied the other's main interest—the defeat of the PKK.

The Kurdish Hizbullah in Turkey was a Sunni Islamist group tracing its origins to the Iranian Revolution.[53] Some youths in Diyarbakır and the surrounding provinces traveled to the Iranian city of Qom for short-term religious training. The pro-Iranian Kurdish youths began to organize in Diyarbakır at the Menzil bookstore. However, after the 1980 military coup, the organization splintered. The moderate faction pursued polit-ical and social activities, while its radical counterpart, having relocated to the Ilim bookstore, argued that armed warfare was the only way to bring about an Islamic revolution in Turkey. What also separated the rad-icals from the moderates was that the former deemed religion, not ethnic identity, the main source of unity. Coincidentally, the Ilim faction leader, Hüseyin Velioğlu, is known to have studied at the Faculty of Political Science, Ankara University, at the same time as Öcalan.[54]

The Ilim faction of the Hizbullah (henceforth referred to as "Hizbullah") was "a mainly urban phenomenon"[55] operating in cities such as Nusaybin, Batman, Diyarbakır, and Van.[56] It began its violent urban campaign against PKK members and sympathizers in October 1991. By 1992, it became "the second most violent and ruthless organization—after the outlawed PKK."[57] The locals began to refer to the organiza-tion as "Hizbul-contra" due to its suspected connection to the state, as evidenced by the high degree of impunity it enjoyed from the Turkish government and military.[58]

The state used the Hizbullah in death squads, pitting "the Kurdish Islamists against the atheist PKK."[59] The Turkish military pursued covert collaboration with select Hizbullah leaders who agreed to work with the state on the common goal of defeating the PKK. State agents also infiltrated the organization. The rank-and-file members likely did not know of their leaders' collaboration with the state.[60]

Much of the Hizbullah's violence was skillfully coordinated. Each operation was carried out by two to four militants, some of whom were under the age of eighteen.[61] Their targets were PKK insurgents and suspected PKK sympathizers.[62] The militants "operated in broad daylight in the mainly Kurdish cities of southeastern Turkey. People who opposed the state were being killed at the rate of two a day; in all, more than a thousand people were assassinated in street shootings from 1992 to 1995."[63]

The state allowed the death squads to operate with impunity in public areas, such as busy streets and coffee houses. Even when the assassins were apprehended by the public and taken into police custody, "they were let go with bogus claims, like they ran away from the second floor of the police station. The people who reported assassins to the police were often then targeted by the Hizbullah."[64] The year 1993 witnessed the largest number of incidents caused by Hizbullah militants. In the town of Silvan, about 300 people were assassinated that year. In the city of Diyarbakır, about 800 individuals and, in the city of Batman, approximately 300 people were killed.[65] As a former parliamentarian who headed the investigation of the state's relationship with the Hizbullah put it, "This is at a time when the area was so securitized that if a kid threw a stone at somebody, he would be immediately surrounded by plainclothes police. But these assassins could walk in broad daylight, shoot someone in the head, and walk away."[66]

The Hizbullah militants were notorious for their execution and torture methods. Their signature execution style was shouting the Takbir and then shooting their victims with one bullet in the head. Their weapon of choice was usually a Makarov pistol.[67] The Hizbullah's signature method of torture was the *domuz bağı* (hogtie). Corpses were frequently found in refrigerators.[68] Court testimonies indicate that the Hizbullah executions usually took place in the morning or evening, when the targets were traveling to or from work.[69]

The Kurdish Hizbullah in the cities and the village guards in the countryside helped upend the local power balance in the state's favor. So successful were the Islamists that, by 1997, the state no longer needed them. Turkey's National Security Policy Document (which was jointly prepared by the government, intelligence units, the military, and the National Security Council) now labeled "religious fundamentalism" and "political Islam" as the country's main national security threats.[70]

The late 1990s witnessed the gradual diminishing of PKK influence in southeastern Turkey. Human rights abuses by the village guards, Islamist militants, and the military personnel continued to scar the region, but the state was emerging as triumphant. The Turkish security forces captured Öcalan in 1999. This marked the beginning of a new PKK strategy that emphasized political participation (i.e., working with the legal Kurdish parties) over violence. The goal of establishing an independent Kurdish state was largely abandoned in favor of a negotiated settlement based on Kurdish rights and autonomy within Turkey's existing borders. The Turkish government lifted the state of emergency law in 2002.

RUSSIA'S FIRST WAR IN CHECHNYA

The Russian military was in organizational disarray throughout the First Chechen War (1994–96). It was not just incapable of effective force employment in Chechnya. It was incapable of effective force employment anywhere. Its ability to carry out combat missions in 1994 was estimated to be five to six times lower than what it was in 1991.[71]

The dissolution of the Soviet Union profoundly influenced the Russian armed forces. Their budget was drastically reduced from its Soviet levels, leaving them with only about 30–40 percent of the required funding and supplies. The army suffered significant shortages of junior officers and had not held divisional or regimental field exercises since 1992. Not a single regiment was functioning at full strength.[72] A journalist stationed in the USSR and Russia describes the breakdown:

Troops were unpaid, training was sparse, equipment went disrepaired; morale collapsed. In the sudden absence of purpose, dramatic lowering of prestige, and multiple day-to-day problems, the armed forces experienced a breakdown of basic discipline, resulting in a sharp rise in offenses ranging from violence and drunkenness to the illegal sale of weaponry.[73]

The case of Russia's performance in the First Chechen War shows that a military needs some basic level of competency to make use of proxies. An army that cannot adequately manage itself is unlikely to manage, be it administratively or operationally, a proxy force. Russia's only attempt during the war to work with local collaborators failed miserably. This section underscores the importance of conventional military strength for successful engagement in unconventional warfare. It shows what happens when this book's scope condition—a strong military—is not satisfied.

Chechnya is one of Russia's twenty-one ethnically-defined republics. Following the dissolution of the Soviet Union in 1991, Chechen leader Dzhokhar Dudayev declared Chechnya's independence from Russia. The move was a product of the unsettling history of Soviet-Chechen relations, Dudayev's personal experiences, and political opportunity. Chechens had been falsely accused of collaborating with the Nazis, and the entire population (hundreds of thousands), along with the Ingush, was deported to Kazakhstan and Siberia in 1944. Between one-third and one-half of the deportees died during the first year of the exile. Dudayev was among those deported, while his aunt, two cousins, and grandmother were massacred for being "untransportable." During the waning years of the USSR, Dudayev served as the commander of a division of nuclear bomber aircraft in Estonia. When the Kremlin ordered him to help suppress Estonia's bid for independence, Dudayev refused. He even flew the Estonian flag at his base. He returned to Chechnya as an anticommunist nationalist leader of the All-National Congress of Chechen Peoples and won a decisive victory in the 1991 presidential elections in Chechnya, which now considered itself independent from Russia.

Russian president Boris Yeltsin responded to Chechnya's declaration of independence by sending troops to Grozny, but Dudayev's forces prevented them from leaving the Grozny airport. Yeltsin feared a "chain reaction of further declarations of independence" by the "more important" republics.[74] The Chechen rebellion followed the formation of independent states in the region after the breakup of the Soviet Union. However, unlike Ukraine, Kazakhstan, or Azerbaijan, Chechnya had not been a distinct Soviet Republic. Its status as an "ethnic republic" within the Russian Soviet Republic (and, later, the Russian Federation) made its self-determination more threatening to Moscow. Yeltsin thought that other ethnic republics could follow, and this could lead to the unraveling of Russia months after the collapse of the USSR.

Over the next three years, Yeltsin tried to declare martial law in Chechnya, but his lack of popularity prevented him from securing the parliament's support. He then initiated an economic blockade and launched several unsuccessful coup attempts against Dudayev. Meanwhile, Chechnya became "a failing de facto independent state and the base for notorious warlords."[75] Mafia activity flourished, and the region became a center of "crime, including the trade in arms, drugs and people."[76]

Given Russia's military disarray, Moscow's proxy policy was limited to exploiting the already existing feuds within the rebel ranks. It was unable to provide significant administrative or operational support to nonstate partners. The haphazard attempt at proxy warfare backfired when the irregulars failed to uphold order and cohesion during the operation.

On November 26, 1994, the Russian security service (then called the Federal Counterintelligence Service, and is now known as the FSB) covertly supported some within the Chechen opposition in their attempt to capture Grozny. The goal of this black operation was to overthrow Dudayev quickly and quietly. The Federal Counterintelligence Service recruited tank drivers from an elite division based near Moscow and supplied them with forty tanks. The tanks and their crew supported the local anti-Dudayev forces which, on November 26, 1994, attempted an assault on Grozny.

Among the local anti-Dudayev forces was Ruslan Labazanov, a former Soviet army physical training instructor who had escaped from prison in

1991 after being sentenced to death for murder. Labazanov had a blood feud with Dudayev, whom he blamed for the death of his close relative. He organized his own armed force and used it in the Grozny assault.[77]

The outcome of the operation has been likened to that of the Bay of Pigs. The anti-Dudayev forces were "spectacularly" defeated, as the infantry "was easily separated from the armor, the tanks were bombed and stopped, and the tank crews were taken prisoner."[78] The failure of this "poorly prepared and disastrously executed" maneuver left the Kremlin with "a difficult choice between an ignominious retreat and a decisive military intervention by Russian federal forces."[79] On December 31, the army launched a full-scale ground assault on the city, with a mission to "restore constitutional order" in the rebellious republic.

The war took place at a historic low point for Russia and its president. The state and military institutions were in dismal condition. The public had little confidence in Yeltsin's leadership. An opinion poll conducted in October 1994 revealed that 95 percent of Russians were under the impression that real power in their country lay in the hands of the "mafia."[80] Real national output was falling rapidly, and, by 1994, the withholding of wages, government pensions, and allowances became "common practice, with arrears for some extending months and even years."[81]

Preparations for war began in the fall of 1994. The plan was for three columns, starting from points north, west, and east of the republic, to converge on Grozny.[82] Between 30,000 and 40,000 Russian troops and several thousand military vehicles (including hundreds of tanks) were to be used. A government spokesman in Moscow initially denied that an invasion was underway, even after columns of vehicles were spotted moving through northwest Chechnya.[83] The military strategy was similar to the one used by the Soviet forces in Hungary in 1956 and in Czechoslovakia in 1968. Victory would be achieved through awe—by intimidating Dudayev's supporters with a show of force. It relied on the assumption that there would be no large-scale armed resistance.

At the onset of the campaign, the Russian armed forces were in such disarray that, as then-journalist Anatol Lieven observed, "there seemed to be a real possibility that the unity of the Russian army would crack, and with it the obedience of junior commanders to the Defense Ministry and the military hierarchy."[84] The Russian strategists calculated that, while Chechnya possessed an enormous arsenal of weapons, only Dudayev's presidential guard stood ready for battle. Moscow did not realize that the civilian population could be quickly mobilized because it "possessed a multitude of weapons."[85]

From early December, Chechen volunteers, expecting a Russian military attack, began arriving in Grozny,[86] which, in 1994, had nearly 490,000 residents.[87] Over 300,000 of them fled Grozny to escape the rocket bombardments by the federal forces. Those who remained were "used as a human shield by the fighters."[88] The city housed many multiple-story buildings and industrial installations covering some 100 square miles. The Chechen resistance had been preparing for the battle of Grozny for at least three to four months prior to the Russian campaign, putting into practice "all the things that the Soviet analysts had identified as key lessons of World War II."[89] The rebels were well-trained, and many were veterans of the Soviet military. Most of them knew Grozny well, and their light weapons facilitated their mobility across closely set buildings and underground passages.

The Russian armed forces were reluctant to get involved in domestic affairs. The western column engaged in a "near mutiny" when it encountered unexpected resistance from the civilian population while advancing to Grozny.[90] On December 13, the column confronted a crowd of Chechen women performing a *zikr* (ritual prayer) on the road. They told the Russian soldiers that to advance they would have to drive over them. The performance of the religious ritual forced the Russian soldiers to consider whether they were willing to use force against peaceful civilians. Moreover, if the Russian soldiers decided to compel the group to disperse, they would not only be using force against civilians but also engaging in symbolic violence against local Muslims. The head of the column announced that he would not harm civilians and refused to advance further. He then walked hand-in-hand down the village high street with a group of elderly women, shouting: "It is not our fault that we are here. We did not want this. This operation contradicts the constitution. It is forbidden to use the army against peaceful civilians."[91]

The roughly 6,000 troops that finally made it to Grozny were not adequately prepared for the "urban battlefield or for any other," as they were composed of "conscripts and haphazardly assembled ad hoc units," most of whom had not trained together before being sent to Grozny.[92] The poor organization was reflected in the high rate of fratricide (mistaken killing of Russian soldiers by Russian soldiers). It accounted for estimated 60 percent of Russian casualties in Chechnya.[93]

Proxies would have certainly been useful to the Russian army, which had remarkably little knowledge of Grozny and the rebellion itself. The army relied on outdated maps and lacked intelligence on centers of resistance. Chechen collaboration could also have signaled Dudayev's lack of legitimacy and justified Yeltsin's intervention. The inability of the Russian military to make effective use of proxy warfare became a significant obstacle to quelling the Chechen rebellion.

The objective of the Chechnya campaign was to depose Dudayev's rule, headquartered in Grozny. There was a marked supply of "pro-Russia" elements inside Chechnya. In fact, by the summer of 1994, Dudayev had little control of the republic outside of Grozny.[94] The pro-Russia armed forces of Dudayev's opposition controlled the republic's northern regions,[95] and some were also stationed east[96] and southwest of the capital.[97] Grozny had historically been a mainly ethnic Russian-inhabited city.[98] It was home to thousands of ethnic Russians who could potentially serve as activist proxies, while, in Moscow alone, the number of ethnic Chechens, who could potentially fill the ranks of irregulars, was roughly 40,000.[99]

A ground assault on Grozny was launched on December 31, the day the Russian media were on a holiday over the New Year, to keep the operation out of the public eye. During the subsequent "siege," which lasted roughly seven weeks, the city was open to the south and east. This allowed the Chechen fighters to receive continuous reinforcement and supplies.[100]

The Russian military failed to overcome the Chechen resistance and, in 1996, withdrew its forces under a peace agreement that gave Chechnya considerable autonomy, though not full independence. The Chechen chief of staff who organized the defense of Grozny, Aslan Maskhadov, was elected president. Under his tenure, Chechnya plunged into political chaos and economic collapse. Maskhadov's political rival, Shamil Basayev, established a network of military officers who then turned into rival warlords. Organized crime and kidnappings became rampant. The number of armed groups active in Chechnya between the years 1996 and 1999 increased to 157. Pro-regime groups controlled oil pipelines and the illegal trade in oil products, while the other organized criminal groups specialized in robberies, kidnappings, and trade in "live" goods. Between 1996 and 1999, over 3,500 Chechens were kidnapped for ransom.[101]

Had the Russian military not been in such disarray, there is good reason to believe that it would have been able to exploit the existing supply of prospective proxies. This good reason is provided by the Second Chechen War, which took place after a major military transformation. The case of the Second Chechen War offers an opportunity to assess the role of this book's principal scope condition—a strong military—in the central argument. It also allows one to evaluate whether the logic driving violence outsourcing in the cases drawn from Pakistan, India, and Turkey may be applied to a case as different as Russia's counterinsurgency campaign in Chechnya.

RUSSIA'S SECOND WAR IN CHECHNYA

The Russian strategists "carefully studied the mistakes of the first war" and made "key improvements" that significantly enhanced Russia's military strength.[102] At the beginning of the first war, the operational group of federal forces in Chechnya numbered 24,000—at the start of the second campaign, it approached 100,000.[103] The principle of volunteer participation of conscript soldiers in combat, which existed during the first war, was abolished.[104] Shifts in the military budget led to improved access to arms and equipment. Military morale and efficiency were also boosted through improved coordination.

The Russian military was not just conventionally stronger, its force employment in the rebellious republic was drastically improved.[105] During the first Chechnya campaign, the multiple ministries and organizations with troops deployed to Chechnya each had their own competing command structures. Coordination between the Ministry of Defense and the Ministry of Internal Affairs units, between ground and air forces, and among troops on the ground was very poorly managed. For the second campaign, command and control was simplified and improved with a single hierarchy under the Ministry of Defense. Force coordination and synchronization of air and land operations were also dramatically improved. So effective was the military's force employment that, within several months of the campaign, the Russian armed forces controlled some 80 percent of Chechen territory.[106]

Moscow's successful projection of its military force in the rebellious republic helped tilt the local power balance away from the rebels. The Russian military was not yet dominating, but neither was it losing. To tilt the balance of power decisively in its favor, it needed to take Grozny. And so the Russian forces headed there. Though, this time, they were not alone. They came with proxies.

In August 1999, Basayev and Saudi-born Ibn al-Khattab led some 1,500 fighters into neighboring Russian republic of Dagestan with the goal of establishing an independent Islamic state. To their surprise, instead of a mass anti-Russia uprising, the village-by-village operation was met with a spontaneous mass mobilization of Dagestani civilians against the invaders. Viewing the invaders not as liberators but as religious fanatics, Dagestani villagers organized themselves into vigilante groups. By mid-September 1999, federal forces, assisted by the local vigilantes and police, succeeded in recapturing the villages that fell under militant control and pushed the invaders back to Chechnya.

During the same month, three Russian cities were rocked by four apartment bombings, which set off a wave of fear across the entire country.

The federal authorities accused Chechen separatists for the bombings, and Putin memorably announced: "If they're in the airport, we'll kill them there. And excuse me, but if we find them in the toilet, we'll exterminate them in their outhouses." The message was clear—anything goes. However, the apartment bombings were not without controversy. Several prominent figures, including former FSB officer Alexander Litvinenko (who died after drinking poisoned tea in London in 2006), accused the FSB of organizing the explosions. Whatever their origins, the bombings significantly helped the Kremlin get public approval for the second Chechnya campaign. As Russia's former Finance Minister Mikhail Kasyanov observed, most of the Russian citizens "simply closed their eyes and let him [Putin] do whatever he wanted as long as he saved them from this threat."[107]

Yeltsin appointed Putin as prime minister and manager of the day-to-day coordination of the military campaign immediately after Basayev had entered Dagestan.[108] On September 23, 1999, the Russian air force bombed Grozny. Maskhadov initially sought to negotiate with the Kremlin and offered to cooperate on cracking down on the warlords proliferating on Chechen territory. His popularity among ordinary Chechens stemmed from his pragmatism and emphasis on peaceful solutions. He had condemned Basayev and Khattab's invasion of Dagestan (as well as the 2004 Beslan school massacre). Maskhadov supported Chechen independence and the rebirth of Chechen religious traditions, and he tried to ban fundamentalist Wahhabism espoused by many of the warlords. But, in the aftermath of the apartment bombings, the Kremlin denounced Maskhadov and proclaimed the Moscow-based State Council of the Republic of Chechnya, which was formed by former members of the Chechen republican legislature, the only legitimate Chechen authority. Maskhadov responded by calling for a *ghazevat*, or holy war, and allied with the warlords against Russia.

In December, the federal troops began a full-scale attack on Grozny, the locus of Chechen resistance.

Alliance between Russia and Gantamirovtsy

One month after the start of the second Chechnya campaign, Yeltsin released from prison a convicted embezzler and ex-mayor of Grozny—Bislan Gantamirov. Gantamirov was jailed for misappropriating federal funds allocated for the restoration of the Chechen capital. He was to lead an irregular military outfit comprising his personal supporters and former rebels. It was tasked with assisting the Russian federal troops in gaining control of Grozny.

Rather than keeping secret or denying the role of the criminals and rebels in the second Chechnya campaign, Russian officials publicly highlighted and sometimes even overemphasized the role of the *gantamirovtsy* (Gantamirov's men). "If anybody is going to enter Grozny, it will be the volunteers of Bislan Gantamirov," pronounced the commander of the unified federal group in the North Caucasus in early December.[109] "The main load of fulfilling tasks in Grozny is on the [Gantamirov] militia," stated a Russian air force commander in late December, though he acknowledged that "the army cannot be totally excluded" from action.[110]

Gantamirov was initially "an active adherent" of Dudayev. However, in 1993, after clashing with the Chechen president over oil business revenues, he became a major figure in the anti-Dudayev movement. He had some 3,000 armed supporters who controlled much of northern Chechnya.[111] Gantamirov's release from prison immediately prompted the Russian newspaper *Kommersant* to speculate that it was intended to help the Russian army to take over Grozny.[112] Gantamirov soon publicly announced his intent "to assume command of all armed forces which will be formed out of Chechen population" and, afterward, to assume an official political post in Chechnya.[113]

Gantamirov's 800-member irregular force was charged with "fighting a way into central Grozny pressing from three directions."[114] However, Russia's interior minister refused to supply the proxies with armored personnel carriers, mortars, or sniper's rifles, and so their combat arsenal was limited to "obsolete AK-47s which jammed after a few shots."[115]

The plan of the Grozny operation envisioned a " 'web-like' pattern of the presence and action of federal troops in Grozny. With Gantamirov's groups in vanguard fighting, the army's special task units and armour will be moving to their rear. After Grozny is under the 'web,' the third stage of the operation will start, which is destruction of the rebel manpower."[116]

As its former mayor, Gantamirov had deep knowledge of the city. Moscow figured that 4,000 out of roughly 10,000 to 12,000 people remaining in Grozny were rebel fighters.[117] Others estimated the number of civilians in Grozny to be as high as 35,000.[118] The proxies were followed in the city proper by an assault force of 4,000–5,000 regulars.[119] They were to help the Russian troops navigate the "local peculiarities" of Grozny, while also serving as "a kind of a buffer between the federal troops and local residents."[120] They were also expected to "save the lives of Russian soldiers by, for example, drawing guerrilla fire so that Russian planes and artillery can lock onto and then pound rebel positions."[121]

The battle concluded with a decisive Russian victory, with the gantamirovtsy playing "a pivotal role."[122] Gantamirov emerged as a war hero. While he was working for the Kremlin, the Russian authorities cultivated an image of him as "a courageous man who has a great authority in Chechnya."[123] The former mayor of Grozny was also associated with normalcy in the capital city. Although many Chechens actually despised Gantamirov for betraying Dudayev, Russian newspapers claimed that Grozny's residents could "still remember that it was under Gantemirov that things got back to normal: The markets began operating, apartment buildings started being rebuilt, and schools and hospitals opened."[124]

Alliance between Russia and Kadyrovtsy

After establishing control in Grozny, Moscow switched its support from Gantamirov to ex-rebel Mufti Akhmad Kadyrov. Kadyrov "practiced a moderate form of Islam and opposed the violent Wahhabism of some Chechen rebels," though he "had no strong political beliefs of his own."[125]

Kadyrov's fighters controlled Gudermes, the second-largest Chechen city, which the Kremlin planned to turn into the republic's temporary capital. The federal forces concluded an agreement with Kadyrov that involved his guerrillas making Gudermes rebel-free without Russian army assistance.[126] What made Kadyrov attractive to the Russian government was that, while he was powerful, he was not too powerful. Kadyrov's influence was at the time limited to Chechnya's northern and northeastern regions, where separatist sentiments had traditionally been weaker and federal controls tighter. Kadyrov had never been supported by the majority within Chechen society,[127] who suspected him of corruption,[128] and so was more dependent on the Kremlin than Gantamirov. Criminals made for particularly appealing allies to Putin, who operated according to the KGB methods he learned in his earlier career: "He [Putin] fostered relationships with people who had compromising material (kompromat) collected about them, who could be prosecuted or blackmailed if it ever became necessary to punish their disloyalty."[129]

Kadyrov was appointed to head the administration in Chechnya, and his kadyrovtsy (Kadyrov's men), a mix of ex-rebels, criminals, and inexperienced hopefuls, helped to establish Moscow's control over the rest of the republic. Kadyrov's personal contacts with insurgents, religious background, and opposition to Wahhabism allowed the Kremlin to carry out a successful amnesty program, which swelled the ranks of the kadyrovtsy. Moreover, the brutality of the federal forces' "cleansings" operations made the irregular military outfit the only source of physical safety for many Chechen men. By 2003, pardoned rebels constituted two-thirds to three-quarters of Kadyrov's personal army.[130] Many of them were coerced to surrender and join the kadyrovtsy. Kadyrov's forces "used severe beatings and torture against those who resisted, and sometimes kidnapped family members to convince individual rebels to surrender."[131] They also burned the family homes of rebels who refused to flip and forced parents "to appear on local television to beg their sons to give in."[132]

The Mufti was assassinated in 2004 by Basayev's forces. Putin then redirected his support to Kadyrov's son, Ramzan, who was the commander of the kadyrovtsy. By 2006, the kadyrovtsy squad boasted at least 5,000 armed members,[133] of whom 1,200 were transformed into the Sever (North) and Yug (South) battalions of the regional law enforcement agency. The control over all Ministry of Internal Affairs structures of Chechnya was gradually transferred to Kadyrov's associates. In 2007, after Kadyrov turned thirty (which made him eligible for presidency), Putin signed a decree installing him as the acting president of the Chechen Republic.[134]

Russia officially ended its "counterterrorism" campaign in Chechnya in April 2009. The kadyrovtsy had become notorious for committing numerous human rights abuses, such as kidnappings, torture, and assassinations, with impunity. According to statistics released by the Chechen government, there were 477 disappearances in 2003, with the kadyrovtsy commonly believed to be responsible for the vast majority of them. The kadyrovtsy were known to pick houses at random and kill some of the inhabitants while abducting others. Kadyrov refused to allow journalists near a former chicken farm outside Gudermes, which human rights activists believed was used as a detention and interrogation center.[135]

CONCLUSION

This chapter shows that civil-wartime alliances between states and nonstate actors have been governed by a balance of interests not only in South Asia but also in Turkey and Russia. States are more likely to seek nonstate partners when the local balance of power favors the rebels or is roughly equal. While opportunists are willing to ally with the state only in the latter scenario, activists may be convinced to join the counterinsurgency through socio-ideological linkages even when the state is very weak.

Despite having a large and relatively well-organized military force that possessed conventional superiority, the Turkish armed forces were hard-pressed to contain the PKK's advances in the second half of the 1980s. The recruitment of activist proxies in embattled regions (pro-state clans in the countryside and the Hizbullah in the cities) and the village guards in the rest of the Kurdistan region enabled the armed forces to tip the local power balance against the PKK's battle-hardened guerrillas in favor of the state.

Russia's experience with proxy warfare in the 1990s underscores how necessary conventional military power is for the effective use of proxies. The dismal condition of the Russian armed forces immediately after the Soviet Union's collapse prevented the state from taking advantage of potential local allies in the first war in Chechnya. As the Russian military reconstituted its strength in the late 1990s, the Kremlin's ability to manipulate the local Chechen forces to its advantage also grew. Moscow's double dealing with Gantamirov and Kadyrov enabled it to impose military control over the restive region and then to impose political control under the aegis of a warlord.

The state-nonstate alliances formed in Turkey and Russia were no less a gamble for all the concerned parties than the alliances formed in Pakistan and India. In each case, the state's counterinsurgency operations depended on civilians who lacked adequate military training or activist nonstate actors who required oversight to contain. Human rights abuses became rampant, and the conflict region reeled under kidnappings, torture, and extra-judicial killings. The nonstate actors also took significant risks. Some of them were betrayed by the state in favor of their local rivals; others became prize targets for the rebel forces.

CONCLUSION

[O]nly the element of chance is needed to make war a gamble, and that element is never absent.

—Carl von Clausewitz, *On War*, 1832[1]

Wars can make for strange allies. The alliance between the US Navy and the New York City mafia during World War II is a case in point.[2] Alliances made in times of civil war can also surprise. Machiavelli forewarns of links between rebels and foreign agents: "When once the people have taken arms against you, there will never be lacking foreigners to assist them."[3] Kautilya similarly cautions that one's people may "join hands with neighboring princes."[4] Neighboring states are not the only ones capable of stoking an insurrection, to which the ties between Libya and the Provisional Irish Republican Army or Lebanon and the Japanese Red Army amply attest.[5]

Civil wars also sometimes make for unexpected allies of a different sort. The embattled states may reach out to unconventional partners, be those partners the ordinary civilians they are expected to protect or the lawbreakers they are expected to reprimand. States as diverse as Britain, Guatemala, Syria, Mozambique, and Afghanistan have outsourced violence to nonstate counterinsurgents. It may not be all that surprising that a militarily weak state would turn to nonstate allies for help quelling an insurgency. But, why would a state with a world-class military do so? Why would it forgo, as Adam Smith put it in *The Wealth of Nations*, "the irresistible superiority which a well regulated standing army has over a militia"?[6]

This book has proposed a novel framework for understanding state-nonstate alliances in times of civil war. It has argued that, when valued territory is at stake, states—be they democratic, semidemocratic, or authoritarian—take the gamble with violence by empowering nonstate actors to fight insurgency on their behalf. The nonstate actors ally with states when doing so satisfies either their immediate material interests (in the case of opportunists) or farsighted goals (in the case of activists). States seek allies only when they need them: when the local power balance is either roughly equal or favors the insurgents. In the former scenario, both the opportunists and the activists could be convinced or compelled to join the counterinsurgency; in the latter, only the activists would take the plunge.

This "balance-of-interests" approach elucidates how different configurations of power and priorities result in distinct alliance patterns. It contributes to the burgeoning scholarship on militias by considering, for the first time, the interests of both the states and the nonstate actors, while also offering a more productive way of operationalizing local power (i.e., beyond just territorial control). In doing so, it both builds on and contributes to the rich alliance literature in the field of international relations and to civil war literature in the fields of comparative politics and security studies.

The book has presented four uniquely in-depth accounts of state-nonstate alliances in South Asia that formed during Pakistan's counterinsurgency campaign in East Pakistan (chapter 3), India's counterinsurgency in Kashmir (chapter 4), and Pakistan's and India's counterinsurgencies in their respective tribal belts (chapter 5). The analysis was then augmented with a paired "out-of-sample" study gauging the implications of the balance-of-interests framework for contexts as diverse as Turkey and Russia (chapter 6).

When it came to Pakistan's and India's outsourcing of violence to nonstate counterinsurgents, neither regime type nor dependence on aid from a democracy made much of a difference. Pakistan used proxies in counterinsurgency operations both as a military dictatorship (in the East Pakistan case) and as a weak democracy (in the FATA-Khyber Pakhtunkhwa case). In both cases, it was heavily dependent on aid from the United States. India used proxies in Kashmir and Chhattisgarh despite its democratic standing. Neither for Pakistan nor for India was plausible deniability the main concern. Tactical calculations trumped appearances. Violence outsourcing was also often quickly publicly exposed—by nongovernmental organizations, the media, and even the celebratory announcements of officials, proud of securing local allies against the insurgents.

The alliances Pakistan and India formed with their nonstate partners were not based on power alone. The different interests each actor brought into play mattered as well. Ideology mattered, but to some more than others. It mattered more to the *al-Badr* activists than the *Razakar* opportunists in East Pakistan in 1971. Identity also mattered, but more to some—like the Hindu villagers in Jammu during India's Kashmir campaign—than to others—like the Muslim renegades in the Kashmir Valley. Those who were willing to forgo immediate benefits, such as protection or patronage, in favor of ideology or identity required cultivation. The state had to draw on existing socio-ideological links, or build new ones, with them. As the six months and the effort it took for the Pakistani army to bring the Islamists into the counterinsurgency in 1971 demonstrate, this can be time-consuming and costly. But, activists were also very valuable when the state was losing, as they were willing to take big risks in assisting their ally. While, with India's support, the Bengali rebels were reclaiming East Pakistan/Bangladesh, the Islamist activists formed death squads that eliminated the prospective future intellectual leaders of Bangladesh.

Opportunists, on the other hand, allied with the state so long as the risks of doing so were low and the benefits of the alliance outweighed the costs. This was when the local balance of power favored the state (i.e., when the state was winning) or when it was roughly equal (i.e., when the state was likely to win, especially with their assistance). State-nonstate alliances formed in the latter scenario but not in the former because, in the former, the state had little need for proxies. It was already succeeding without them.

State interests also sometimes varied. In the East Pakistan/Bangladesh and Kashmir cases, the state was interested, first and foremost, in reasserting its sovereignty over the rebellious region. But, as chapter 6 shows, this is not always the case. It was not the case for the government in central India in the 1990s and in Pakistan's northwest in 2001–2016. New Delhi became very interested in the Naxalite-controlled tribal areas when private companies developed plans to exploit their mineral deposits. For Islamabad, the slow realization that what happened in the tribal areas could actually destroy the entire country may have made the difference, though that remains to be seen.

When the state is not interested in (re-)claiming the rebel-controlled territory, a robust state-nonstate alliance cannot form. This is why the *Salwa Judum* congealed in the central Indian state of Chhattisgarh in the early 2000s and not in the 1990s, despite the earlier grassroots efforts to resist the rebels. And, it is why, despite having a reputation for indiscriminately outsourcing violence, the Pakistani army offered so little support to the lashkars of the tribal northwest.

The cases of Turkey and Russia tell a remarkably similar story. When, in the mid-1980s, the Kurdish rebels came to dominate the Kurdish countryside, the Turkish army allied with activists—nationalist (pro-Turkish) clans who were ideologically at odds with the separatists. They helped tilt the local power balance in favor of the state, which facilitated the enrollment of opportunists—those who joined the counterinsurgency for money and security. The opportunists helped shift the power balance in the Kurdish countryside further in favor of the state. But, as in the case of India's operations in Kashmir, Turkey's recapture of the rebellious areas resulted in rebel relocation. The separatists moved to urban areas. There, the Turkish army turned to Islamists for assistance. By the late 1990s, these activist proxies helped shift the balance of power in the region decisively in favor of the Turkish state. The proxy policy was then abandoned.

It was not until the Russian army achieved parity with the Chechen rebels that the likes of Bislan Gantamirov and Akhmad Kadyrov opportunistically joined the Russian side. The former—a convicted criminal—helped Moscow to take back the capital city of Grozny. The latter—a rebel leader—helped the Russian army to recapture much of the rest of the region.

As did the fates of Motiur Rahman Nizami in Bangladesh, Kuka Parrey in Kashmir, Abdul Malik in Khyber Pakhtunkhwa, and Mahendra Karma in Chhattisgarh, the fates of Gantamirov and Kadyrov demonstrate the serious risks nonstate actors take when allying with the state. Moscow abandoned Gantamirov after using him, reneging on its promise to let him lead Chechnya once victory had been achieved. Kadyrov was assassinated.

The risks states take in outsourcing violence may be separated into three types: tactical, strategic, and societal. The tactical risks stem from the principal-agent problem underlying state-proxy relations on the ground. Proxies may act against state interests by supplying information to the rebels or intentionally misidentifying the target. Proxy misadventures often stoke resentment and even militancy within the local population. This may compel outsiders, as was the case with India in 1971, to get involved in the conflict. The strategic risks of violence outsourcing include loss of prestige and condemnation at regional and international levels. This is how Pakistan came to be viewed as "the world's largest assembly line of terrorists."[7] Societal risks include human rights abuses and politically destabilizing controversies over who played what role in the conflict. This is why India's Supreme Court described the Salwa Judum as a practice that "could divide and destroy society."[8]

POLICY RECOMMENDATIONS

Formulating policy prescriptions based on research of a security problem requires considering three important issues. The first is that of audience. *To whom* are the recommendations being made? Who is meant to be listening and taking action? US researchers typically target the US security establishment. The targeted audience may also be the governments of the countries from which the study draws its data. But what does it mean to offer policy recommendations to the very entities that carry out or turn a blind eye to the illicit and abusive activities under investigation?

Researchers sometimes instead aim advice to the "international community." But how can countries effectively unite to challenge a practice that is ubiquitous among the world's most powerful states? National and international nongovernmental organizations, such as Human Rights Watch, may perhaps be the answer. But these organizations are usually well aware of the problem and are the ones trying to make it public. Yet, the problem persists.

What about the public? A scholar could target her policy recommendations toward the constituents of the culpable state or of a state powerful enough to influence it. Yet, the collective action problem plaguing the international community is no less acute for the general public, assuming it could be convinced to care about the issue.

Another consideration is *for whom* the recommendations are made. Is it for the security apparatus to more effectively carry out its counterinsurgency operations? Is it for the victimized civilian population? Or, could it be for the nonstate counterinsurgents, many of whom are, technically, prisoners of war? What is good for the goose is not, in this case, necessarily good for the gander: what benefits the military does not automatically benefit the civilian population or the prisoners of war.

With all this in mind, it is useful to reflect on why this book endeavors to provide policy recommendations in the first place. Its goal is not to advise states on how to make violence outsourcing less costly and more efficient. It is not to speculate about what it would take to make their nonstate allies behave better. The objective is to understand the conditions under which states stop instrumentalizing civilians in violent conflicts. Not all is fair in love and war. Violence outsourcing violates international humanitarian law. It is not just risky. It is unethical and unlawful.

This section first addresses the military commanders, especially those serving the world's most powerful armed forces, the misbehavior of which is particularly disturbing and harmful. The target audience includes the so-called strategic corporals. These individuals are the ones whose judgment and behavior ultimately make the difference between a state outsourcing violence or not. As the highly influential US counterinsurgency field manual puts it, these "young leaders"

> often make decisions at the tactical level that have strategic consequences. Senior leaders set the proper direction and climate with thorough training and clear guidance; then they trust their subordinates to do the right thing. Preparation for tactical-level leaders requires more than just mastering Service doctrine; they must also be trained and educated to adapt to their local situations, understand the legal and ethical implications of their actions, and exercise initiative and sound judgment in accordance with their senior commanders' intent.[9]

My recommendation to military commanders is to act professionally. Samuel Huntington reminds us that what "distinguishes the military officer of today from the warriors of previous ages" is professionalism.[10] Professionalism not only entails a specific type of expertise, or specialized knowledge and skills, but also a set of responsibilities. Modern military officers are guided by "certain values and ideals" in their dealings with others.[11] Among their professional responsibilities is the protection of civilians and humane treatment of prisoners of war.[12] To treat either as cheap weapons or cannon fodder violates the values and ideals of the modern officer corps.

What if the state cannot win without nonstate allies? In all of the cases examined in this book, nonstate allies gave states, at best, a tactical advantage, not outright victory. The case of the 1971 war in East Pakistan/Bangladesh shows that nonstate allies do not necessarily help states win. Cases in which militias served as the necessary condition for military victory—in Kashmir, Chhattisgarh, Chechnya, and Turkish Kurdistan—are hardly poster children of peace. In these regions life is very far from back to normal. Kashmir, Sameer Lalwani observed in 2016, "looks worryingly similar to the Kashmir of the 1980s, just before the region erupted into a bloody insurgency."[13] The conflict in Chhattisgarh has "intensified."[14] Chechnya's leader, Ramzan Kadyrov, the son of the slain former rebel-turned-Russian ally, "commands the full obedience of Chechnya's citizens thanks to widespread violations of rights and a climate of fear around the republic's powerful security services."[15] A recent confrontation between the Turkish government and the PKK has claimed thousands of lives.[16]

In sum, the victories states achieved with the help of nonstate allies were either ephemeral or incomplete. They may have given states territorial control but not legitimacy or peace. It may be that peace sometimes requires compromise, not destroying the enemy at any cost. The Colombian government's negotiations with the rebel Revolutionary Armed Forces of Colombia (FARC), which resulted in a peace deal in 2016 and demobilization of the FARC,[17] is an instructive example. Though, even in Colombia, it may prove that sustainable peace requires not just compromising with the most powerful rebel group but also making changes to the structural conditions that engendered the uprising in the first place.

The next target audience is security scholars. Sometimes we find ourselves crafting policy advice with the implicit goal of helping powerful governments better fight wars that are difficult, if not impossible, to justify and win. Offering recommendations about tactics and strategies can also be highly problematic. For example, to advise states how they can more effectively recruit and use militias comprising civilians or former combatants would be to condone violation of international humanitarian law. A renaissance in security scholarship is occurring in the backdrop of the global war on terrorism. Much of the policy advice it offers would, if effective, help powerful states remain powerful, notwithstanding how that power is wielded. Rather than taking a stand against a given policy that involves violence, our recommendations sometimes inadvertently advise how the violence can be carried out more effectively and at a lower cost. The human cost is too often conceived solely in terms of the lives of the citizens of the powerful states.

Challenging the status quo has not traditionally been one of the main goals of political science. The discipline unabashedly traces its intellectual origins to a self-appointed adviser to a prince. But the persistence of uprisings that we are so desperately trying to end once and for all shows that, while life in the twenty-first century may be good for some, it is not good for many.

This does not mean that we should not offer advice to policy practitioners. In fact, for those of us who do policy-relevant work, doing so may be our best bet for having any "real-world" influence. It does mean not crafting our research specifically to address the kinds of questions we think the policy practitioners, especially those of powerful states, want us to answer. It means crafting our research to address the underlying problems that led to those questions in the first place. And sometimes these fundamentally stem not from the defiant nonstate actors, but from how states exercise their monopoly on "legitimate" violence. Not all "security" policies result in actual security.

DIRECTIONS FOR FUTURE RESEARCH

This book calls attention to three problems that have so far received insufficient attention in civil war research but bear important theoretical and policy implications. The first concerns actors' motivations. The second is analyzing covert and illicit state behavior. The third is the problem identified by Clausewitz in the chapter's epigraph. It is the problem of chance, and it makes every war a gamble.

The existing civil war literature typically treats actors' motivations as constant or inconsequential. Ironically, it is the popular "micro-level" scholarship that especially black-boxes the micro, or individual, level of analysis.[18] In his pathbreaking *The Logic of Violence in Civil War*, Stathis Kalyvas cautions that "motives are typically subject to (strategic or unselfconscious) reinterpretation and ex post rationalization by the subjects. Even when fully revealed, intentions often turn out to be mixed or even contradictory."[19]

The dominant large-N scholarship on political violence is not well-equipped for studying changes and hierarchies in actors' motivations. Doing so requires carrying out fine-grained qualitative research.[20] It requires building relationships through prolonged and recurring contact with subjects.[21] This is difficult for any research conducted in conflict settings. Attempts to get inside the minds of violent actors have at times fallen victim to "theoretical speculation based on subjective interpretation of anecdotal observations."[22] A popular research program—on "ethnic war"—may have gravely misinterpreted the main motivations of its subjects. In an in-depth analysis of the violence that took place in the former Yugoslavia and Rwanda in the 1990s, John Mueller shows that the main perpetrators were not driven by ethnic hatred. They were, in effect, "opportunistic, sadistic, and often distinctly nonideological marauders" who were "recruited and permitted free rein by political authorities."[23]

The motivations we attribute to violent actors carry serious policy implications. For example, seeing perpetrators of genocidal violence as driven primarily by ethnic hatred may "discourage policing because it implies that the entire ethnic group—rather than just a small, opportunistic, and often cowardly subgroup—must be brought under control."[24] But, if Mueller is correct, the international community could help prevent another Yugoslavia or Rwanda type of conflict by assisting countries in making their police forces more coherent and unbiased.

Motivations matter, and accurately measuring them requires fine-grained studies of actors' beliefs and behaviors across time. More research is needed to understand why and when actors prioritize some interests over others. Activists who forgo material rewards and even safety for a long-term vision are particularly intriguing. They defy our expectations of "rational," or purely structurally determined, behavior. How are activists made and unmade? What causes opportunists to transform into activists and activists into opportunists?

This book shows that disaggregating actors by their motivations provides a better understanding of alliance patterns. For example, separating activists into moderates and extremists may, as the recent work of Barbara F. Walter suggests,[25] prove productive. The empirical implications of such research are evidenced by the failed US partnership with "moderate" Syrian rebels against the regime of Bashar al-Assad.[26]

The second problem this book draws attention to is the need to study more closely, systematically, and cross-nationally covert and illicit state behavior. This type of work has been limited for the same reason research on motivations has been scarce—it is difficult to do. Theories of state behavior at both the international and national levels overwhelmingly rely on observable conduct. Meanwhile, a vast repertoire of unconventional and unlawful behaviors—from assassinations to regime change attempts—lies hidden and underexplored. The study of covert behavior is particularly important because powerful states are increasingly using special operations forces to carry out military tasks.[27] Important systematic work is emerging on the covert behavior of the United States.[28] Cross-national studies are needed if our theories are to travel to the less powerful but still highly active states. Such research would enhance theories of international security and counterinsurgency. By giving scholars a more complete picture of state conduct, it would also deepen their policy perspectives.

Finally, there is the problem of chance. In *War and Peace*, Leo Tolstoy (a former artillery officer) reflects on the relationship between agency, structure, and chance in one of the most historically consequential campaigns—Napoleon's invasion of Russia:

> [A]ll of the countless persons who participated in this war acted . . . as a result of their personal qualities, habits, conditions, and aims. They feared, boasted, rejoiced, resented, supposing that they knew what they were doing and that they were doing it for themselves, and yet they were all involuntary instruments of history, and performed work hidden from them but comprehensible to us. Such is the inevitable fate of all men of action, and the higher they stand in the human hierarchy, the less free they are . . . The facts say the obvious thing, that Napoleon did not foresee the danger of moving on Moscow, nor did Alexander and the Russian commanders think then about luring Napoleon, but both thought the opposite. The drawing of Napoleon into the depths of the country occurred not according to someone's plan (no one even believed in such a possibility), but occurred as a result of the most complex interplay of intrigues,

aims, and desires of the people participating in war, who did not perceive what was to happen and what would be the only salvation of Russia. It all occurs by chance.[29]

Chance generates "friction"—the accidents and unanticipated complications (e.g., fog) occurring during conflict. Friction can reduce, intensify, or altogether thwart the influence of our explanatory factors. It can also be a cause in itself. Despite, as Clausewitz reminds us, chance being present in every war, social scientists are particularly poor at recognizing and accounting for its significance. This is because treating friction as a cause, not just a residual, complicates our "scientific" inquiry. It also requires deep knowledge of and close attention to the context in which the conflict takes place. War is not one domino knocking over the next in neat succession. Better methodological and analytical tools are needed to help us understand how friction interacts with and transforms the context in which it occurs.

IMPLICATIONS FOR SOUTH ASIAN SECURITY

The in-depth case studies of Pakistan's and India's civil-wartime alliances with nonstate actors challenge three powerful narratives. The first is that Pakistan is uniquely and pathologically addicted to outsourcing violence. The second is that democratic India represents a model great power. Third, the book challenges the notion that, if they just devote enough resources, powerful countries like the United States can carry out successful counterinsurgency operations on foreign soil, in places like Afghanistan, with limited backlash or unintended consequences. It also casts doubt on the effectiveness with which Pakistan and India can use proxies against each other.

The first narrative the book challenges is that which deems Pakistan an "abnormal state" for outsourcing violence to armed nonstate actors.[30] What the book shows is that violence outsourcing is a common practice not just for Pakistan. That India uses it less than Pakistan as a foreign policy tool is a product of its conventional military superiority rather than moral ascendancy. When it came to counterinsurgency, the same logic applied to state-nonstate alliances in both countries.

Indian officials are understandably concerned about Pakistan's relations with anti-India militant organizations such as Lashkar-e-Taiba. But, naming and shaming Pakistan without taking responsibility for its own misconduct in Kashmir and Chhattisgarh—or Punjab, Andhra Pradesh, and Assam, or Pakistan's Balochistan province[31] and Sri Lanka[32]—will not help India make violence outsourcing taboo, which is what eliminating the practice likely requires.[33]

India aspires to great power status.[34] Its commitment to democratic values makes it a particularly sympathetic great-power aspirant, as opposed to China or Russia. India being "the world's largest democracy" makes it a strong candidate for permanent membership in the United Nations Security Council.[35]

But the mechanisms by which India's coercive apparatus pursues security in its "frontiers" and "ghettos" have been deeply problematic.[36] They often reflect a continuation of the institutional mechanisms by which the British Empire ruled India.[37] These mechanisms engender grave human rights abuses. For example, the policy of rewarding officers who arrest or kill suspected rebels in Kashmir has led to ordinary civilians being encouraged by the security forces to join rebel groups so that they could then be turned in or killed to receive rewards.[38] This system of material rewards inevitably attracts opportunists who prioritize personal enrichment over professionalism and basic humanity.

India's achievement of great power status hinges not only on its "soft" or "hard" power but also on its ability to resolve its internal conflicts. The persistence of the Maoist insurgency and the conflict in Kashmir suggest that the existing measures, including the outsourcing of violence, are failing. The willingness and ability of the Indian government to address the underlying social, economic, and political conditions that engender unrest will not just help India become a great power. It will also show what it means to be a great power in the twenty-first century.

Finally, this book reveals the degree to which indigenous military establishments use knowledge, linkages, and political acumen to forge the kinds of relationships necessary to manipulate subnational violent competition. No matter how "strong" it may be, it seems unlikely that a foreign army, diplomatic corps, or intelligence apparatus could comprehend, let alone manipulate, another country's politics well enough to play this game effectively.

NOTES

CHAPTER 1

1. Mark Bowden, "The Killing Machines: How to Think about Drones," *The Atlantic*, September 2013, 60.
2. National Commission on Terrorist Attacks Upon the United States, *The 9/11 Commission Report* (New York: W.W. Norton, 2004), 132–33.
3. Nonstate actors operating in such environments are expected to prioritize immediate payoffs. See Lee J. M. Seymour, "Why Factions Switch Sides in Civil Wars: Rivalry, Patronage, and Realignment in Sudan," *International Security* 39, no. 2 (Fall 2014), 94.
4. Belgin San-Akca, *States in Disguise: Causes of State Support for Rebel Groups* (New York: Oxford University Press, 2016); Daniel Byman, *Deadly Connections: States that Sponsor Terrorism* (Cambridge: Cambridge University Press, 2005).
5. Carl von Clausewitz, *On War*, trans. and ed. Michael Howard and Peter Paret (Princeton: Princeton University Press, 1976), 85.
6. Niccolò Machiavelli, *The Prince*, ed. and trans. Peter Bondanella (Oxford: Oxford University Press, 2005), 43 and 54.
7. Adam Smith, *An Inquiry into the Nature and Causes of the Wealth of Nations* (Edinburgh: Thomas Nelson, 1843), 292.
8. George Washington, "Letter, George Washington to the President of Congress," September 24, 1776, American Archives, http://amarch.lib.niu.edu/islandora/object/niu-amarch%3A84896; Leon Trotsky, *How the Revolution Armed: The Military Writings and Speeches of Leon Trotsky*, vol. 2 (London: New Park, 1979).
9. Yelena Biberman, Farhan Zahid, and Philip Hultquist, "Bridging the Gap between Policing and Counterinsurgency in Pakistan," *Military Review* (November–December 2016), 37–43.
10. Supreme Court of India, *Nandini Sundar & Org. versus State of Chhattisgarh Order*, July 5, 2011, 18.
11. They are China (Xinjiang), Russia (North Caucasus), India (Northeast), Pakistan (Northwest and Balochistan), Turkey (Southeast), Syria (Civil War), Eritrea (Southeast Red Sea Coast), Iran (Sistan and Baluchestan), Egypt (North Sinai), Israel (West Bank), and Ukraine (Donbass). Of the world's fifteen militarily

strongest states that did not experience an insurgency inside their borders were the United States, South Korea, Saudi Arabia, and Vietnam. Military strength is assessed using a comparative scale. States are ranked based on their prioritization of resources for military use and the size of their militaries (data source: World Bank). The percentage of GDP committed to military spending was multiplied by the number of military personnel, and the resultant figure was converted to a 1–100 scale to facilitate comparison.

12. "Pro-government militias" are defined as groups that (1) are identified by media sources as pro-government or sponsored by the government (national or subnational); (2) are identified as not being part of the regular security forces; (3) are armed; and (4) have some level of organization. Sabine C. Carey, Neil J. Mitchell, and Will Lowe, "States, the Security Sector, and the Monopoly of Violence: A New Database on Pro-Government Militias," *Journal of Peace Research* 50, no. 2 (March 2013), 250.

13. Ibid., 253.

14. Pakistan is a case in point. "Snake Country," *Economist*, October 1, 2011.

15. Sumit Ganguly and S. Paul Kapur, "The Sorcerer's Apprentice: Islamist Militancy in South Asia," *Washington Quarterly* 33, no. 1 (January 2010), 47–59.

16. Kimberly Marten, "The Danger of Tribal Militias in Afghanistan: Learning from the British Empire," *Journal of International Affairs* 63, no. 1 (Fall–Winter 2009), 157–74.

17. Ahsan I. Butt, *Secession and Security: Explaining State Strategy against Separatists* (Ithaca: Cornell University Press, 2017), 59–63.

18. Amnesty International, "Guatemala: The Civil Defence Patrols Re-emerge," 2002, http://www.unhcr.org/refworld/docid/3d99cd394.html.

19. Regina Bateson, "How Local Institutions Emerge from Civil War," Working Paper, Massachusetts Institute of Technology (October 2, 2015), 4.

20. Human Rights Watch, " 'Just Don't Call It a Militia': Impunity, Militias, and the 'Afghan Local Police,' " September 2011, 3.

21. US Department of the Army, *Counterinsurgency*, Field Manual 3-24, December 2006 (Washington, DC), 3–1.

22. Corinna Jentzsch, Stathis N. Kalyvas, and Livia Isabella Schubiger, "Militias in Civil Wars," *Journal of Conflict Resolution* 59, no. 5 (August 2015), 755–69; Kristine Eck, "Repression by Proxy: How Military Purges and Insurgency Impact the Delegation of Coercion," *Journal of Conflict Resolution* 59, no. 5 (August 2015), 924–46; Tomáš Šmíd and Miroslav Mareš, " 'Kadyrovtsy': Russia's Counterinsurgency Strategy and the Wars of Paramilitary Clans," *Journal of Strategic Studies* 38, no. 5 (2015), 674; Jason Lyall, "Are Coethnics More Effective Counterinsurgents? Evidence from the Second Chechen War," *American Political Science Review* 104, no. 1 (February 2010), 1–20; Sunil Dasgupta, "Paramilitary Groups: Local Alliances in Counterinsurgency Operations," *Brookings Counterinsurgency and Pakistan Paper Series* 6 (June 2009); Stathis N. Kalyvas, *The Logic of Violence in Civil War* (New York: Cambridge University Press 2006), 109.

23. Mark Mazzetti, "C.I.A. Study of Covert Aid Fueled Skepticism About Helping Syrian Rebels," *New York Times*, October 14, 2014.

24. International Committee of the Red Cross, "Protocols I and II Additional to the Geneva Conventions" (Geneva: January 1, 2009).

25. Charu Sudan Kasturi, "Unease at Terror-for-Terror Slip," *The Telegraph*, May 26, 2015, http://www.telegraphindia.com/1150526/jsp/nation/story_22196.jsp#. VXr9-0aN0QQ.

26. Author's interviews with security experts, New Delhi, October 2011.

27. Sadiq Ahmed, Saman Kelegama, and Ejaz Ghani (World Bank), *Promoting Economic Cooperation in South Asia* (New Delhi: Sage, 2010), 3–27.

28. Vipin Narang, "Posturing for Peace? Pakistan's Nuclear Postures and South Asian Stability," *International Security* 34, no. 3 (Winter 2009/10), 38–78; Sumit Ganguly, "Nuclear Stability in South Asia," *International Security* 33, no. 2 (Fall 2008), 45–70; S. Paul Kapur, "Ten Years of Instability in a Nuclear South Asia," *International Security* 33, no. 2 (Fall 2008), 71–94.

29. Among the prominent writings in this vast literature are Max Weber, "Politics as a Vocation," in eds. H. H. Garth and C. Wright Mills, *Essays in Sociology* (New York: Macmillian, 1946), 26-45; Charles Tilly, "War Making and State Making as Organized Crime," in eds. Peter B. Evans, Dietrich Rueschemeyer, and Theda Skocpol, *Bringing the State Back In* (Cambridge: Cambridge University Press, 1985), 169-191; Michael Mann, *States, War and Capitalism: Studies in Political Sociology* (Oxford: Basil Blackwell, 1988); Charles Tilly, *Coercion, Capital, and European States, AD 990–1990* (Cambridge: Basil Blackwell, 1990); Hendrik Spruyt, "The Origins, Development, and Possible Decline of the Modern State," *Annual Review of Political Science* 5 (2002), 127–49.

30. Max Weber, "The Bureaucratization of the Army by the State and by Private Capitalism," in eds. H.H. Garth and C. Wright Mills, *Economy and Society*, vol. 2 (Berkeley: University of California Press, 1978), 981.

31. Ahmed Rashid, *Pakistan on the Brink: The Future of America, Pakistan, and Afghanistan* (New York: Penguin Books, 2013), 27.

32. C. Christine Fair, *Fighting to the End: The Pakistan Army's Way of War* (Oxford: Oxford University Press, 2014), 5. Also, see Sumit Ganguly, *Deadly Impasse: Indo-Pakistani Relations at the Dawn of a New Century* (Cambridge: Cambridge University Press, 2016).

33. Robert I. Rotberg, "Failed States, Collapsed States, Weak States: Causes and Indicators," in ed. Robert I. Rotberg, *State Failure and State Weakness in a Time of Terror* (Cambridge, MA: World Peace Foundation, 2003); James D. Fearon and David D. Laitin, "Ethnicity, Insurgency, and Civil War," *American Political Science Review* 97, no. 1 (February 2003), 75–90; William I. Zartman, *Collapsed States: The Disintegration and Restoration of Legitimate Authority* (London: Lynne Rienner, 1995).

34. Miguel Centeno, "Limited War and Limited States," in eds. Diane E. Davis and Anthony W. Pereira, *Irregular Armed Forces and Their Role in Politics and State Formation* (Cambridge: Cambridge University Press, 2003), 82-95.

35. Ariel I. Ahram, *Proxy Warriors: The Rise and Fall of State-Sponsored Militias* (Stanford: Stanford University Press, 2011).

36. John Stevens, "The Stevens Inquiry: Overview and Recommendations," Metropolitan Police Service, United Kingdom, BBC, April 17, 2003, http://news. bbc.co.uk/2/shared/spl/hi/northern_ireland/03/stephens_inquiry/html/.

37. "Unrest Catches China's Police by Surprise," *Financial Times*, February 6, 2012, 3.

38. For an overview of the state's illicit practices in the global economy, see Peter Andreas, "Illicit Globalization: Myths, Misconceptions, and Historical Lessons," *Political Science Quarterly* 126, no. 3 (Fall 2011), 406–25. For the role of illicit economic activity in state formation, see Peter Andreas, *Smuggler Nation: How Illicit Trade Made America* (Oxford: Oxford University Press, 2013).

39. Thomas S. Wilkins, "'*Alignment,*' Not '*Alliance*'—the Shifting Paradigm of International Security Cooperation: Toward a Conceptual Taxonomy of Alignment," *Review of International Studies* 38 (2012), 54.

40. Among the prominent writings in this vast literature are Steven R. David, "Explaining Third World Alignment," *World Politics* 43, no. 2 (January 1991), 233–56; Thomas J. Christensen and Jack Snyder, "Chain Gangs and Passed Bucks: Predicting Alliance Patterns in Multipolarity," *International Organization* 44, no. 2 (Spring 1990), 137–68; Walt, *The Origins of Alliances*; Kenneth N. Waltz, *Theory of International Politics* (Reading, MA: Addison-Wesley, 1979).

41. Randall L. Schweller, "Bandwagoning for Profit: Bringing the Revisionist State Back In," *International Security* 19, no. 1 (Summer 1994), 103–4.

42. Fotini Christia, *Alliance Formation in Civil Wars* (Cambridge: Cambridge University Press, 2012), 239. Similarly, Posen uses basic neorealist assumptions to explain the behavior of ethnic groups when states break down. Barry R. Posen, "The Security Dilemma and Ethnic Conflict," *Survival* 35, no. 1 (Spring 1993), 27–47.

43. Posen, "The Security Dilemma."

44. Kalyvas, *The Logic of Violence in Civil War*; Ana Arjona, Nelson Kasfir, and Zachariah Mampilly, *Rebel Governance in Civil War* (New York: Cambridge University Press, 2015).

45. For example, Lyall shows that Russia's use of Chechen nonstate counterinsurgents reduced insurgent violence in Chechnya. Jason Lyall, "Are Coethnics More Effective Counterinsurgents? Evidence from the Second Chechen War," *American Political Science Review* 104, no. 1 (February 2010), 1–20.

46. Jeremy M. Weinstein, "Resources and the Information Problem in Rebel Recruitment," *Journal of Conflict Resolution* 49, no. 4 (August 2005), 599–600.

47. Ibid., 599.

48. Lee J. M. Seymour, "Why Factions Switch Sides in Civil Wars: Rivalry, Patronage, and Realignment in Sudan," *International Security* 39, no. 2 (Fall 2014), 94.

49. Matt Zapotosky, "American ISIS Fighter Captured by Kurds: 'I Found It Hard,'" *Washington Post*, March 18, 2016, https://www.washingtonpost.com/world/ national-security/virginia-man-captured-by-kurds-claims-in-video-he-escaped-islamic-state/2016/03/17/c151ed70-ec88-11e5-a6f3-21ccdbc5f74e_story.html.

50. Jentzsch, Kalyvas, and Schubiger, "Militias in Civil Wars," 756.

51. Ariel I. Ahram, *Proxy Warriors: The Rise and Fall of State-Sponsored Militias* (Stanford: Stanford University Press, 2011); Janet Klein, *The Margins of Empire: Kurdish Militias in the Ottoman Tribal Zone* (Stanford: Stanford University

Press, 2011); Bruce B.Campbell and Arthur D. Brenner, *Death Squads in Global Perspective: Murder with Deniability* (New York: Pelgrave Macmillan, 2002); Janice E. Thomson, *Mercenaries, Pirates, and Sovereigns: State-Building and Extraterritorial Violence in Early Modern Europe* (Princeton: Princeton University Press, 1994).

52. Neil J. Mitchell, Sabine C. Carey, and Christopher K. Butler, "The Impact of Pro-Government Militias on Human Rights Violations," *International Interactions* 40, no. 5 (2014): 812-36.

53. Corinna Jentzsch, "Auxiliary Armed Forces and Innovations in Security Governance in Mozambique's Civil War," *Civil Wars* 19, no. 3 (2017): 325-47; Goran Peic, "Civilian Defense Forces, State Capability, and Government Victory in Counterinsurgency Wars," *Studies in Conflict and Terrorism* 37, no. 2 (January 2014): 162-84; Stephen Biddle, Jeffrey A. Friedman, and Jacob N. Shapiro, "Testing the Surge: Why Did Violence Decline in Iraq in 2007?" *International Security* 37, no. 1 (Summer 2012): 7-40.

54. Staniland's study of the role of ideology in state-militia relations shows how ideology influences the state's choice of nonstate partner, but surprisingly neglects to consider whether and, if so, how ideology matters to the nonstate actors themselves. Paul Staniland, "Militias, Ideology, and the State," *Journal of Conflict Resolution* 59, no. 5 (August 2015), 770–93.

55. Ibid.

56. Paul Staniland, "Between a Rock and a Hard Place: Insurgent Fratricide, Ethnic Defection, and the Rise of Pro-State Paramilitaries," *Journal of Conflict Resolution* 56, no. 1 (February 2012), 16–40.

57. The term *opportunist* is not used as a pejorative label. It applies to individuals who seek to improve their material lot or avoid harm. Opportunists prioritize immediate concerns. Activists prioritize farsighted preferences.

CHAPTER 2

1. Kautilya, *The Arthashastra*, trans. and ed. L. N. Rangarajan (New Delhi: Penguin Books, 1992), 568.

2. Ibid., 521.

3. Alan Zuckerman, "Political Cleavage: A Conceptual and Theoretical Analysis," *British Journal of Political Science* 5, no. 2 (April 1975), 231.

4. Gary Goertz, *Social Science Concepts: A User's Guide* (Princeton: Princeton University Press, 2006), 5.

5. Michael Mann, "The Autonomous Power of the State: Its Origins, Mechanisms, and Results," in ed. John A. Hall, *States in History* (Oxford: Blackwell, 1986), 112.

6. Theda Skocpol, *States and Social Revolutions: A Comparative Analysis of France, Russia, and China* (Cambridge: Cambridge University Press, 1979), 29–30.

7. Joel S. Migdal, *State in Society: Studying How States and Societies Transform and Constitute One Another* (Cambridge: Cambridge University Press, 2001).

8. With the possible (and problematic) exception of private military contractors. See P. W. Singer, *Corporate Warriors: The Rise of the Privatized Military Industry* (Ithaca: Cornell University Press, 2007), 8–18.

9. Glenn H. Snyder, *Alliance Politics* (Ithaca: Cornell University Press, 1997), 6.

10. Kautilya, *The Arthashastra*, 569–70.

11. Stephen W. Walt, *The Origins of Alliances* (Ithaca: Cornell University Press, 1987), 1, fn. 1.

12. Sabine C. Carey, Neil J. Mitchell, and Will Lowe, "States, the Security Sector, and the Monopoly of Violence: A New Database on Pro-Government Militias," *Journal of Peace Research* 50, no. 2 (March 2013), 250–51.

13. Robert J. McCartney, "El Salvador Transfers Death Squad Suspects," *Washington Post*, November 30, 1983.

14. Corinna Jentzsch, Stathis N. Kalyvas, and Livia Isabella Schubiger, "Militias in Civil Wars," *Journal of Conflict Resolution* 59, no. 5 (August 2015), 756.

15. Ibid.

16. For example, see Sumit Ganguly and S. Paul Kapur, "The Sorcerer's Apprentice: Islamist Militancy in South Asia," *Washington Quarterly* 33, no. 1 (January 2010), 53.

17. Reservists and veterans, who are civilians with military experience, do not fall under the nonstate actor category because they are formally associated with the state's military institutions through regular compensation and, in the case of the reservists, expectation of service.

18. Theda Skocpol, "Bringing the State Back In: Strategies of Analysis in Current Research," in eds. Peter B. Evans, Dietrich Rueschemeyer, and Theda Skocpol, *Bringing the State Back In* (Cambridge: Cambridge University Press, 1985), 15.

19. US Department of the Army, *Operational Terms and Graphics*, Field Manual 1-02, 2010 (Washington, DC), 1–105.

20. "Unnecessary Killing in West Bank," *Haaretz*, May 6, 2012, http://www.haaretz.com/opinion/unnecessary-killing-in-west-bank-1.428439.

21. Samuel P. Huntington, *The Soldier and the State: The Theory and Politics of Civil-Military Relations* (Cambridge: Belknap Press, 1957), 10.

22. Yelena Biberman, "Self-Defense Militias, Death Squads, and State Outsourcing of Violence in India and Turkey," *Journal of Strategic Studies* 41, no. 5 (2018): 751-81.

23. For example, see Ali Seraj, "The Arbaki Can Secure Afghanistan Better Than the US," *Al Jazeera*, November 5, 2014.

24. I use the term "nonstate" heuristically while remaining cognizant of this fact.

25. Arnold van Gennep, *The Rites of Passage*, trans. Manika B. Vizedom and Gabrielle L. Caffee (Chicago: University of Chicago Press, 1960), 11.

26. Thomas Barfield, *The Dictionary of Anthropology* (Oxford: Blackwell, 1997), 288.

27. Carl Schmitt, *Theory of the Partisan: Intermediate Commentary on the Concept of the Political* (New York: Telos, 2007), 10.

28. I thank Erica De Bruin for drawing my attention to this distinction. US Department of the Army, *Operations*, Field Manual 3-0, February 2008 (Washington, DC).

29. I include assistance with logistics in administrative collaboration. For more on the importance of logistics in war, see Martin van Creveld, *Supplying War: Logistics from Wallenstein to Patton* (New York: Cambridge University Press, 2004).

30. Carl von Clausewitz, *On War*, trans. and ed. Michael Howard and Peter Paret (Princeton: Princeton University Press, 1976), 95.

31. For example, see K. P. S. Gill, "Endgame in Punjab: 1988–93," in eds. K. P. S. Gill and Ajai Sahni, *Terror and Containment Perspectives of India's Internal Security* (New Delhi: Gyan, 2001).

32. For example, see "A Spectre Haunting India," *The Economist*, August 17, 2006, http://www.economist.com/node/7799247.

33. For example, see Ali Akbar, "Five Peace Committee Members Shot Dead in Khyber Agency," *Dawn*, September 7, 2015, http://www.dawn.com/news/1205468.

34. For usefulness of ideal types, see Max Weber, "Definitions of Sociology and of Social Action," in eds. H. H. Garth and C. Wright Mills, *Economy and Society*, vol. 2 (Berkeley: University of California Press, 1978), 20–22.

35. David K. Yelton, *Hitler's Volkssturm: The Nazi Militia and the Fall of Germany, 1944–1945* (Lawrence: University Press of Kansas, 2002), 8.

36. Guangqiu Xu, "Militia," in ed. Xiaobing Li, *China at War: An Encyclopedia* (Santa Barbara: ABC-CLIO, 2012), 276.

37. Elizabeth J. Perry, *Patrolling the Revolution: Worker Militias, Citizenship, and the Modern Chinese State* (Lanham: Rowman and Littlefield, 2006), 18.

38. Ibid., 324.

39. Xu, "Militia," 277.

40. John Stevens, "The Stevens Inquiry: Overview and Recommendations," Metropolitan Police Service, United Kingdom, BBC, April 17, 2003, http://news.bbc.co.uk/2/shared/spl/hi/northern_ireland/03/stephens_inquiry/html/.

41. Peter Andreas, *Blue Helmets and Black Markets: The Business of Survival in the Siege of Sarajevo* (Ithaca: Cornell University Press, 2008).

42. Guillermo A. O'Donnell, "Why the Rule of Law Matters," *Journal of Democracy* 15, no. 4 (October 2004), 41.

43. Stephen Tankel, *Storming the World Stage: The Story of Lashkar-e-Taiba* (Oxford: Oxford University Press, 2014).

44. Sabine C. Carey, Michael P. Colaresi, and Neil J. Mitchell, "Governments, Informal Links to Militias, and Accountability," *Journal of Conflict Resolution* 59, no. 5 (August 2015), 850–76.

45. Dara Kay Cohen and Ragnhild Nordas, "Do States Delegate Shameful Violence to Militias? Patterns of Sexual Violence in Recent Armed Conflicts," *Journal of Conflict Resolution* 59, no. 5 (August 2015), 877–98; Jessica A. Stanton, "Regulating Militias: Governments, Militias, and Civilian Targeting in Civil War," *Journal of Conflict Resolution* 59, no. 5 (August 2015), 901.

46. Eitan Shamir and Eyal Ben-Ari, "The Rise of Special Operations Forces: Generalized Specialization, Boundary Spanning and Military Autonomy," *Journal of Strategic Studies* 41, no. 3 (2018): 335-71.

47. Paul Staniland, "Militias, Ideology, and the State," *Journal of Conflict Resolution* 59, no. 5 (August 2015), 771.

48. Ibid., 777.

49. Fotini Christia, *Alliance Formation in Civil Wars* (New York: Cambridge University Press, 2012), 6–7.

50. Lee J. M. Seymour, "Why Factions Switch Sides in Civil Wars: Rivalry, Patronage, and Realignment in Sudan," *International Security* 39, no. 2 (Fall 2014), 92–131;

Paul Staniland, "Between a Rock and a Hard Place: Insurgent Fratricide, Ethnic Defection, and the Rise of Pro-State Paramilitaries," *Journal of Conflict Resolution* 56, no. 1 (February 2012), 16–40.

51. Biberman, "Self-Defense Militias, Death Squads, and State Outsourcing of Violence in India and Turkey."

52. James C. Scott, *Weapons of the Weak: Everyday Forms of Peasant Resistance* (New Haven: Yale University Press, 1985), 29.

53. Author's interview with Quazi Sajjad Ali Zahir, Dhaka, August 2015.

54. Jeremy M. Weinstein, *Inside Rebellion: The Politics of Insurgent Violence* (New York: Cambridge University Press, 2006), 8.

55. The Crimean Tatars are a case in point. It would have been very difficult, if not outright impossible, for Russia to recruit activist proxies among the Crimean Tatars to facilitate the annexation of Crimea in 2014. This group is still nursing wounds from the forced deportation its predecessors endured in 1944.

56. John Lynn, *The Bayonets of the Republic: Motivation and Tactics in the Army of Revolutionary France, 1791–94* (Urbana: University of Illinois Press, 1984), 21.

57. Barry R. Posen, "Nationalism, the Mass Army, and Military Power," *International Security* 18, no. 2 (Fall 1993), 83.

58. Fair, *Fighting to the End.*

59. Ben Oppenheim, Abbey Steele, Juan F. Vargas, and Michael Weintraub, "True Believers, Deserters, and Traitors: Who Leaves Insurgent Groups and Why," *Journal of Conflict Resolution* 59, no. 5 (2015), 794–823.

60. Roger R. Reese, *Why Stalin's Soldiers Fought: The Red Army's Military Effectiveness in World War II* (Lawrence: University of Kansas Press, 2011), 151.

61. Dipali Mukhopadhyay, *Warlords, Strongman Governors, and the State in Afghanistan* (New York: Cambridge University Press, 2014), 2

62. Gideon Rose, "Review: Neoclassical Realism and Theories of Foreign Policies," *World Politics* 51, no. 1 (October 1998), 146–52.

63. For example, when interviewing the actors is not possible, one may interview their family members. Günes Murat Tezcür, "Ordinary People, Extraordinary Risks: Participation in an Ethnic Rebellion," *American Political Science Review* 110, no. 2 (May 2016), 251.

64. Randall L. Schweller, "Bandwagoning for Profit: Bringing the Revisionist State Back In," *International Security* 19, no. 1 (Summer 1994), 72–107.

65. Jeffrey W. Taliaferro, Steven E. Lobell, and Norrin M. Ripsman, "Introduction: Neoclassical Realism, the State, and Foreign Policy," in eds. Steven E. Lobell, Norrin M. Ripsman, and Jeffrey W. Taliaferro, *Neoclassical Realism, The State, and Foreign Policy* (Cambridge, Cambridge University Press, 2009), 7–8.

66. Kenneth N. Waltz, *Theory of International Politics* (Reading, MA: Addison-Wesley, 1979), 71–72, fn. 1.

67. Philip Hultquist, "Power Parity and Peace? The Role of Relative Power in Civil War Settlement," *Journal of Peace Research* 50, no. 5 (September 2013), 627.

68. US Department of the Army, *Counterinsurgency*, Field Manual 3-24, December 2006 (Washington, DC).

69. The microdynamics of civil war research program involves "the systematic collection of data at the subnational level and its sophisticated analysis." Stathis N. Kalyvas, "Promises and Pitfalls of an Emerging Research Program: The Microdynamics of Civil War," in eds. Stathis N. Kalyvas, Ian Shapiro, and Tarek Masoud, *Order, Conflict, and Violence* (Cambridge: Cambridge University Press, 2008), 387.

70. Christia, *Alliance Formation in Civil Wars*, 11.

71. Christopher K. Butler and Scott Gages, "Asymmetry, Parity, and (Civil) War: Can International Theories of Power Help Us Understand Civil War?" *International Interactions* 35, no. 3 (2009), 330–40.

72. Vera Nikolaevna Figner, *Memoirs of a Revolutionist* (DeKalb: Northern Illinois University Press, 1991).

73. Carlotta Gall, *The Wrong Enemy: America in Afghanistan, 2001–2014* (Boston: Houghton Mifflin Harcourt, 2014).

74. Mao Tse-tung, *On Guerrilla Warfare* (New York: Classic House Books, 2009), 41.

75. US Department of the Army, *Counterinsurgency*.

76. Kalyvas, *The Logic of Violence in Civil War*, 192.

77. Stephen Biddle, *Military Power: Explaining Victory and Defeat in Modern Battle* (Princeton: Princeton University Press, 2004), 2.

78. Mao Tse-Tung, *On the Protracted War* (Peking: Foreign Languages Press, 1954), 87.

79. Relative power in this sense should not be confused with (a) an overall assessment of power of a given side that falls outside the theater of war, or (b) a form of currency that enables its bearer to achieve any number of other ends.

80. Michael Mann, "The Autonomous Power of the State: Its Origins, Mechanisms, and Results," in ed. John A. Hall, *States in History* (Oxford: Blackwell, 1986), 113.

81. Ibid.

82. Shivaji Mukherjee, "Why Are the Longest Insurgencies Low Violence? Politician Motivations, Sons of the Soil, and Civil War Duration," *Civil Wars* 16, no. 2 (2014), 173.

83. Stathis N. Kalyvas and Laia Balcells, "International System and Technologies of Rebellion: How the End of the Cold War Shaped Internal Conflict," *American Political Science Review* 104, no. 3 (August 2010), 421.

84. Jason Lyall, "Process Tracing, Causal Inference, and Civil War," in eds. Andrew Bennett and Jeffrey Checkel, *Process Tracing: From Metaphor to Analytic Tool* (Cambridge: Cambridge University Press, 2014), 186.

85. Ibid.

86. David Collier, "Understanding Process Tracing," *PS: Political Science and Politics* 44, no. 4 (2011), 823.

87. Mukherjee, "Why Are the Longest Insurgencies Low Violence?" 173.

88. What we may see instead is the phenomenon of vigilantism, as exemplified by the *lashkars* in Pakistan in 2003–2008 and in India in the 1990s.

89. Diana Kapiszewski, Lauren Morris MacLean, and Benjamin L. Read, *Field Research in Political Science: Practices and Principles* (Cambridge: Cambridge University Press, 2015), 29.

90. Romain Malejacq and Dipali Mukhopadhyay, "The 'Tribal Politics' of Field Research: A Reflection on Power and Partiality in 21st-Century Warzones," *Perspectives on Politics* 14, no. 4 (December 2016), 1017.

91. For more on reflexivity, see Lee Ann Fujii, "Politics of the 'Field,'" *Perspectives on Politics* 14, no. 4 (December 2016), 1150–51.

92. While reflexivity had not been part of my formal training as a political scientist, it came from my preoccupation with impartiality and anything that might hinder it. It was also a legacy of my former occupation as a journalist operating in a journalism-unfriendly environment.

CHAPTER 3

1. Rabindranath Tagore, "The Communal Award" (originally the Presidential Address at a conference held in Calcutta in 1936), in ed. Sisir Kumar Das, *The English Writings of Rabindranath Tagore: A Miscellany* (New Delhi: Sahitya Akademi, 2006), 702.

2. Human Rights Watch, "Bangladesh: Charge or Release Detained Counsel," October 26, 2015, https://www.hrw.org/news/2015/10/26/bangladesh-charge-or-release-detained-counsel.

3. Author's interview with Mohammad Shishir Manir (advocate of the Supreme Court of Bangladesh and ex-secretary general of Jamaat student wing), Dhaka, August 2015.

4. Jamaat leader Ghulam Azam reportedly quoted in the *Daily Sangram* in 1971. Julfikar Ali Manik, "Focus Back On, 8 Years After," *The Daily Star*, May 12, 2009, http://www.thedailystar.net/newDesign/news-details.php?nid=87828.

5. Archer K. Blood, *The Cruel Birth of Bangladesh: Memoirs of an American Diplomat* (Dhaka: University Press Limited, 2006), 213.

6. Henry Kissinger, *White House Years* (Boston: Little, Brown, 1979), 855.

7. C. Christine Fair, *Fighting to the End: The Pakistan Army's Way of War* (Oxford: Oxford University Press, 2014).

8. Paul Staniland, "Militias, Ideology, and the State," *Journal of Conflict Resolution* 59, no. 5 (August 2015), 17.

9. Stephen Philip Cohen, *The Idea of Pakistan* (Washington, DC: Brookings Institution Press, 2004), 112.

10. Even Soviet leader Joseph Stalin can be observed using religion for political ends. For example, he made religious appeals during World War II to mobilize the Soviet citizenry against the German invasion. A popular Soviet song released in 1941 describes the struggle against Germany as "a holy war." But it would be erroneous to conclude that the Soviet establishment actually believed that religion should play a prominent role in politics.

11. Mona Kanwal Sheikh, *Guardians of God: Inside the Religious Mind of the Pakistani Taliban* (Delhi: Oxford University Press, 2016), 53–54.

12. Despite its "untiring efforts," the Jamaat-e-Islami won only four of the 151 national assembly seats it contested (all in West Pakistan) and four of the 331 provincial assembly seats. All the Islamist parties "taken together did poorly in both parts of Pakistan." Seyyed Vali Reza Nasr, *The Vanguard of the Islamic Revolution: The*

Jama'at-i Islami of Pakistan (Berkeley: University of California Press, 1994), 165–66.

13. Following the 1971 war, Pakistan's Prime Minister Zulfikar Ali Bhutto also sought to draw closer to the Arab oil countries for aid by emphasizing their common Islamic identity and bond. John L. Esposito, "Islamization: Religion and Politics in Pakistan," *The Muslim World* 72, nos. 3–4 (October 1982), 199.

14. Charge No. 16 (Death) against Motiur Rahman Nizami, Supreme Court of Bangladesh.

15. Since 1945, the average length of a civil war has been about ten years. Barbara F. Walter, "The Four Things We Know About How Civil Wars End (and What This Tells Us About Syria)," *Political Violence @ a Glance*, October 18, 2013.

16. Author's interview with Quazi Sajjad Ali Zahir (former Pakistan army officer who defected to become a Mukti Bahini commander), Dhaka, August 2015.

17. Ashutosh Sarkar, "Liberation War Denial Crimes Act Drafted: 5-Year Jail for Denial of Historically Established Facts," *Daily Star*, March 23, 2016, http://www.thedailystar.net/backpage/liberation-war-denial-crimes-act-drafted-1198240.

18. David Bergman, "The Politics of Bangladesh's Genocide Debate," *New York Times*, April 5, 2016, http://www.nytimes.com/2016/04/06/opinion/the-politics-of-bangladeshs-genocide-debate.html.

19. A hitherto most exhaustive and award-winning account of the conflict does not even mention the Razakar and al-Badr phenomena. Gary J. Bass, *The Blood Telegram: Nixon, Kissinger, and a Forgotten Genocide* (New York: Vintage Books, 2013). Neither are they discussed in the critically acclaimed Srinath Raghavan, *1971: A Global History of the Creation of Bangladesh* (Cambridge: Harvard University Press, 2013).

20. Richard Sisson and Leo E. Rose, *War and Secession: Pakistan, India, and the Creation of Bangladesh* (Berkeley: University of California Press, 1990), 144.

21. "Operation Searchlight," copy of original document, in Siddiq Salik, *Witness to Surrender* (Dhaka: University Press Limited, 1997), appendix III, 228.

22. From American Consul, Dacca [Archer K. Blood] to US Department of State, "East Pakistan: Qualitative Appraisal of the Awami League" (Confidential), Airgram, January 29, 1971, in Roedad Khan, *The American Papers: Secret and Confidential India-Pakistan-Bangladesh Documents, 1965–1973* (Oxford: Oxford University Press, 1999), 457.

23. From American Embassy, Islamabad, to US Department of State, "Conversations with West Paks and Bengalis" (Confidential), Airgram, June 4, 1971, in Khan, *The American Papers*, 599. Henry Kissinger, who served at the time as the US National Security Advisor, also observed, "Mujib's version of autonomy seemed indistinguishable from independence." Kissinger, *White House Years*, 852.

24. US Central Intelligence Agency (CIA), Directorate of Intelligence, "East Pakistan: An Independent Nation?" Intelligence Memorandum (Secret), March 1, 1971, 3; National Archives at College Park, College Park, MD.

25. The per capita income in West Pakistan was 61 percent higher than that in East Pakistan. Husain Haqqani, *Pakistan: Between Mosque and Military* (Washington, DC: Brookings Institution Press, 2005), 61.

26. CIA, "East Pakistan: An Independent Nation?" 4.

27. Muhammad Anisur Rahman, *My Story of 1971: Through the Holocaust That Created Bangladesh* (Dhaka: Liberation War Museum, 2001), 17.

28. CIA, "East Pakistan: An Independent Nation?" 8.

29. Salik, *Witness to Surrender*, 3.

30. Sarmila Bose, *Dead Reckoning: Memories of the 1971 Bangladesh War* (London: Hurst, 2011), 23.

31. Ibid., 30.

32. Salik, *Witness to Surrender*, 63

33. Operation Blitz involved enforcing martial law in its classical role. It was planned for the worst-case scenario (e.g., the declaration of East Pakistan's independence) during the elections but deemed no longer relevant after the elections. Bose, *Dead Reckoning*, 48.

34. Ibid., 21.

35. J. F .R. Jacob, *Surrender at Dacca: Birth of a Nation* (Dhaka: University Press Limited, 2004), 31.

36. Haqqani, *Pakistan*, 78.

37. Sisson and Rose, *War and Secession*, 159.

38. Ibid., 158–59.

39. "Chronology: Foreign Office Files for India, Pakistan and Afghanistan, 1947–1971," Archives Direct, British National Archives at Kew, accessed at Public Workstation at Library of Congress, Washington, DC, November 21, 2011.

40. Rahman, *My Story of 1971*.

41. "A partial transcript of the tape recording of some conversations between some of the Pakistani Army units operating in Dacca on the night of March 25, 1971" (1:30 a.m. to 9:00 a.m., March 26, 1971), in *1971: Documents on Crimes Against Humanity Committed by Pakistan Army and Their Agents in Bangladesh during 1971* (Dhaka: Liberation War Museum, 1999), 169.

42. Abu Salah Mohammed Nasim, *Bangladesh Fights for Independence* (Dhaka: Columbia Prokashani, 2002), 29.

43. Bose, *Dead Reckoning*, 53.

44. Haqqani, *Pakistan*, 71–72.

45. "A partial transcript of the tape recording," 167.

46. On January 30, 1971, two Kashmiri Muslims hijacked an Indian Airlines Fokker Friendship aircraft and ordered it to land in Lahore, West Pakistan. When, on February 3, the hijackers destroyed the aircraft, the Indian government prohibited flights over India by Pakistan until the question of compensation was satisfactorily settled. The Pakistan government claimed that the hijacking and destruction of the aircraft was an Indian plot, while Mujib described it as "a conspiracy by the Pakistan government to postpone the transfer of power." Talukder Maniruzzaman, *The Bangladesh Revolution and Its Aftermath* (Dhaka: University Press Limited, 2009), 102, fn. 36. The mystery of the hijacking has not been solved, but the ban forced Pakistani aircrafts to fly via Sri Lanka and added 2,000 miles to their normal flight route.

47. Nasr, *The Vanguard of the Islamic Revolution*, 168.

48. Ibid., 169.

49. Ibid.

50. S. N. Prasad, *Official History of the 1971 India Pakistan War* (New Delhi: History Division, Ministry of Defense, Government of India, 1992), 185.

51. CIA, "East Pakistan: An Independent Nation?" 7.

52. Bose, *Dead Reckoning*, 30.

53. Sarmila Bose, "Anatomy of Violence: Analysis of Civil War in East Pakistan in 1971," *Economic and Political Weekly* 40, no. 41 (October 8–14, 2005), 4466.

54. Sisson and Rose, *War and Secession*, 166.

55. Sukumar Biswas, *Bangladesh Liberation War Mujibnagar Government Documents, 1971* (Dhaka: Mowla Brothers, 2005), 149.

56. Rafiqul Islam, *A Tale of Millions: Bangladesh Liberation War—1971* (Dhaka: Ananya, 2011), 222–23.

57. A. R. Siddiqi, *East Pakistan: The Endgame, An Onlooker's Journal 1969–1971* (Oxford: Oxford University Press, 2004), 145.

58. "Belonia Bulge," brief shared electronically with the author by Mofidul Hoque, director of the Liberation War Museum, Dhaka, July 28, 2016. This document describes the Battle of the Belonia Bulge in June 1971 as "the first major offensive launched by the Muktibahini." Though many of the details are similar, the document contradicts the defense story, which is based on both Pakistani and Bangladeshi sources. It does, however, agree that the battle was a major turning point: "a great moral victory [for the rebels] in the early phase of the liberation war" that signaled a sudden weakening of the Pakistan army's force employment capacity vis-à-vis the rebels.

59. Siddiqi, *East Pakistan*, 144.

60. Sisson and Rose, *War and Secession*, 142. The authors' uniquely insightful account of the conflict is based on their interviews in 1978 with key political leaders and their principal advisers in India, Pakistan, and Bangladesh.

61. Maniruzzaman, *The Bangladesh Revolution and Its Aftermath*, 110.

62. Quote from Raghavan, *1971*, 70.

63. Sisson and Rose, *War and Secession*, 143.

64. Ibid., 144.

65. Islam, *A Tale of Millions*, 222.

66. Maniruzzaman, *The Bangladesh Revolution and Its Aftermath*, 107.

67. Sisson and Rose, *War and Secession*, 182.

68. Siddiqi, *East Pakistan*, 145–46.

69. Ibid., 146.

70. The term "razakar" means "volunteer" in Urdu. It was originally used to describe the private militia employed in 1947–48 by the Nizam (ruler) of Hyderabad to resist the princely state's accession to India. The estimated 150,000 Razakars were affiliated with the Muslim political party Ittehad-ul-Muslimeen, which advocated Hyderabad's independence. On September 13, 1948, India invaded Hyderabad with a military campaign code named Operation Polo. The Razakars were outmatched by the Indian army, and Hyderabad—famous for its abundant polo grounds—was soon incorporated into the Indian Union.

71. "Guidelines Regarding East Pakistan Razakars Organization," Secret Memo from K. A. Khabir, Deputy Secretary to the Government of East Pakistan, to Deputy Commissioner, Mymensingh; July 7, 1971, Liberation War Museum Archives, Dhaka, Bangladesh.

72. "Guidelines Regarding East Pakistan Razakars Organization." The popular claim that the Pakistani government had planned to recruit 100,000 Razakars (Prasad, *Official History of the 1971 India Pakistan War*, 187; Salik, *Witness to Surrender*, 105; Muniruzzaman *The Bangladesh Revolution*, 96) is not supported by the official Pakistani government documents. The same sources cite 50,000 as the final number of recruits; the former Commander of Eastern Military High Command A. A. K. Niazi has identified the number as 40,000. Prasad, *Official History of the 1971 India Pakistan War*, 253, fn. 10.

73. "Enrolment [*sic*] of Razakars," Secret Memo to ASMILA Tangail, etc. July 17, 1971 Liberation War Museum Archives, Dhaka, Bangladesh.

74. CIA, "Memorandum: The Indo-Pakistani Crisis: Six Months Later," 2.

75. Nasim, *Bangladesh Fights for Independence*, 118.

76. Salik, *Witness to Surrender*, 105; Prasad, *Official History of the 1971 India Pakistan War*, 185.

77. "Guidelines Regarding East Pakistan Razakars Organization," July 7, 1971.

78. Ibid.

79. Ibid.

80. "Enrolment [*sic*] of Razakars," July 17, 1971, Liberation War Museum Archives.

81. Ibid.

82. "Guidelines Regarding East Pakistan Razakars Organization," July 7, 1971.

83. Nasim, *Bangladesh Fights for Independence*, 118.

84. Ibid.

85. Muniruzzaman, *The Bangladesh Revolution*, 114.

86. Ibid.

87. Interview with Qamrul Hassan Bhuiyan (a.k.a. Quamrul Islam) (former Mukti Bahini rebel and Chairman, Center for Bangladesh Liberation War Studies), Dhaka, March 14, 2012.

88. Author's interview with Kamrul Hassan, Dhaka, July 2015.

89. Author's interview with a Bangladeshi general (retired), Dhaka, June 2015.

90. A former Pakistani officer of Bengali ethnic origin recounted numerous incidents of discrimination. His West Pakistani counterparts often referred to him as a "rice eater," thereby implying that he, as a Bengali, was weak. Author's interview with Major General K. M. Shafiullah (second in command of Second East Bengal Regiment; brigade commander of S-force of the Bangladesh Forces during the 1971 war, and chief of army staff of the Bangladesh army, 1972–1975), Dhaka, March 2012. East Pakistanis constituted over half (roughly 54 percent) of the total population of Pakistan, but less than 10 percent of the military establishment. CIA, "East Pakistan: An Independent Nation?" 12.

91. Blood, *The Cruel Birth of Bangladesh*, 218.

92. Haqqani, *Pakistan*, 76.

93. Yelena Biberman and Rachel Castellano, "Genocidal Violence, Nation-Building, and the Bloody Birth of Bangladesh," *Asian Security* 14, no. 2 (2018): 106-18.
94. Author's interview with Major General K. M. Shafiullah, March 2012; Siddiqi, *East Pakistan*, 146.
95. Author's interview with Sarwar Ali (former Mukti Bahini recruiting officer), Dhaka, March 2012.
96. Prasad, *Official History of the 1971 India Pakistan War*, 164.
97. Muniruzzaman, *The Bangladesh Revolution*, 109.
98. Author's interview with Mofidul Hoque (former Mukti Bahini and Liberation War Museum director), Dhaka, March 2012.
99. Prasad, *Official History of the 1971 India Pakistan War*, 164.
100. Ibid.
101. Ibid., 153.
102. Muniruzzaman, *The Bangladesh Revolution*, 108–9.
103. Praveen Swami, "India's Secret War in Bangladesh," *The Hindu*, February 11, 2012.
104. Prasad, *Official History of the 1971 India Pakistan War*, 167.
105. Ibid.
106. Ibid., 168.
107. Fair, *Fighting to the End*, 148.
108. Maniruzzaman, *The Bangladesh Revolution*, 112.
109. Prasad, *Official History of the 1971 India Pakistan War*, 170.
110. Author's interview with M. A. Hasan (former Mukti Bahini and chairperson of War Crimes Facts Finding Committee in Bangladesh), Dhaka, August 2015.
111. Manik, "Focus Back On, 8 Years After."
112. Niazi, *The Betrayal of East Pakistan*, 78–79.
113. Memorandum, Coordinator of US Disaster Relief for East Pakistan Maurice J. Williams to Secretary of State Rogers, Washington, September 3, 1971, Foreign Relations, 1969–1976, Volume E-7, South Asia, 1969–1972, Released by the Office of the Historian, US Department of State Online Archives.
114. Author's interview with M.A. Hasan, August 2015; Maniruzzaman, *The Bangladesh Revolution*, 97.
115. Nasim, *Bangladesh Fights for Independence*, 118.
116. *A Killing Squad of Pakistan Army*, documentary film, Laser Vision Exclusive; Dhaka, Bangladesh.
117. Author's interview with Quazi Sajjad Ali Zahir, August 2015.
118. Author's interview with Mofidul Hoque, August 2015.
119. Nasr, *The Vanguard of the Islamic Revolution*, 66.
120. Ibid., 169.
121. Ibid., 76–77.
122. Ibid., 169.
123. Prasad, *Official History of the 1971 India Pakistan War*, 187; Nasim, *Bangladesh Fights for Independence*, 118.
124. Author's interview with Mofidul Hoque, August 2015.
125. Nasr, *The Vanguard of the Islamic Revolution*, 169.
126. Author's interview with Mohammad Shishir Manir, August 2015.

127. Author's interview with Mofidul Hoque, August 2015.
128. Letter from Malcolm W. Browne to James Greenfield, November 14, 1971; *New York Times Company Records. Foreign Desk Records, 1948–1993,* Manuscripts and Archives Division, New York Public Library, box 13, folder 4, "Browne, Malcolm W., Foreign Desk, 1971."
129. Charge No. 16 (Death) against Motiur Rahman Nizami, Supreme Court of Bangladesh.
130. Sisson and Rose, *War and Secession,* 214.
131. Author's interview with Imtiaz Ahmed (former Mukti Bahini rebel), Dhaka, March 2012.
132. Browne to Greenfield, November 14 1971.
133. Bass, *The Blood Telegram.*
134. G. W. Choudhury, *The Last Days of United Pakistan* (Dhaka: University Press Limited, 2011), 206.
135. Kissinger, *White House Years,* 689.
136. Romania was the alternative. William Burr, "The Beijing-Washington Back-Channel and Henry Kissinger's Secret Trip to China," September 1970–July 1971, Electronic Briefing Book No. 66, February 27, 2002; The National Security Archive, George Washington University, http://www.gwu.edu/~nsarchiv/NSAEBB/NSAEBB66/#3.
137. Kissinger, *White House Years,* 854.
138. "Meeting between the President and Pakistan President Yahya," White House Oval Office, October 25, 1970, Memo (Top Secret/Sensitive); National Security Archive, George Washington University, http://www.gwu.edu/~nsarchiv/NSAEBB/NSAEBB66/ch-03.pdf.
139. "Chinese Communist Initiative," Memorandum (Top Secret/Sensitive) from Henry Kissinger to President Richard Nixon, December 1970; National Security Archive, George Washington University, http://www.gwu.edu/~nsarchiv/NSAEBB/NSAEBB66/ch-06.pdf.
140. Kissinger video interview, "Nixon's China Game," PBS, Special Feature, 2000, http://www.pbs.org/wgbh/amex/china/sfeature/kissinger.html.
141. Kissinger recalls that, when he and his Secret Service staff boarded the plane, they encountered four Chinese men in Mao suits sitting there. Zhou had sent them to escort Kissinger to China. Kissinger was not aware of this, and so "our Secret Service people nearly had a heart attack," likely thinking that this was a kidnapping. Kissinger video interview, "Nixon's China Game."
142. See memoir by US consul general in East Pakistan who was recalled by Nixon after protesting the atrocities committed in East Pakistan by the Pakistani troops. Blood, *The Cruel Birth of Bangladesh.*
143. Lawrence Lifschultz and Kai Bird, "Bangladesh: Anatomy of a Coup," *Economic and Political Weekly* 14, no. 49 (December 8, 1979), 2004.
144. Blood, *The Cruel Birth of Bangladesh,* 213–16.
145. Kissinger, *White House Years,* 854.
146. Ibid., 849.

147. Richard Nixon, *The Memories of Richard Nixon* (New York: Grosset and Dunlap, 1978), 526.
148. Kissinger, *White House Years*, 852.

CHAPTER 4

1. Interview with Abdul Gani Bhat in Jammu Kashmir Coalition of Civil Society, in *Structures of Violence: The Indian State in Jammu and Kashmir* (Srinagar: International Peoples' Tribunal on Human Rights and Justice in Indian-Administered Kashmir and the Association of Parents of Disappeared Persons, 2015), 543–44.
2. Interviewee's name changed to protect his identity. Author's interview in Srinagar, Jammu, and Kashmir, March 2012.
3. Many of the young men who worked for the Muslim United Front (MUF), a coalition of local political parties, were imprisoned for months without charge or trial; some were tortured. Sumantra Bose, "The Kashmir Conflict in the Early 21st Century" in ed. Sanjib Baruah, *Ethnonationalism in India* (New York: Oxford University Press, 2009), 215.
4. Steve Coll, "Kashmir: The Time Has Come," *New York Review of Books*, September 30, 2010.
5. Ashutosh Varshney, *Battles Half Won: India's Improbable Democracy* (Gurgaon: Penguin, 2014), 45.
6. Human Rights Watch/Asia, "India's Secret Army in Kashmir: New Patterns of Abuse Emerge in the Conflict," 8, no. 4, May 1996.
7. Some in the Indian government vehemently denied any collaboration with the militants, while others publicly acknowledged it. For example, in a March 1996 report in the national daily *Hindu* (prior to the Human Rights Watch exposé), Jammu and Kashmir Chief Secretary Ashok Kumar denied allegations that the government was providing arms to surrendered militants, stating, "[t]he government will not be party to such a racket. We are not giving arms to the illegal persons." At the same time, an adviser to the state governor told reporters that the government was going to provide the surrendered militants with licenses for shotguns. In a *Times of India* report on March 9, 1996, Colonel K. P. Ramesh of the Rashtriya Rifles stated that surrendered militants were provided arms for their protection and given reward money for information.
8. In addition, the regular armed forces appear to have committed significantly more human rights abuses than the irregulars. Parvez Imroz, Kartik Murukutla, Khurram Parvez, and Parvaiz Mata, *Alleged Perpetrators: Stories of Impunity in Jammu and Kashmir* (Srinagar: International Peoples' Tribunal on Human Rights and Justice in Indian-Administered Kashmir and Association of Parents of Disappeared Persons, 2012), 289–321.
9. Shivani Sharma, "Paradise Lost—the Kashmiri Pandits," BBC World Service, http://www.bbc.co.uk/worldservice/specials/1246_land/page9.shtml.
10. Praveen Swami, "A Beleaguered Force," *Frontline* 16, no. 3 (January 30–February 12, 1999).

11. The term "piling-on bandwagoning" refers to opportunistic behavior in which actors join the winning side "because they fear the victors will punish them if they do not actively side against the losers" or "to claim an unearned share of the spoils." Randall L. Schweller, "Bandwagoning for Profit: Bringing the Revisionist State Back In," *International Security* 19, no. 1 (Summer 1994), 95.

12. Human Rights Watch, *The Human Rights Crisis in Kashmir: A Pattern of Impunity* (New York, 1993), 68–69.

13. Harinder Baweja, "Breaching a Bastion," *India Today*, December 31, 1993.

14. Sanjoy Hazarika, "Indian Army Troops Crush Revolt by Police in Kashmir," *New York Times*, April 29, 1993.

15. Author's interview with an Indian army officer who served in Kashmir in the 1990s, New Delhi, August 2015.

16. Author's interview with Radhavinod Raju (who served as Indian police service officer of the Jammu and Kashmir and in the Central Bureau of Investigation; first director-general of National Investigation Agency, federal agency approved by the Indian government to combat terror in India formed in 2009, following 2008 Mumbai terror attacks; headed special investigation team that investigated the assassination of Rajiv Gandhi), New Delhi, October 10, 2011.

17. Sumit Ganguly, *The Crisis in Kashmir: Portents of War, Hopes of Peace* (New York: Woodrow Wilson Center Press and Cambridge University Press, 1997), 102.

18. Yateendra Singh Jafa, "Defeating Terrorism: A Study of Operational Strategy and Tactics of Police Forces in Jammu & Kashmir (India)," *Police Practice and Research* 6, no. 2 (May 2005), 145.

19. Sumantra Bose, *Kashmir: Roots of Conflict, Paths to Peace* (Cambridge: Harvard University Press, 2003), 296.

20. Nitasha Kaul, "Kashmir: A Place of Blood and Memory," in ed. Sanjay Kak, *Until My Freedom Has Come: The New Intifada in Kashmir* (Chicago: Haymarket Books, 2013), 205.

21. Victoria Schofield, *Kashmir in Conflict: India, Pakistan and the Unending War* (London: I. B. Tauris, 2003), 198.

22. Sumit Ganguly, "Explaining the Kashmir Insurgency: Political Mobilization and Institutional Decay," *International Security* 21, no. 2 (Fall 1996), 76.

23. Bose, *Kashmir*, 121.

24. The Jammu and Kashmir Disturbed Areas Act, 1990 (Governor's Act No. 12 of 1990).

25. The Armed Forces (Jammu & Kashmir) Special Power Act, 1990 No. 21 of 1990.

26. C. Christine Fair, "Military Operations in Urban Areas: The Indian Experience," *India Review* 2, no. 1 (January 2003), 62.

27. Ibid.

28. Sati Sahni, "The Birth of the Hizbul Mujahideen," *Rediff*, July 31, 2000, http://www.rediff.com/news/2000/jul/31hizb.htm.

29. Navnita Chadha Behera, *Demystifying Kashmir* (Washington, DC: Brookings Institution Press, 2006), 154.

30. Schofield, *Kashmir in Conflict*, 198.

31. Author's interview with an Indian army officer stationed in Kashmir, New Delhi, August 2015.
32. Author's interview with an Indian army officer stationed in Kashmir, New Delhi, August 2015.
33. Ibid.
34. Ibid.
35. Author's interview with former Indian police officer in Kashmir and in the Central Bureau of Investigation, New Delhi, October 2011.
36. Author's interview with Manoj Joshi, New Delhi, August 2015.
37. Author's interview with Praveen Swami, New Delhi, August 2015.
38. Praveen Swami, "India's Forgotten Army," *The Hindu*, September 14, 2003.
39. Basharat Peer, *Curfewed Night: One Kashmiri Journalist's Frontline Account of Life, Love, and War in His Homeland* (New York, Scribner, 2010), 171.
40. Interview with Kuka Parrey in Pradeep Thakur, *Militant Monologues: Echoes from the Kashmir Valley* (New Delhi: Parity, 2003), 43.
41. Ibid., 46–47.
42. Manoj Joshi, *The Lost Rebellion* (New Delhi: Penguin Books, 1999), 58–59.
43. Asia Watch and Physicians for Human Rights, *The Human Rights Crisis in Kashmir: A Pattern of Impunity* (New York: Human Rights Watch, June 1993), 196.
44. Joshi, *The Lost Rebellion*, 59.
45. Interview with Liyaqat Ali Khan in Jammu Kashmir Coalition of Civil Society, *Structures of Violence*, 547.
46. Author's interview with Manoj Joshi, New Delhi, August 2015.
47. Interview with Liyaqat Ali Khan in Thakur, *Militant Monologues*, 88–89.
48. Adrian Levy and Cathy Scott-Clark, *The Meadow: Kashmir 1995—Where the Terror Began* (London: Harper Press, 2012), 387–88.
49. Interview with Kuka Parrey in Thakur, *Militant Monologues*, 53.
50. Ibid., 55.
51. Ibid., 56.
52. Author's interview with Praveen Swami, New Delhi, August 2015.
53. Interview with Kuka Parrey in Thakur, *Militant Monologues*, 59.
54. Interview with Liyaqat Ali Khan in Jammu Kashmir Coalition of Civil Society, *Structures of Violence*, 548.
55. Interview with Liyaqat Ali Khan in Thakur, *Militant Monologues*, 89.
56. Ibid., 90.
57. Interview with Liyaqat Ali Khan in Jammu Kashmir Coalition of Civil Society, *Structures of Violence*, 548.
58. Levy and Scott-Clark, *The Meadow*, 388–89.
59. Interview with Liyaqat Ali Khan in Jammu Kashmir Coalition of Civil Society, *Structures of Violence*, 549.
60. Ibid., 550.
61. Human Rights Watch/Asia, *India's Secret Army in Kashmir*.
62. Schofield, *Kashmir in Conflict*, 199.
63. Author's interview with an Indian army officer, New Delhi, August 2015.

64. Interview with Sameer Darzi in Jammu Kashmir Coalition of Civil Society, *Structures of Violence*, 555

65. Author's interview with an Indian army officer, August 2015.

66. Matthew Fuhrmann and Todd S. Sechser, "Signaling Alliance Commitments: Hand-Tying and Sunk Costs in Extended Nuclear Deterrence," *American Journal of Political Science* 58, Issue 4 (October 2014), 919.

67. "Separatists in Kashmir Take Journalists Hostage," *New York Times*, July 9, 1996.

68. Human Rights Watch/Asia, *India's Secret Army in Kashmir*.

69. Author's interview with a Baramulla resident, New Delhi, August 2015.

70. Author's interview with an Indian military official, August 2015.

71. Human Rights Watch/Asia, *India's Secret Army in Kashmir*.

72. Levy and Scott-Clark, *The Meadow*, 389.

73. The SOG was the special counterinsurgency division of the Jammu and Kashmir police. It was formed in June 1994 and was initially called the Special Task Force.

74. Interview with Bashir Colonel in Jammu Kashmir Coalition of Civil Society, *Structures of Violence*, 552.

75. Interview with Liyaqat Ali Khan in Jammu Kashmir Coalition of Civil Society, *Structures of Violence*, 548.

76. Human Rights Watch/Asia, *India's Secret Army in Kashmir*.

77. Interview with Zafar Salati in Jammu Kashmir Coalition of Civil Society, *Structures of Violence*, 557.

78. Author's interview with an Indian army officer August 2015.

79. Human Rights Watch/Asia, *India's Secret Army in Kashmir*.

80. "Kashmir Police Officer Suspected of Recruiting Rebels Then Killing Them," *The Guardian*, June 5, 2013, http://www.theguardian.com/world/2013/jun/05/kashmir-police-recruiting-rebels-killing.

81. Ibid.

82. Jamaat's apprehension about being involved in the insurgency resurfaced in the late 1990s, as it "tried to distance itself from the militant groups, partly because hundreds of its members were arrested and killed by the Indian troops and many more during the campaign by Ikhwan counterinsurgents." Peer, *Curfewed Night*, 171. Murtaza Shibli, "Kashmir: Islam, Identity and Insurgency," *Kashmir Affairs* (January 2009), 23.

83. Most Jamaat members, including the supreme leader, "had reservations and wanted to publicly distance itself from the alliance [with militants]." However, "massive Indian repression and human rights violations changed the climate and gave rise to unprecedented public approval for the brand of armed insurgency that the HM advocated and to which the JIK [Jamaat] informally, but reluctantly gave its support." In early 1991, sensing an opportunity, Dar announced that the Hizb was now the military wing of the party. Jamaat would then have to decide whether it was in or out. Murtaza Shibli, "Kashmir: Islam, Identity and Insurgency," *Kashmir Affairs* (January 2009), 23.

84. Ibid.

85. Interview with Mohammad Ahsan Dar in Jammu Kashmir Coalition of Civil Society, *Structures of Violence*, 547.

86. Interview with Bilal Siddiqui in Jammu Kashmir Coalition of Civil Society, *Structures of Violence*, 567.
87. Interview with Abdul Gani Bhat in Jammu Kashmir Coalition of Civil Society, *Structures of Violence*, 544.
88. Ibid.
89. Interview with Fayaz Ahmad Bhat in Jammu Kashmir Coalition of Civil Society, *Structures of Violence*, 553.
90. Interview with Bilal Siddique in Jammu Kashmir Coalition of Civil Society, *Structures of Violence*, 567.
91. Interview with Mohammad Syed Shah in Jammu Kashmir Coalition of Civil Society, *Structures of Violence*, 567.
92. Levy and Scott-Clark, *The Meadow*, 396.
93. Ibid.
94. Interview with Fayaz Ahmad Bhat in Jammu Kashmir Coalition of Civil Society, *Structures of Violence*, 553.
95. Levy and Scott-Clark, *The Meadow*, 396–97.
96. Jammu Kashmir Coalition of Civil Society, *Structures of Violence*, 52.
97. Interview with Abdul Gani Bhat in Jammu Kashmir Coalition of Civil Society, *Structures of Violence*, 544.
98. Levy and Scott-Clark, *The Meadow*, 396.
99. Interview with Abdul Gani Bhat in Jammu Kashmir Coalition of Civil Society, *Structures of Violence*, 544.
100. Interview with Ghulam Nabi Sumji in Jammu Kashmir Coalition of Civil Society, *Structures of Violence*, 543.
101. Jammu Kashmir Coalition of Civil Society, *Structures of Violence*, 52.
102. Ibid.
103. Ibid.
104. Interview with Shabir Dar in Jammu Kashmir Coalition of Civil Society, *Structures of Violence*, 568.
105. Praveen Swami, "The Tanzeems and Their Leaders," *Frontline* 17, no. 17 (August 19–September 01, 2000), http://www.frontline.in/static/html/fl1717/17170200.htm.
106. Jammu Kashmir Coalition of Civil Society, *Structures of Violence*, 21.
107. Interview with Fayaz Ahmad Bhat in Jammu Kashmir Coalition of Civil Society, *Structures of Violence*, 553.
108. Ibid., 21–22.
109. Ibid., 22–23.
110. Ibid., 553.
111. Ibid.
112. Author's interview with Praveen Swami, August 2015.
113. Shibli, "Kashmir," 25.
114. Interview with Kuka Parray, *Rediff*, July 19, 2002, http://www.rediff.com/news/2002/jul/19inter.htm.
115. Author's interview with an Indian army officer, August 2015.
116. Kenneth J. Cooper, "Troops Force Kashmiris to Vote," *Washington Post*, May 24, 1996.

117. Jammu Kashmir Coalition of Civil Society, *Structures of Violence*, 95.
118. Interview with Liyaqat Ali Khan in Jammu Kashmir Coalition of Civil Society, *Structures of Violence*, 549.
119. Human Rights Watch, *Human Rights Watch World Report 1997: Events of 1996* (New York: Human Rights Watch, 1996), 159.
120. Author's interview with Praveen Swami, August 2015.
121. Author's interview with an Indian army officer, August 2015.
122. Swami, "A Beleaguered Force."
123. Joshi, *Lost Rebellion*, 427–28.
124. Author's interview with a Kashmir-based activist, Srinagar, Jammu and Kashmir, March 2012.
125. Author's interview with an Indian army officer, August 2015.
126. "Rules for the Enrolment and Re-Employment of the Special Police Officers," document shared by Jammu Kashmir Coalition of Civil Society during visit, Srinagar, Jammu and Kashmir, March 2012.
127. Supreme Court of India, *Nandini Sundar & Org. versus State of Chhattisgarh Order*, July 5, 2011, 28.
128. The insurgents claim to represent the peasants and tribals who were displaced when mining and land rights over their resource-rich land were granted to Indian and multinational companies. Between 1951 and 1990, 8.5 million individuals were displaced by the developmental projects, while only 25 percent of them were rehabilitated. Supreme Court of India, *Nandini Sundar & Org. versus State of Chhattisgarh Order*, 13.
129. Praveen Swami, "Tackling Terror," *Frontline* 15, no. 10 (May 9–22, 1998).
130. Ganguly, *The Crisis in Kashmir*, 132.
131. Author's interview with an Indian journalist, New Delhi, August 2015.
132. Swami, "Tackling Terror."
133. "Composition of VDCs Has Led to Communal Polarization, Increase in Militarization: JKCCS," *KSN Kashmir*, January 1, 2016, http://www.knskashmir.com/news.aspx?news=Composition-of-VDCs-has-led-to-communal-polarization--increase-in-militarization--JKCCS--4021. Also see Bose, *Kashmir*, 152.
134. Sumantra Bose, "Session 3—Geography, Politics and the Fighters of Kashmir: An Eyewitness Account," Conflict in Kashmir Seminar, London School of Economics and Political Science, http://fathom.lse.ac.uk/Seminars/10701013/10701013_session3.html/.
135. Author's interview with an Indian army officer, August 2015.
136. Ibid.
137. Ibid.
138. Author's interview with Praveen Swami, August 2015.
139. Sumantra Bose, *Kashmir*, 152.
140. "475 Special Police Officers Killed in Kashmir Militancy," *Indo Asian News Service*, March 31, 2012, https://in.news.yahoo.com/475-special-police-officers-killed-kashmir-militancy-100356335.html.

141. Public Commission on Human Rights, *State of Human Rights in Jammu and Kashmir, 1990–2005* (Srinagar: Coalition of Civil Society, Bund, Amira Kadal, 2006), 247.

142. Author's interview with a Kashmir-based journalist, March 2012.

143. "Jammu and Kashmir Police Takes Stock of Village Defence Committees," *Indo-Asian News Service*, September 7, 2012, http://www.sify.com/news/jammu-and-kashmir-police-takes-stock-of-village-defence-committees-news-national-mjhqE8ghccg.html?ref=false.

144. International Crisis Group, "Nepal: Dangerous Plans for Village Militias," ASIA Briefing (Kathmandu/Brussels, February 17, 2004), 4–5; "Four Village Defence Committee Men Killed in JK," Reuters, June 9, 2002, http://www.expressindia.com/news/fullstory.php?newsid=11379.

145. Public Commission on Human Rights, *State of Human Rights in Jammu and Kashmir*, 247.

146. Ibid.

147. Author's interview with an Indian army officer, August 2015.

148. Martin Regg Cohn, "Kashmiris Go to Polls amid Fear, Bloodshed," *Toronto Star*, September 21, 2002, A1.

149. Author's interview with an Indian army officer who served in Kashmir in the 1990s, August 2015.

150. Interview with Bashir Colonel in Jammu Kashmir Coalition of Civil Society, *Structures of Violence*, 552.

151. Interview with Liyaqat Ali Khan in Jammu Kashmir Coalition of Civil Society, *Structures of Violence*, 548.

152. "Kuka Parrey Shot Dead," *The Hindu*, September 14, 2003.

153. Interview with Sameer Darzi in Jammu Kashmir Coalition of Civil Society, *Structures of Violence*, 556.

CHAPTER 5

1. Quoted in Ramachandra Guha, *Makers of Modern India* (Cambridge: Belknap Press, 2014), 69.

2. Supreme Court of India, *Nandini Sundar & Org. versus State of Chhattisgarh Order*, July 5, 2011, 18.

3. Daud Khattak, "The Risks of Supporting Tribal Militias in Pakistan," *CTC Sentinel* 4, no. 3 (March 2011), 17.

4. Orla Guerin, "Lone Stand of Surrounded Pakistan anti-Taliban Militia," BBC News, March 9, 2010, http://news.bbc.co.uk/2/hi/south_asia/8537127.stm (accessed January 10, 2017).

5. Sabrina Tavernise, "Pakistan Blast Kills Anti-Taliban Mayor," *New York Times*, November 8, 2009.

6. Zahid Hussain, "Pakistan Turns to Tribal Militias," *Wall Street Journal*, September 30, 2008, http://www.wsj.com/articles/SB122270429796586073.

7. Farhat Taj, "Anti-Taliban Lashkar in North Waziristan?" *Daily Times*, June 17, 2011.

8. The Pakistani state here refers primarily to the military-intelligence establishment that, throughout the examined period, dominated the country's security policy.

9. Rohan Gunaratna and Khuram Iqbal, *Pakistan: Terrorism Ground Zero* (London: Reaktion Books, 2011), 72; Farhat Taj, *Taliban and Anti-Taliban* (Newcastle upon Tyne: Cambridge Scholars, 2011), 41.

10. Author's interviews in Islamabad, Pakistan, December 2014.

11. Ibid.

12. The British pursued a "Close Border" arrangement in colonial India's Northwest Frontier until the end of the nineteenth century. They governed the plains while leaving the hills as a sort of a human "nature reserve." On occasion, they sent punitive expeditions into a hostile tribe's territory. In what was known as "Butcher and Bolt," they usually "killed a few of the men, blew up the fortified towers, pulled down the terraces of the fields, extracted a fine in cash and firearms, and then withdrew." Charles Chenevix Trench, *The Frontier Scouts* (London: Jonathan Cape, 1985), 2. The alternative approach, the "Forward Policy," involved occupying and administering the country right up to the Durand Line—the international boundary agreed on and demarcated with Afghanistan in 1893. This worked only in Baluchistan through a loose system of indirect rule by means of tribal chiefs. But it proved too costly and required a large, permanently employed army to protect the disarmed tribes. What resulted was a compromise policy, consisting of an administered border to the east of which prevailed law and order based on the Indian Penal Code and Criminal Procedure Code. To the west, up to the Durand Line, was an area known as Tribal Territory. The army was stationed in cantonments in British India, while the Tribal Territory was the domain of political agents. There were six political agents, each responsible for selected tribes and backed by scouts. The scouts were not regular soldiers, though organized like the Indian army in platoons and commanded by junior officers (most of whom were locals). Meanwhile, the Khassadars, whom the British employed mostly to keep open the local roads, comprised only the tribesmen.

13. Ismail Khan, "Reforms Proposed for Fata's Merger into KP," *Dawn*, June 13, 2016.

14. Anatol Lieven, *Pakistan: A Hard Country* (New York: PublicAffairs, 2011), 8; Robert L. Grenier, *88 Days in Kandahar: A CIA Diary* (New York: Simon and Schuster, 2015), 362.

15. C. Christine Fair, *Fighting to the End: The Pakistan Army's Way of War* (Oxford: Oxford University Press, 2014); Sumit Ganguly, *Deadly Impasse: Indo-Pakistani Relations at the Dawn of a New Century* (Cambridge: Cambridge University Press, 2016).

16. Stephen Philip Cohen, "India and Pakistan: The Armed Forces," in *The South Asia Papers: A Critical Anthology of Writings by Stephen Philip Cohen* (Washington, DC: Brookings Institution Press, 2016), 240.

17. Husain Haqqani, *Magnificent Delusions: Pakistan, the United States, and an Epic History of Misunderstanding* (New York: PublicAffairs, 2013), 2.

18. T. V. Paul develops the concept of the "geostrategic curse" to explain Pakistan's condition of a *rentier* state living off the rents provided by external benefactors for supporting their particular geostrategic goals—a status made possible by the

country's geostrategic importance and willingness of the elite to play the geo-strategic games. T. V. Paul, *The Warrior State: Pakistan in the Contemporary World* (Oxford: Oxford University Press, 2014), 18. Stephen P. Cohen has also argued that Pakistan's decades-long sociopolitical crisis is linked to its history of alliances, especially with the United States. Stephen Philip Cohen, "How a Botched US Alliance Fed Pakistan's Crisis," in *The South Asia Papers*, 292.

19. Yelena Biberman, "Reimagining Pakistan's Militia Policy," *Atlantic Council Issue Brief*, April 27, 2015.

20. Secret Memorandum on Aid to Pakistan for Secretary of State, October 28, 1947; Dominions Office, Records of the Asian Divisions and Departments of the Commonwealth Relations Office: DO 196/360, Rann of Kutch Dispute, 1965, February 1965–April 1965; National Archives, Kew, United Kingdom.

21. Ayesha Siddiqa, *Military Inc.: Inside Pakistan's Military Economy* (London: Pluto Press, 2017), 27.

22. Ahmed Rashid, *Pakistan on the Brink: The Future of America, Pakistan, and Afghanistan* (New York: Penguin Books, 2013), 65.

23. Though, there was also concern that India may be supporting some of them. Author's interviews in Islamabad, Pakistan, December 2014.

24. Grenier, *88 Days in Kandahar*, 5.

25. Seth G. Jones, *In the Graveyard of Empires: America's War in Afghanistan* (New York: W. W. Norton, 2010), 323.

26. Grenier, *88 Days in Kandahar*, 362–63.

27. Carlotta Gall, *The Wrong Enemy: America in Afghanistan, 2001–2014* (Boston: Houghton Mifflin Harcourt, 2014), 159.

28. Jones, *In the Graveyard of Empires*, 323.

29. Gall, *The Wrong Enemy*, 160–61.

30. Lieven, *Pakistan*, 8.

31. Ibid., 8–9.

32. Daniel S. Markey, *No Exit from Pakistan: America's Tortured Relationship with Islamabad* (New York: Cambridge University Press, 2013), 25.

33. Rashid, *Pakistan on the Brink*, 50–51.

34. Ibid.

35. Ibid., 53.

36. Hassan Abbas, "A Profile of Tehrik-i-Taliban," *CTC Sentinel* 1, no. 2 (2008), 1–4.

37. Yelena Biberman and Farhan Zahid, "Why Terrorists Target Children: Outbidding, Desperation, and Extremism in the Peshawar and Beslan School Massacres," *Terrorism and Political Violence*, February 2016.

38. Author's interviews in Islamabad, December 2014.

39. Mona Kanwal Sheikh, *Guardians of God: Inside the Religious Mind of the Pakistani Taliban* (New Delhi: Oxford University Press, 2016), 3.

40. Ibid., 7.

41. Rashid, *Pakistan on the Brink*, 53.

42. Grenier, *88 Days in Kandahar*, 341.

43. Daud Khattak, "Evaluating Pakistan's Offensives in Swat and FATA," *CTC Sentinel* 4, 10 (October 2011): 9-11.

44. Sheikh, *Guardians of God*, 24.
45. Ibid.
46. Grenier, *88 Days in Kandahar*, 385.
47. A similar institution exists in Afghanistan called the *arbaki* (guardian). Ali Seraj, "The Arbaki Can Secure Afghanistan Better Than the US," *Al Jazeera*, November 5, 2014.
48. Taj, *Taliban and Anti-Taliban*, 35.
49. Ibid.
50. Niaz A. Shah, *Islamic Law and the Law of Armed Conflict: The Conflict in Pakistan* (Abingdon: Routledge, 2011), 129.
51. Taj, *Taliban and Anti-Taliban*, 35–36.
52. Mukhtar A. Khan, "The Role of Tribal Lashkars in Winning Pakistan's War on Terror," *Terrorism Focus* 5, no. 40 (November 26, 2008), 9.
53. Hussain, "Pakistan Turns to Tribal Militias."
54. Bill Roggio, "Anti-Taliban Tribal Militia Leader Assassinated in Pakistan's Northwest," *Long Wars Journal*, July 30, 2009.
55. For details about the 1947 events, see Shuja Nawaz, "The First Kashmir War Revisited," *India Review* 7, no. 2 (2008), 115–54.
56. Khattak, "The Risks of Supporting Tribal Militias in Pakistan," 16.
57. Zia Ur Rehman, "Tribal Militias are Double-Edged Weapons," *Friday Times*, September 30, 2011.
58. Salman Yousafzai, "Death by Lashkar: The Forgotten Protectors of Adezai Village," *Dawn*, May 9, 2016.
59. Khattak, "The Risks of Supporting Tribal Militias in Pakistan," 16.
60. Yousafzai, "Death by Lashkar."
61. Taj, "Anti-Taliban Lashkar in North Waziristan?"
62. Yousafzai, "Death by Lashkar."
63. Ibid.
64. Guerin, "Lone Stand of Surrounded Pakistan anti-Taliban Militia."
65. Hussain, "Pakistan Turns to Tribal Militias."
66. Christophe Jaffrelot, *Pakistan at the Crossroads: Domestic Dynamics and External Pressures* (New York: Columbia University Press, 2016), 130.
67. Khan, "The Role of Tribal Lashkars in Winning Pakistan's War on Terror," 10.
68. Seth G. Jones and C. Christine Fair, *Counterinsurgency in Pakistan* (Santa Monica, CA: RAND, 2010), 34.
69. Ibid.
70. Ibid., xiv.
71. Author's interviews in Islamabad, December 2014.
72. Jane Perlez and Pir Zubair Shah, "Pakistan Uses Tribal Militias in Taliban War," *New York Times*, October 23, 2008.
73. Taj, *Taliban and Anti-Taliban*, 38–39.
74. Tayyab Ali Shah, "Pakistan's Challenges in Orakzai Agency," *CTC Sentinel* 3, no. 7 (July 2010), 13.
75. Ashutosh Varshney, "Three Compromised Nationalisms: Why Kashmir Has Been a Problem" in ed. Raju Thomas, *Perspectives on Kashmir* (Boulder: Westview Press, 1992).

76. Strikingly, S. Mahmud Ali's masterful study of the insurgencies beleaguering South Asia does not contain a single section (let alone chapter) devoted to the Naxalite movement. S. Mahmud Ali, *The Fearful State: Power, People and Internal War in South Asia* (London: Zed Books, 1993).

77. Tilak D. Gupta, "Maoism in India: Ideology, Programme and Armed Struggle," *Economic and Political Weekly* 41, no. 29 (July 22–28, 2006), 3174.

78. Central Committee, Communist Party of India (Maoist), "Party Constitution," September 21, 2004, available at http://www.satp.org/satporgtp/countries/india/maoist/documents/papers/partyconstitution.htm.

79. K. Balagopal, "Physiognomy of Violence," *Economic and Political Weekly* 41, no. 22 (June 3–9, 2006), 2183–84.

80. Ranajit Guha, *Elementary Aspects of Peasant Insurgency in Colonial India* (Durham: Duke University Press, 1999), 2.

81. For a critical evaluation of the terms "indigenous" and "tribal," see Virginius Xaxa, "Tribes as Indigenous People of India," *Economic and Political Weekly* 34, no. 51 (December 18–24, 1999), 3589–95.

82. Sameer Lalwani, "India's Approach to Counterinsurgency and the Naxalite Problem," *CTC Sentinel* 4, 10 (October 2011): 5-9.

83. Sudeep Chakravarti, *Red Sun: Travels in Naxalite Country* (New Delhi: Viking, 2008), 24.

84. Dantewada district was formerly part of Bastar district.

85. Randeep Ramesh, "Inside India's Hidden War," *Guardian*, May 8, 2006.

86. Aruna Kashyap, *Dangerous Duty: Children and the Chhattisgarh Conflict* (Human Rights Watch, 2008).

87. Chakravarti, *Red Sun*.

88. People's Union for Civil Liberties, *Where the State Makes War on Its Own People* (New Delhi: PUCL 2006), 11.

89. Asian Centre for Human Rights, *The Adivasis of Chhattisgarh: Victims of the Naxalite Movement and Salwa Judum Campaign*, Delhi, 2016, 13–14.

90. Asian Centre for Human Rights, "The Adivasis of Chhattisgarh: Victims of Naxalite Movement and Salwa Judum Campaign. Excerpts from the Main Report," Delhi, March 22, 2006.

91. Office of the Registrar General and Census Commissioner, India, *Basic Data Sheet: District Dantewada, Chhattisgarh. Source: Census of India 2001*, http://www.censusindia.gov.in/Dist_File/datasheet-2216.pdf.

92. Ibid.

93. Ibid., 222.

94. Jonathan Kennedy, "Gangsters or Gandhians? The Political Sociology of the Maoist Insurgency in India," *India Review* 13, no. 3 (2014), 220–21.

95. Sreenivas Janyala, "When They Talked, and Failed," *Indian Express*, March 14, 2010, http://indianexpress.com/article/print/when-they-talkedand-failed/.

96. Nandini Sundar, "Insurgency, Counter-insurgency, and Democracy in Central India," in eds., Robin Jeffrey, Ronojoy Sen, and Pratima Sen, *More than Maoism: Politics and Policies of Insurgency in South Asia* (New Delhi: Manohar, 2013), 149.

97. Ministry of Coal and Mines, Government of India, *Annual Report: 2003–2004* (New Delhi, 2004), 1.

98. Sundar, "Insurgency, Counter-insurgency, 153.

99. Ibid., 150.

100. Ministry of Coal and Mines, *Annual Report: 2003–2004*, 1.

101. In 2003, the government announced a plan to start a separate CRPF strike force against the Naxalites in Chhattisgarh, Jharkand, Andhra Pradesh, Orissa, and parts of Uttar Pradesh. "CRPF to Raise Battalions to 205 by 2004," *Times of India*, December 16, 2003.

102. People's Union for Civil Liberties, *Where the State Makes War on Its Own People*, 13. Prior to 2005, nineteen India Reserve battalions were raised in the nine Naxalite-affected states. Gautam Navlakha, "Maoists in India," *Economic and Political Weekly* 41, no. 22 (June 3–9, 2006), 2187.

103. Ministry of Home Affairs, Government of India, *Annual Report: 2004–2005* (New Delhi, 2005), 48.

104. Ibid.

105. Eight slots in total. Ministry of Home Affairs, Government of India, *Annual Report: 2005–2006* (New Delhi, 2006), 27.

106. Sanjay Kak, "Fire with Fire: Ten Years of the Chhattisgarh School of Counter-Insurgency," *The Caravan*, August 1, 2015, http://www.caravanmagazine.in/reportage/fire-with-fire-chattisgarh-school-counter-insurgency.

107. Nandini Sundar, "Bastar, Maoism and Salwa Judum," *Economic and Political Weekly* 41, no. 29 (July 22–28, 2006), 3187.

108. Jason Miklian, "The Purification Hunt: The Salwa Judum Counterinsurgency in Chhattisgarh, India," *Dialectical Anthropology* 33, no. 3/4 (December 2009), 443.

109. Nandini Sundar, "At War with Oneself: Constructing Naxalism as India's Biggest Security Threat," in ed., Michael Kugelman, *India's Contemporary Security Challenges* (Washington, DC: Woodrow Wilson International Center, 2013), 15.

110. Supreme Court of India, *Nandini Sundar & Org. versus State of Chhattisgarh Order*, July 5, 2011, 4.

111. Despite the ban, a new movement comprising former proxies was launched in Chhattisgarh in 2015, drawing both strong public criticism and support. Priyanka Kaushal, "'We Have No Regard for Those against Development of Bastar'— Chavindra Karma," *Tehelka*, February 6, 2016, http://www.tehelka.com/2016/02/we-have-no-regard-for-those-against-development-chavindra-karma/.

112. People's Union for Civil Liberties, *Where the State Makes War on Its Own People*, 12.

113. Suvojit Bagchi, "The Rise and Fall of Mahendra Karma—the Bastar Tiger," *The Hindu*, May 27, 2013, http://www.thehindu.com/news/national/the-rise-and-fall-of-mahendra-karma-the-bastar-tiger/article4753665.ece.

114. People's Union for Civil Liberties, *Where the State Makes War on Its Own People*, 12.

115. Bagchi, "The Rise and Fall of Mahendra Karma."

116. Kak, "Fire with Fire."

117. Ministry of Home Affairs, *Annual Report: 2004–2005*, 47.

118. Sundar, "At War with Oneself," 15.
119. Bert Suykens, "Diffuse Authority in the Beedi Commodity Chain: Naxalite and State Governance in Tribal Telangana, India," *Development and Change* 41, no. 1 (January 2010), 158.
120. Bagchi, "The Rise and Fall of Mahendra Karma."
121. Kashyap, *Dangerous Duty*, 5.
122. "Indian State 'Backing Vigilantes,'" BBC News, July 15, 2008.
123. Sundar, "Insurgency," 161.
124. Author's interview with a local expert, New Delhi, August 2015.
125. People's Union for Civil Liberties, *Where the State Makes War on Its Own People*, 19.
126. Asian Centre for Human Rights, *The Adivasis of Chhattisgarh*, 18.
127. Author's interview with Indian journalist, New Delhi, August 2015.
128. Kak, "Fire with Fire."
129. Supreme Court of India, *Nandini Sundar & Org. versus State of Chhattisgarh Order*, July 5, 2011, 23.
130. Ibid., 25.
131. Asian Centre for Human Rights, *The Adivasis of Chhattisgarh*, 34.
132. Miklian, "The Purification Hunt," 447–48.
133. International Labour Organization, *The International Labour Organization's Fundamental Conventions* (Geneva: International Labour Office, 2003), 44.
134. Kashyap, *Dangerous Duty*, 5.
135. People's Union for Civil Liberties, *Where the State Makes War on Its Own People*, 24.
136. Somini Sengupta, "In Villages Across India, Maoist Guerrillas Widen 'People's War,'" *New York Times*, April 13, 2006.
137. Asian Centre for Human Rights, *The Adivasis of Chhattisgarh*, 4.
138. Ibid. These observations were confirmed in an interview with a local expert who requested anonymity due to the sensitivity of the subject. Author's interview with a local expert, New Delhi, August 2015.
139. People's Union for Civil Liberties, *Where the State Makes War on Its Own People*, 24.
140. Ibid., 13.
141. Ministry of Home Affairs, *Annual Report: 2005–2006*, 28.
142. Ibid., 25–30.
143. Author's interview with Ajai Sahni, New Delhi, August 2015.
144. Miklian, "The Purification Hunt," 447.
145. Joseph Marianus Kujur, "Development-Induced Displacement in Chhattisgarh: A Case Study from a Tribal Perspective," *Social Action* 58 (January–March 2008), 36.
146. Asian Centre for Human Rights, *The Adivasis of Chhattisgarh*, 17.
147. Ibid., 16.
148. People's Union for Civil Liberties, *Where the State Makes War on Its Own People*, 15 and 17.
149. Asian Centre for Human Rights, *The Adivasis of Chhattisgarh*, 34.

150. Ibid., 26.
151. See People's Union for Civil Liberties, *Where the State Makes War on Its Own People*, 15.
152. Kashyap, *Dangerous Duty*, 17.
153. Sundar, "At War with Oneself," 16.
154. Arundhati Roy, "Gandhi, but with Guns," *The Guardian*, March 27, 2010.
155. Miklian, "The Purification Hunt," 442.
156. Report of an Expert Group to Planning Commission, *Development Challenges in Extremist Affected Areas* (New Delhi: Government of India, 2008), 77.
157. Ramachandra Guha, "Will India Become A Superpower?" *Outlook India*, June 30, 2008.
158. Perlez and Shah, "Pakistan Uses Tribal Militias in Taliban War."

CHAPTER 6

1. Human Rights Watch, "Turkey," *Human Rights Watch World Report 1992* (1992), https://www.hrw.org/reports/1992/WR92/HSW-06.htm#TopOfPage.
2. For example, Turkey actively supported the United States during the 1991 Persian Gulf conflict.
3. Human Rights Watch, "Turkey."
4. İlnur Cevik, "Kurdish Village Guards Face Uncertain Future," *Al-Monitor*, April 11, 2013, http://www.al-monitor.com/pulse/originals/2013/04/turkey-village-guards-pkk-fight-peace-process-kurdish-issue.html.
5. Paul Staniland, "Militias, Ideology, and the State," *Journal of Conflict Resolution* 59, no. 5 (August 2015), 12.
6. Thomas Grove, "Analysis: Chechnya: How Did Putin's Party Win 99 Percent?" Reuters, December 21, 2011, http://www.reuters.com/article/us-russia-chechnya-elections-idUSTRE7BK1CA20111221.
7. Shaun Walker, "Boris Nemtsov Murder: Chechen Chief Kadyrov Confirms Link to Prime Suspect," *The Guardian*, March 8, 2015.
8. Andrei Shleifer and Daniel Treisman, "A Normal Country," *Foreign Affairs* 83, no. 2 (March-April 2004), 22 and 31–35.
9. Yelena Biberman, "Violence by Proxy: Russia's Ex-Rebels and Criminals in Chechnya," in ed. Bettina Koch, *State Terror, State Violence: Global Perspectives* (Wiesbaden: Springer, 2016): 135-50.
10. Jason Lyall, "Are Coethnics More Effective Counterinsurgents? Evidence from the Second Chechen War," *American Political Science Review* 104, no. 1 (February 2010), 3.
11. Kimberly Marten, *Warlords: Strong-Arm Brokers in Weak States* (Ithaca: Cornell University Press, 2012), 106.
12. In the 1980s, 62 percent of the population lived in villages, and roughly 36,000 settlements had less than 2,000 inhabitants. Matthew Kocher, "The Decline of PKK and the Viability of a One-State Solution in Turkey," *International Journal on Multicultural Societies* 4, no. 1 (2002), 4.

13. Stathis N. Kalyvas, *The Logic of Violence in Civil War* (New York: Cambridge University Press 2006), 136.

14. The scheme was reminiscent of the Hamidiye corps, the local militia system used in the late Ottoman period. For a detailed account of the Hamidiye, see Janet Klein, *The Margins of Empire: Kurdish Militias in the Ottoman Tribal Zone* (Stanford: Stanford University Press, 2011). On the long tradition of state-nonstate collaboration and nonstate violence in Turkey and the Ottoman Empire, see Ugur Ümit Üngör, *The Making of Modern Turkey: Nation and State in Eastern Anatolia, 1913–1950* (Oxford: Oxford University Press, 2012); Barkey, *Bandits and Bureaucrats.*

15. Cevik, "Kurdish Village Guards Face Uncertain Future."

16. Ceren Belge, "State Building and the Limits of Legibility," *International Journal of Middle East Studies* 43, no. 1 (Feb 2011), 106.

17. Author's interview with a former Turkish security official, Istanbul, August 2013.

18. Author's interview with an official from Turkish Ministry of Interior, Ankara, August 16, 2013.

19. David McDowall, *A Modern History of the Kurds* (New York: I. B. Tauris 2004), 424.

20. Ünal, *Counterterrorism in Turkey,* 54.

21. Human Rights Watch, "Turkey," 28.

22. Ibid., 56.

23. Author's interview with an official of the Human Rights Association, Diyarbakır Branch, Diyarbakır, Turkey, August 2013.

24. A reputable Turkish NGO, the Turkish Economic and Social Studies Foundation (TESEV), describes that the figure of 3 to 4 million as "a rather high estimate." A. Tamer Aker, Betül Çelik, Dilek Kurban, Turgay Ünalan, and Deniz Yükseker, *The Problem of Internal Displacement in Turkey: Assessment and Policy Proposals* (Istanbul: Turkish Economic and Social Studies Foundation 2005), 4.

25. John S. Pustay, *Counterinsurgency Warfare* (New York: Free Press 1965), 100.

26. Ayse Aslihan Celenk, "Democratization of the National Security Discource and the Political Parties in Turkey," *Erciyes Üniversitesi Iktisadi ve Idari Bilimler Fakültesi Dergisi* 33 (July–December 2009), 121.

27. Human Rights Watch, "Weapons Transfers and Violations of the Laws of War in Turkey," November 1995, https://www.hrw.org/reports/1995/Turkey.htm.

28. Evren Balta, "Causes and Consequences of the Village Guard System in Turkey," conference paper, Mellon Fellowship for Humanitarian and Security Affairs Conference, CUNY Graduate Center, New York, December 2, 2004, 11.

29. Cited in ibid., 11–12.

30. McDowall, *A Modern History of the Kurds,* 424.

31. Nadir Gergin, Fatih Balci, and I. Sevki Eldivan, "Turkey's Counter Terrorism Policies Against the PKK: The 'Fish' or the 'Water'?" in eds. Sıddık Ekici, Ahmet Ekici, David A. McEntire, Richard H. Ward, and Sudha S. Arlikatti, *Building Terrorism Resistant Communities* (Amsterdam: IOS Press 2008), 274.

32. Holly Cartner, "Turkey: Letter to Minister Aksu calling for the Abolition of the Village Guards Human Rights Watch," Human Rights Watch, June 7, 2006, http://www.hrw.org/news/2006/06/07/turkey-letter-minister-aksu-calling-abolition-village-guards.

33. Author's interview with a lawyer and member of Goc-Der migrant's association and a lawyer associated with the Diyarbakır Bar Association, Diyarbakır, Turkey, August 2013.

34. Gergin, Balci, and Eldivan, "Turkey's Counter Terrorism Policies Against the PKK," 269–70.

35. Author's interview with Mesut Değer (former parliamentarian from Diyarbakır on Republican People's Party [CHP] ticket), Ankara, Turkey, August 17, 2013. Değer led the investigation of the government's relationship with the village guards and illicit organizations, especially the Hizbullah.

36. US Department of State, "Country Reports on Human Rights Practices," Bureau of Democracy, Human Rights, and Labor, March 31, 2003, http://www.state.gov/j/drl/rls/hrrpt/2002/18396.htm.

37. Gergin, Balci, and Eldivan, "Turkey's Counter Terrorism Policies Against the PKK," 274.

38. GIS map created using the data provided by Minister of Internal Affairs Nahit Menteşe to Mehmet Emin Sever of the Social Democratic People's Party at the April 18, 1995, Turkish parliamentary session, in response to a parliamentary inquiry about the village guards. In Şemsa Özar, Nesrin Uçarlar, and Osman Aytar, *From Past to Present, a Paramilitary Organization in Turkey: Village Guard System* (Diyarbakır, Turkey: Institute for Political and Social Research, 2013).

39. The gendarmerie is formally under the control of the Turkish Minister of Interior. Its members are trained as soldiers and spread across a network of police stations and outposts to control rural areas, patrol villages, and gather intelligence. During conflict, the gendarmerie is under the jurisdiction of the military.

40. Author's interview with an official from the Turkish Ministry of Interior, Ankara, August 16, 2013.

41. Human Rights Watch, *Turkey: Forced Displacement of Ethnic Kurds from Southeastern Turkey* 6, no. 12 (Helsinki: Human Rights Watch, October 1994), 27.

42. Author's interview with a Kurdish academic and field researcher who interviewed dozens of village guards, Ankara, August 17, 2013.

43. The absolute size of the rural population in the OHAL provinces fell by 11.9 percent from 1990 to 1997, despite a population growth of 14 percent. The population of district centers in the same region increased by 45 percent. The rural depopulation in the OHAL region proceeded nearly three times faster than in the rest of Turkey, while the OHAL population grew faster. Kocher, "The Decline of PKK and the Viability of a One-State Solution in Turkey," 6–9.

44. Author's interview with an official of Mazlum-Der (religiously conservative human rights association), Diyarbakır, Turkey, August 15, 2013. Author's interview with a Kurdish academic and field researcher, Ankara, August 17, 2013.

45. Author's interview with a former subprovincial governor in southeastern Turkey (name of province withheld for anonymity), Ankara, August 16, 2013.

46. Author's interview with an official of Mazlum-Der, August 15, 2013.

47. Author's interview with an official from Turkish Ministry of Interior, August 16, 2013.

48. Author's interview with an official of Mazlum-Der, August 15, 2013.

49. Author's interview with an official from Turkish Ministry of Interior, August 16, 2013.

50. Author's interview with an official of Mazlum-Der, August 15, 2013.

51. Author's interview with an official from Turkish Ministry of Interior, August 16, 2013.

52. The Kurdish Hizbullah, comprising Sunni members, is not linked to the Shia organization operating under the same name in Lebanon.

53. The Iranian Revolution inspired a variety of Islamist movements in the Middle East in the early 1980s, including some Sunni groups such as the Kurdish Hizbullah.

54. İsmet G. İmset, *The PKK: A Report on Separatist Violence in Turkey* (Ankara: Turkish Daily News 1992), 123.

55. Human Rights Watch, "What Is Turkey's Hizbullah?" February 16, 2000, http://www.hrw.org/legacy/english/docs/2000/02/16/turkey3057_txt.htm.

56. Henri J. Barkey and Graham Fuller, *Turkey's Kurdish Question* (Lanham: Rowman and Littlefield, 1998), 73.

57. İmset, *The PKK*, 124.

58. Author's interview with Değer, August 17, 2013.

59. Author's interview with an official of Mazlum-Der, August 15, 2013.

60. Author's interview with a lawyer who handled legal cases involving the Hizbullah, Diyarbakır, August 2013.

61. İmset, *The PKK*, 123.

62. Human Rights Watch, "What Is Turkey's Hizbullah?"

63. Ibid.

64. Author's interview with a former state official, Ankara, August 2013.

65. Author's interview with Değer, August 17, 2013.

66. Ibid.

67. Author's interview with a Diyarbakır lawyer, Diyarbakır, August 2013.

68. Author's interview with Değer, August 17, 2013.

69. Author's interview with a Diyarbakır lawyer, August 2013.

70. Whereas the 1992 documents listed separatism and terrorism and did not mention of Islamism. Pina Bilgin, "Turkey's Changing Security Discourses: The Challenge of Globalization," *European Journal of Political Research* 44 (2005), 188.

71. Timothy L. Thomas, "The Battle of Grozny: Deadly Classroom for Urban Combat" (article first appeared in *Parameters* [Summer 1999]: 87–102), http://fmso.leavenworth.army.mil/documents/battle.htm.

72. Olga Oliker, *Russia's Chechen Wars 1994–2000: Lessons from Urban Combat* (Santa Monica, CA: Arroyo Center, RAND, 2001), 14.

73. Robert Seely, *Russo-Chechen Conflict, 1800–2000: A Deadly Embrace* (London: Frank Cass, 2001), 220.

74. Anna Politkovskaya, *A Small Corner of Hell: Dispatches from Chechnya* (Chicago: University of Chicago Press, 2003), 17–18.

75. Simon Saradzhyan, "Chechnya Vow Cast a Long Shadow," *Moscow Times*, February 26, 2008.

76. Steven Eke, "Yeltsin's Chechen Nightmare," BBC News, April 24, 2007, http://news.bbc.co.uk/2/hi/europe/6588221.stm.

77. Ali Askerov, *Historical Dictionary of the Chechen Conflict* (Lanham: Rowman and Littlefield, 2015), 147.
78. Labazanov was killed in 1996. Ilyas Akhmadov and Miriam Lanskoy, *The Chechen Struggle: Independence Won and Lost* (New York: Palgrave Macmillan, 2010), 14
79. Dmitri V. Trenin and Aleksei V. Malashenko, *Russia's Restless Frontier: The Chechnya Factor in Post-Soviet Russia* (Washington, DC: Carnegie Endowment for International Peace, 2004), 21.
80. Anatol Lieven, *Chechnya: Tombstone of Russian Power* (New Haven: Yale University Press, 1999), 213.
81. Timothy J. Colton, *Yeltsin: A Life* (New York: Basic Books, 2008), 230.
82. Seely, *Russo-Chechen Conflict*, 223.
83. Ibid., 225
84. Lieven, *Chechnya*, 102
85. Valery Tishkov, *Chechnya: Life in a War-Torn Society* (Berkeley: University of California Press, 2004), 69.
86. Seely, *Russo-Chechen Conflict*, 170
87. Thomas, "The Battle of Grozny."
88. Richard Sakwa, "Introduction: Why Chechnya?" in ed. Richard Sakwa, *Chechnya: From Past to Future* (London: Anthem Press, 2005), 28.
89. Oliker, *Russia's Chechen Wars 1994–2000*, 16.
90. Lieven, *Chechnya*, 103.
91. Seely, *Russo-Chechen Conflict*, 226–27.
92. Oliker, *Russia's Chechen Wars 1994–2000*, 14.
93. Ibid., 16
94. Seely, *Russo-Chechen Conflict*, 163–67.
95. Trenin and Malashenko, *Russia's Restless Frontier*, 20.
96. Yury Golotyuk, "On the Eve: Bad Peace Before a Good Quarrel," *Current Digest of the Russian Press* 46, no. 31, August 31, 1994, 1.
97. Seely, *Russo-Chechen Conflict*, 163.
98. Anatol Lieven, "Gracious Grozny," *National Interest*, September 18, 2008, http://nationalinterest.org/article/gracious-grozny-2865.
99. Tishkov, *Chechnya*, 69.
100. Lieven, *Chechnya*, 109.
101. Dzhabrail Gakaev, "Chechnya in Russia and Russia in Chechnya," in ed. Richard Sakwa, *Chechnya: From Past to Future* (London: Anthem Press, 2005), 31–32.
102. Oliker, *Russia's Chechen Wars 1994–2000*, xi.
103. Trenin and Malashenko, *Russia's Restless Frontier*, 131–32.
104. Ibid., 132.
105. As the Pakistani, Indian, and Turkish cases show, a strong military does not automatically translate into effective force employment, especially in counterinsurgency operations.
106. Trenin and Malashenko, *Russia's Restless Frontier*, 35.
107. Quoted in Simon Shuster, "How the War on Terrorism Did Russia a Favor," *Time*, September 19, 2011, http://content.time.com/time/world/article/0,8599,2093529,00.html.

108. Colton, *Yeltsin*, 433.
109. "Federals Unlikely to Storm Grozny, Warlords Ready to Pay Anything for Escape," *Military News Agency*, December 12, 1999.
110. "Russia-Chechnya-Grozny," *Itar-Tass Weekly News*, December 25, 1999.
111. Leonid Berres, "Russia's First Guerrilla," *Defence & Security*, November 11, 1999.
112. "Russia-Press-Review," *Itar-Tass Weekly News*, November 6, 1999.
113. "Russia-Chechnya-New-Man," *Itar-Tass Weekly News*, November 14, 1999.
114. "Russia-Chechnya-Grozny," *Itar-Tass Weekly News*, December 25, 1999.
115. Erik Batuev, "Grozny's Maverick Mayor Resigns," Institute for War and Peace Reporting, May 21, 2001, https://iwpr.net/global-voices/groznys-maverick-mayor-resigns.
116. "Russia-Chechnya-Grozny."
117. "Russia-Chechnya," *Itar-Tass Weekly News*, December 11, 1999.
118. Aslan Ramazanov and Maxim Stepenin, "Feds Begin to Launch Assault against Chechen Capital," *Kommersant-Daily*, December 15, 1999, 1.
119. Oliker, *Russia's Chechen Wars 1994–2000*, 44.
120. Olga Alenova and Musa Muradov, "The Efficiency of Gantamirov's Regiment Has Been Tested in Combat," *Kommersant Daily*, December 3, 1999, 3.
121. Colin McMahon, "Moscow Caught Off Guard by Dagestan Rebels," *Chicago Tribune*, September 7, 1999, http://articles.chicagotribune.com/1999-09-07/news/9909070170_1_dagestani-chechnya-russian-warplanes.
122. Batuev, "Grozny's Maverick Mayor Resigns."
123. Loris Gukasyan, "Russia-Chechnya-Voluntee," *Itar-Tass Weekly News*, December 10, 1999.
124. "Russia's No. 1 Guerrilla—Yeltsin Pardons Beslan Gantemirov – He Might Be Useful," *Current Digest of the Russian Press* 51, no. 45, December 8, 1999.
125. Kimberly Marten, *Warlords: Strong-Arm Brokers in Weak States* (Ithaca: Cornell University Press, 2012), 106.
126. Making the area surrounding Gudermes rebel-free was accomplished with the help of another, less-known, rebel commander, Sulim Yamadayev. Yamadayev and his four brothers had previously fought for the Chechen secessionist government but were disillusioned with the movement when the moderate Chechen government of Maskhadov allied with the Islamists. The Yamadayevs and their followers turned to Moscow when "the Chechen war for national independence came to resemble a jihad." Brian Glyn Williams, "Fighting with a Double-Edged Sword? Proxy Militias in Iraq, Afghanistan, Bosnia, and Chechnya," in ed. Michael Innes, *Making Sense of Proxy Wars: States, Surrogates & the Use of Force* (Dulles: Potomac Books, 2012), 85. Sulim Yamadayev frequently clashed with Ahkmad Kadyrov's son, Ramzan, and was killed in Dubai in 2009.
127. Trenin and Malashenko, *Russia's Restless Frontier*, 37.
128. Marten, *Warlords*, 107.
129. Ibid.
130. Emil Souleimanov, "An Ethnography of Counterinsurgency: Kadyrovtsy and Russia's Policy of Chechenization," *Post-Soviet Affairs* 31, no. 2 (March 2015), 105.
131. Marten, *Warlords*, 111.

132. Ibid., 112.

133. Emil Souleimanov, "Russian Chechnya Policy: 'Chechenization' Turning into 'Kadyrovization'?" *Central Asia-Caucasus Analyst* 8, no. 11 (May 31, 2006), 4.

134. Human Rights Center Memorial, "The Chechen Republic: Consequences of 'Chechenization' of the Conflict," 2006, http://www.memo.ru/eng/memhrc/texts/6chechen.shtml.

135. Simon Ostrovsky, "Kadyrov Jr. Flexes His Muscles in Chechnya," *Moscow Times*, February 27, 2004.

CHAPTER 7

1. Carl von Clausewitz, *On War*, trans. and ed. Michael Howard and Peter Paret (Princeton: Princeton University Press, 1976), 85.

2. See US Department of the Army, *Urban Operations*, Field Manual 3-06, October 2006 (Washington, DC), 3–16.

3. Niccolo Machiavelli, *The Prince*, ed. and trans. Peter Bondanella (Oxford: Oxford University Press, 2005), 87.

4. Kautilya, *The Arthashastra*, ed. and trans. L. N. Rangarajan (New Delhi: Penguin Books, 1992), 134.

5. Daniel Byman, *Deadly Connections: States That Sponsor Terrorism* (Cambridge: Cambridge University Press, 2007), 1.

6. Adam Smith, *An Inquiry into the Nature and Causes of the Wealth of Nations* (Edinburgh: Thomas Nelson, 1843), 293.

7. Ayesha Jalal cited in Maleeha Lodhi, *Pakistan: Beyond the 'Crisis State'* (London: Hurst, 2011), 7.

8. Supreme Court of India, *Nandini Sundar & Org. versus State of Chhattisgarh Order*, July 5, 2011, 18.

9. US Department of the Army, *Counterinsurgency*, Field Manual 3-24, December 2006 (Washington, DC), 1–28.

10. Samuel P. Huntington, *The Soldier and the State: The Theory and Politics of Civil-Military Relations* (Cambridge: Belknap Press, 1957), 7.

11. Ibid., 10.

12. United Nations Human Rights Office of the Commissioner, "Geneva Convention Relative to the Treatment of Prisoners of War," August 12, 1949, http://www.ohchr.org/EN/ProfessionalInterest/Pages/TreatmentOfPrisonersOfWar.aspx.

13. Sameer Lalwani, "Valley of the Brawls: Tensions Rise in Kashmir," *Foreign Affairs*, February 11, 2016.

14. Author's interview with expert who regularly visits the region, New Delhi, August 2015. Also see Nandini Sundar, "No End in Sight for India's Bloody Maoist Conflict," *Al Jazeera*, May 9, 2017.

15. Ekaterina Sokirianskaia, "Is Chechnya Taking over Russia?" *New York Times*, August 17, 2017.

16. Berkay Mandıracı, "Turkey's PKK Conflict Kills almost 3,000 in Two Years," *International Crisis Group*, July 20, 2017.

17. With the notable exception of some of the branches linked to drug trafficking.

18. Stathis Kalyvas, "Micro-Level Studies of Violence in Civil War: Refining and Extending the Control-Collaboration Model," *Terrorism and Political Violence* 24, no. 4 (September 2012): 658-68.

19. Stathis N. Kalyvas, *The Logic of Violence in Civil War* (New York: Cambridge University Press 2006), 24.

20. Kai M. Thaler, "Mixed Methods Research in the Study of Political and Social Violence and Conflict," *Journal of Mixed Methods Research* 11, no. 1 (2017), 69.

21. For excellent examples of this type of work with a focus on rebels, see Mona Kanwal Sheikh, *Guardians of God: Inside the Religious Mind of the Pakistani Taliban* (Delhi: Oxford University Press, 2016); Elisabeth Jean Wood, *Insurgent Collective Action and Civil War in El Salvador* (Cambridge: Cambridge University Press, 2003).

22. Jeff Victoroff, "The Mind of the Terrorist: A Review and Critique of Psychological Approaches," *Journal of Conflict Resolution* 49, no. 1 (February 2005), 3.

23. John Mueller, "The Banality of 'Ethnic War,'" *International Security* 25, no. 1 (Summer 2000), 43.

24. Ibid., 70.

25. Barbara F. Walter, "The Extremist's Advantage in Civil Wars," *International Security* 42, no. 2 (Fall 2017), 7–39.

26. Karen DeYoung, "U.S.-Trained Fighters in Syria Gave Equipment to al-Qaeda Affiliate," *Washington Post*, September 25, 2015.

27. Nick Turse, "Documents Show US Military Expands Reach of Special Operations Programs," *The Intercept*, September 8, 2016; Nick Turse, "American Special Ops Forces Have Deployed to 70 Percent of the World's Countries in 2017," *The Nation*, June 26, 2017; Eitan Shamir and Eyal Ben-Ari, "The Rise of Special Operations Forces: Generalized Specialization, Boundary Spanning and Military Autonomy," *Journal of Strategic Studies* 41, no. 3 (2018): 335-71.

28. Lindsey O'Rourke, "Covert Calamities: American-Backed Covert Regime Changes and Civil War," *Canadian Foreign Policy Journal* 23, no. 3 (2017), 232–45.

29. Leo Tolstoy, *War and Peace*, trans. Richard Pevear and Larissa Volokhonsky (New York: Vintage Books, 2008), 682 and 684.

30. Ahmed Rashid, *Pakistan on the Brink: The Future of America, Pakistan, and Afghanistan* (New York: Penguin Books, 2013), 27.

31. Anatol Lieven, *Pakistan: A Hard Country* (New York: PublicAffairs, 2011), 8.

32. Paul Staniland, "Between a Rock and a Hard Place: Insurgent Fratricide, Ethnic Defection, and the Rise of Pro-State Paramilitaries," *Journal of Conflict Resolution* 56, no. 1 (February 2012), 30.

33. Nina Tannenwald, "The Nuclear Taboo: The United States and the Normative Basis of Nuclear Non-Use," *International Organization* 53, no. 3 (Summer 1999), 433–68.

34. Bharat Karnad, *Why India Is Not a Great Power (Yet)* (New Delhi: Oxford University Press, 2015).

35. Frank Pallone, "Pallone and Bera Introduce Resolution Supporting India's Bid for Permanent U.N. Security Council Seat," Press Release, September 26, 2017, https://pallone.house.gov/press-release/pallone-and-bera-introduce-resolution-supporting-indias-bid-permanent-un-security-0.

36. For more on these important concepts, see James Ron, *Frontiers and Ghettos: State Violence in Serbia and Israel* (Berkeley: University of California Press, 2003).
37. Shivaji Mukherjee, "Colonial Origins of Maoist Insurgency in India: Historical Institutions and Civil War," *Journal of Conflict Resolution* 62, no. 10 (2018): 2232-74.
38. Associated Press in Srinagar, "Kashmir Police Officer Suspected of Recruiting Rebels Then Killing Them," *The Guardian*, June 5, 2013, https://www.theguardian.com/world/2013/jun/05/kashmir-police-recruiting-rebels-killing?CMP=Share_iOSApp_Other.

INDEX

Tables and figures are indicated by an italic *t* and *f*, respectively, following the page number.

Abdullah, Farooq, 89–91
activist rebel, 10
activists. *See also specific types*
  balance-of-interests theory, 12
  balance-of-interests theory, new, 25, 26
  balance-of-interests theory, new, *vs.*
    opportunists, 26–28
  interests, 25, 26
  nonstate actors' interests, 25, 26
  relational alliances, 26–28
  state-nonstate alliances, civil war, 12
  state preference, *vs.* opportunists, 28
Adezai Aman Lashkar, 97–98,
  108–9
administrative collaboration, 19, 20*f*
Afghanistan tribal fighters, against
  al-Qaeda, 5
Aham, Ariel, 7–8
al-Assad, Bashar, 5
al-Badr activists–Pakistan alliance,
  56–59, 159
Al Baraq, Indian, 78
al-Ikhwan, 78
al-Khattab, Ibn, 150
alliances. *See also specific types, countries,*
  and wars
  asymmetrical, 28
  coalitions, 16–17
  collaboration, 19, 20*f*
  ideology, choices, 24

  Kautilya on, 16
  nonstate, typology, 15–23
  rebel, existing research, 9–10
  relational, 26–28
  state, 9
  state-nonstate, 158 (*see also* state-
    nonstate alliances)
  transactional, 26–28
  wartime, 16–17
alliances, balance-of-interests theory, 16
  ideology in choice of, 24
  new, 16
  power distribution and formation, 24
  state-nonstate, 16, 158
  wartime, 16–17
Alpha (Naba Azad), 85, 86, 88
al-Shams, 56–57, 58
Anbar Awakening, 98, 100
Andhra Pradesh, Cobras, 6
anti-Naxalite "awakening," Chhattisgarh,
  112–28. *See also* India, anti-Naxalite
  "awakening," Chhattisgarh
Armed Forces (Jammu and Kashmir)
  Special Powers Act, 69–70
army. *See also specific armies and countries*
  standing, necessity, 7
  "volunteer," Razakars, 29–52, 53–54
Arthashastra (Kautilya), 14–15, 16,
  19, 157
Assam, SULFA, 6

asymmetrical alliances, 28
auxiliary, 20–21
    China, People's Liberation Army
      Militia, 20–21
    Germany, Second World War, 20
    history, 21
Awami League, 40, 42, 43
    leaders' escape to India, 44
    Mujib Bahini, 55–56
    Rahman, Sheikh Mujibur (Mujib),
      42, 43–44
    support, high, 43–44
Awami National Party (ANP), 111
Azad, Ghulam Nabi, 85, 86, 88

Babloo, 96
Baig, Hilal Ahmed, 74
balance-of-interests theory, 12
    Pakistan army–Islamist militant
      alliance, 40
    state-nonstate alliances, 158
    state-nonstate alliances, Pakistan and
      India, 158–60
balance-of-interests theory, new, 14–24
    activist-opportunist choice and
      alliance differences, 26–28
    administrative and operational
      collaboration, state-militia, 19, 20f
    alliance, 16
    alliance, wartime, 16–17
    "apolitical" (tactics-focused)
      approach, 24
    argument summary, 26–30, 27f
    asymmetrical alliances, 28
    auxiliary, 20–21
    balance, importance, 28
    collaboration, administrative and
      operational, 19, 20f
    data collection, 34–36
    democracy, weak, 23
    framework, 24–30, 27f
    freelancer, 22–23
    ideology, in alliance choices, 24
    insurgency, robust, 30–31
    Kautilya, *Arthashastra,* 14–15
    literature explanations, potential, 23–24

lower power balance, socio-ideological
    links, and state-nonstate alliance
    outcomes, 27f
    militia, 17–19 (*see also* militia)
    neoclassical realism, 8–9, 28–29
    nonstate actors' interests,
      activists, 25, 26
    nonstate actors' interests,
      opportunists, 25
    nonstate actors' interests, varying, 25
    nonstate allies, typology, 15–23
    power, distribution and alliance
      formation, 24
    power, operationalizing, 29–30
    proxy, 21–22, 30, 31
    research design and case
      selection, 32–34
    research needs, comparative
      qualitative, 32
    scope conditions, 30–32
    state, conceptualization, 15
    state-militia collaboration forms and
      militia types, 20f
    state-nonstate alliance, 16
    violence outsourcing, 16
    war and balance of power, Mao on, 30
bandwagoning, piling-on, 66–67,
    130, 139
Bangladesh
    1971 Pakistan war (*See* Pakistan,
      1971 war)
    birth, bloody, 39–40
    war crimes tribunal, 37
Basayev, Shamil, 149, 150, 151
Bastar Tiger, 119–22, 125, 161
Battle of the Belonia Bulge, 47–49
Bhat, Abdul Gani, 64, 83–84
Bhat, Fayaz Ahmad (Tanveer), 84–86
Bhat, Maqbool, 82
Bhutto, Benazir, 111
Bhutto, Zulfikar Ali, 43
Biddhu (Scorpion) Squads, 55
Bihari, 46
bin Laden, Osama, Afghanistan tribals
    capture deal for, 1–2
Bodo Liberation Tigers, Assam, 6

Britain, 8
Bush, George H. W., Turkey
    relations, 131
Bush, George W., 102

Cats, Punjab, 6
Centeno, Miguel, 7–8
Chechnya
    as ethnic republic, 144–45
    Russian wars, 132–33, 143–55 (*see also* Russia, Chechnya wars)
    Russia relations, history, 144
    Yeltsin and, 144–45
Chhattisgarh
    anti-Naxalite "awakening," 112–28
        (*see also* India, anti-Naxalite
        "awakening," Chhattisgarh)
    current status, 163–64
    formation, 116–17
    India's weakness to parity, 117–19
    lands and tribes, 115
    mineral-rich land, 116–17
    population densities and
        residents, 115
    Salwa Judum (*see* Salwa Judum)
China, 8
    People's Liberation Army
        Militia, 20–21
Christia, Fotini, 9
civil defense force. *See* militias,
    pro-government
civil war. *See also specific countries
    and wars*
    ally, unexpected, 157–58
civil war, state-nonstate alliances
    balance-of-interests theory, 16, 158
    Pakistan and India, 158–60
    Turkey and Russia, 160–61
    understanding, 158
civil wars, scholarship, 8
    rebel alliances, 9–10
    state alliances, 9
coalition, 16–17. *See also specific types*
Cobras, Andhra Pradesh, 6
coercion, of opportunists, 25–26
Cohen, Stephen P., 39

collaboration
    administrative, 19, 20*f*
    alliances, 19, 20*f*
    operational, 19, 20*f*
    operational, proxy, 21–22, 30, 31
Colonel, Bashir, 95
Communist Party of India, 116, 117
Communist Party of India People's War,
    114, 116
concepts. *See also specific types*
    applicable, 15
    definition, 15
    state, 15
    state, Weberian, 16
counterinsurgency field manual,
    U.S., 162–63
counterinsurgent, nonstate. *See also
    specific countries and types*
    effectiveness, 5–6
    legal issues, 6
    South Asia, 6
    usefulness *vs.* national and
        international norms, 6

Dadayev, Zaur, 132
Dar, Mohammad Ahsan. *See also* Hizbul
    Mujahideen
    capture, 84, 85
    Hizbul Mujahideen, 82–83
    Mujahideen-e-Islam, 83–84
Darzi, Sameer (Babloo), 96
data collection and sources, 34–36
    local networks, 35
    Pakistan war, 1971, 41
    tribes, 35
democracy, weak
    balance-of-interests theory, new, 23
    India's weakness to parity in
        Chhattisgarh, 117–19
    plausible deniability, 23, 61
deniability, plausible. *See* plausible
    deniability
Dudayev, Dzhokhar, 144–45, 148
    Gantamirov betrayal, 153
Duvdevan unit, Israel Defense
    Forces, 18, 23

East Pakistan, Pakistan regaining control
(March–May, 1971)
Biharis, 46
demographics, 42
guerrilla refugee force, 41
military regime and martial law, 46–47
Operation Blitz, 43
Operation Searchlight and Awami
League, 42, 43–46
politics: Mujib, Bhutto, and Yahya, 43
population and settlement area, 42
poverty, 42–43
proxy assistance, lack, 45–46
West Pakistani Army killing innocents,
Dhaka University, 44–45
ethnic war research, 165–66

Federally Administered Tribal Areas
(FATA), 105, 106–7
Khassadars (tribal police force), 107
flexible discipline, 35
freelancer, 22–23

Gall, Carlotta, 103
Gano Bahini, 55
Gantamirov, Bislan, 132–33, 161
Dudayev betrayal, 153
postwar spoils, 132–33
Russia alliance, 152–53
Geelani, Syed Ali Shah, 82–83
Germany, Second World War, auxiliary
forces, 20
Grenier, Robert, 102–3, 105, 106
Guatemala
Patrullas de Autodefensa Civil, 5
U.S. proxies, 21
Guha, Ramachandra, 126–27
Guha, Ranajit, 114
guns, as balance of power, 66
Güreş, Doğan, 138

Hannibal's troops, Battle of Cannae, 21
Hizbul Mujahideen, 83–86
Dar, Mohammad Ahsan, 82–83
emergence, 70
founding, 83

infiltrators from, 75
Jamaat partnership, 83
Liyaqat, surrounding, 77
Muslim Mujahideen, main target, 88
Muslim Mujahideen, reconciliation
attempt, 86
in Parrey's territory, 76
rise and proxy cultivation, 72–73
on the run, 89
slogan, 70
training, 83
Huntington, Samuel, 163

ideology, in alliance choices, 24
ideology hypothesis, 131–32
Ikhwan, Jammu and Kashmir, 6,
66–67
Ikhwan-ul-Muslimoon, 72–73
atrocities, 74
balance of power, shifting,
66–67, 72–73
Colonel, Bashir, 95
commanders, assassination
attempt, 96
difficult lives, 81
Jammu and Kashmir Awami League
and Kashmir Assembly elections,
89, 90f
Liyaqat, Ali Khan, 74–75,
76–78, 80–81
opportunists, India alliance, 73–82
Parrey, Kuka, 76, 78–79
performance anxiety and
abuses, 81–82
post-1996 elections, 91
Sopore rajdhani, Indian army
action, 67–69
Wagay, Basir Ahmad ("the Tiger"), 75,
77–78, 79–80
India
East Pakistani refugees entering, daily
number, 49–50, 50f
Kashmir war, 64–96, 159 (see also
Kashmir, India's war)
security implications, 168–69
state-nonstate alliances, 158–60

India, anti-Naxalite "awakening,"
    Chhattisgarh, 112–28
    background, 99–100
    conclusions, 127–28
    fundamentals, 112–13
    India's interests, context, 115–17
    India's weakness to parity in
        Chhattisgarh, 117–19
    Naxalite (Maoist) insurgency,
        background, 113–15
    Salwa Judum "awakening," 100 (see
        also Salwa Judum, Chhattisgarh)
    Salwa Judum opportunists alliance, 6,
        119–27, 123t, 160
India–Ikhwan-ul-Muslimoon
    opportunists alliance, 73–82
India–Muslim Mujahideen opportunists
    alliance, 82–88
Indian Al Baraq, 78
India–Village Defense Committee
    activists alliance, 92–94
insurgency. See also specific types
    robust, 30–31
international relations (IR) theory
    neorealist, 8
    realist, 8
    rebel alliances, 9
    state alliances, 8–9
Inter-Services Intelligence (ISI), Taliban
    links, 103–4
Ireland, Northern, 8
Islami Jamiat-e -Tulabah, 57
Islamist militants, Pakistan
    outsourcing violence to, 7
    Pakistani army alliance, 28, 38–39
Islamists, Pakistan
    counterinsurgent atrocities, U.S.
        on, 38–39
    parties, 39
    Razakars, 53–54
Israel Defense Forces, Duvdevan unit, 18, 23

Jalaluddin Haqqani network, 105
Jamaat-e-Islami, 37–38, 82–83
    Hizbul Mujahideen partnership, 83
    Pakistani army alliance, 37–38, 45–46

Jammu and Kashmir Awami League,
    40, 42, 43
    Ikhwan-ul-Muslimoon political wing,
        89, 90f
    Kashmir Assembly elections, 89, 90f
    Parrey, Kuka, 89, 90f
Jammu and Kashmir Disturbed Areas
    Act, 69–70
Jammu and Kashmir Ikhwan, 66–67
Jammu and Kashmir Liberation Front
    (JKLF), 65
    decline, 70
    Parrey, Kuka, 74
    Students Liberation Front, 74
Jammu war, 92
    India–Village Defense Committee
        activists alliance, 92–94
    Village Defense Committees, 92
Jirki clan, Hakkari, 135–36
Joshi, Manoj, 72, 74–75

Kader Bahini, 56
Kadyrov, Akhmad, 132–33, 161
    Russia alliance, 153–55
Kadyrov, Ramzan, 154–55, 163–64
Kalvas, Stathis, Logic of Violence, The, 165
Karma, Mahendra (Bastar Tiger), 119–
    22, 125, 161
Kashmir
    1989–1993, from insurgent control to
        parity, 67–72
    current status, 163–64
    Ikhwan, 6
Kashmir, India's war, 64–96, 128, 159
    1980s Kashmir crisis, 65
    1996 elections, turning point,
        88–92, 90f
    Abdullah, Farooq, 89–91
    al-Ikhwan, 78
    Armed Forces (Jammu and Kashmir)
        Special Powers Act, 69–70
    Azad, Ghulam Nabi, 85, 86, 88
    Bhat, Abdul Gani, 64, 83–84
    Bhat, Fayaz Ahmad (Tanveer), 84–86
    Colonel, Bashir, 95
    conclusion, 94–96

Kashmir, India's war (*Cont.*)
Dar, Mohammad Ahsan, 82–84, 85
ex-rebel proxies, 65–66
"get them by their balls"
approach, 94–95
guns (balance of power) and
balance-of-interests, 66
Hizbul Mujahideen, 70, 72–73, 75, 76,
77, 83–86, 88
Ikhwan-ul-Muslimoon (*see*
Ikhwan-ul-Muslimoon)
India, outsourcing violence, 65
India army–Hindu villagers
relationship, 65–66
India–Ikhwan-ul-Muslimoon
opportunists alliance, 73–82
India–Muslim Mujahideen
opportunists alliance, 82–88
Indian Al Baraq, 78
Jammu and Kashmir Awami League,
40, 42, 43
Jammu and Kashmir Disturbed Areas
Act, 69–70
Jammu and Kashmir Ikhwan, 66–67
Jammu and Kashmir Liberation
Front, 65, 70
Jammu theater of war, 92
Jammu theater of war, India–Village
Defense Committee activists
alliance, 92–94
Kashmiri Pandits, 31, 66, 69
Kashmir Liberation Jehad, 78
Kashmir Valley, 1989–1993, from
insurgent control to parity, 67–72
Kashmir Valley, 1989–1996, from
parity to India's control, 72–88
Khan, Reyaz Ahmad, 87–88
Liyaqat, Ali Khan, 74–75,
76–78, 80–81
Lok Sabha elections, 88–89
Mujahideen-e-Islam, 83–85
Muslim Liberation Army, 78
Muslim Mujahideen, 66–67, 72–73, 96
Parrey, Kuka, 73–79
piling-on bandwagoning, 66–67
proxy–Indian state alliances, proxy
commanders' fate, 95–96

proxy–Indian state alliances, proxy
rebels' fate, 95
Rashtriya Rifles, 71, 73, 79–80
Salati, Zafar, 80–81
Siddique, Bilal Ahmad, 83–84
Special Police Officers, 91–92
Taliban, 78
Wagay, Basir Ahmad ("the Tiger"), 75,
77–78, 79–80
Kashmiris, Nehru on, 69
Kashmir Liberation Jehad, 78
Kashmir Pandits, 31, 66, 69
Kashmir Valley, 1989–1996, from parity
to India's control, 72–88
India–Ikhwan-ul-Muslimoon
opportunists alliance, 73–82
India–Muslim Mujahideen
opportunists alliance, 82–88
Kasyanov, Mikhail, 150–51
Kautilya, *Arthashastra (The Science of
Politics)*, 14–15, 16, 19, 157
Kayani, Ashfaq Pervaiz, 105, 106, 110
Khan, Ayub, 43–44
Khan, Khushdil, 108
Khan, Mohammad Ayub, 39
Khan, Reyaz Ahmad, 87–88
Khan, Syed Ahmad, 97, 127–28
Khan, Tikka, 45–46
Khan, Yahya, 43
Koel. *See* Parrey, Kuka
Kurdish clans–Turkey alliance,
135–39, 139*f*
Kurdish Hizbullah–Turkey
alliance, 140–43
Kurdish rebels, Turkey war against, 133–
43, 160. *See also* Turkey, Kurdish
rebels war
Kurdistan Workers' Party (PKK)
Turkey–Kurdish clans alliance against,
135–39, 139*f*
Turkey–Kurdish Hizbullah alliance
against, 140–43
Turkish armed forces, opposition
to, 155
violent campaign and advance
against Turkish armed
forces, 133–35

Labazanov, Ruslan, 145–46
large-N scholarship, 165–66
lashkars, Pakistan, 100. *See also* Pakistan,
    anti-Taliban tribal "awakening"
    Adezai Aman Lashkar, 97–98, 108–9
    background, 106–7
    government support, early
        withholding, 98–99
    jirgas (tribal councils), 106–7
    rise (Anbar Awakening), 98, 100
    Salarzai, 110
    weak government alliance and
        misalignment of interests, 106–12
Lieven, Anatol, 146–47
liminality, of militias, 18–19
Litvinenko, Alexander, 150–51
Liyaqat, Ali Khan, 74–75, 76–78, 80–81
local networks, as data sources, 35
Logic of Violence, The (Kalyvas), 165

Machiavelli, Niccolò, 2, 157
mafia, NYC–US Navy alliance, World
    War II, 157
Malik, Abdul, 97–98, 161
Manir, Mohammad Shishir, 37–38
Mao Zedong, on war and balance of
    power, 30
Maskhadov, Aslan, 149, 151
militia, 17–19. *See also specific types*
    ad hoc and not trained, 18
    anti-rebel, 17
    collaboration with state, active, 18
    conceptualization, 17–18
    definition, 17
    as irregular forces, 17–18
    as liminal agents, 18–19
    nonstate actors as, 17–18
    organization title, 17
    Salvadoran right-wing death
        squads, 17
    vs. state's regular armed forces, 18
    working *for* but not *of* state, 18
militias, pro-government
    prevalence, 3, 4*f*
    research, existing, 11
minbing, 20–21
Mueller, John, 165–66

Mujahideen-e-Islam, 83–85
Mujib Bahini, 55–56
Mukhopadhyay, Dipali, 28, 35
Mukti Bahini, 37, 48–51, 54–55, 55*f*, 58
Musharraf, Pervez, 101, 104, 105–6
Muslim Liberation Army, 78
Muslim Mujahideen, 66–67, 72–73, 96
    founding, 83–84
    Hizbul Mujahideen, as main target, 88
    Hizbul Mujahideen, as reconciliation
        attempt, 86
    India alliance, as opportunists, 82–88

Naba Azad, 85, 86
National Socialist Council of
    Nagaland-Khaplang (NSCN-K),
    Nagaland, 6
Naxalbari, 113
Naxalites, 113–14
    Andhra Pradesh Greyhounds
        counterinsurgency operations, 116
    anti-Naxalite "awakening," 112–28
    (*see also* India, anti-Naxalite
        "awakening," Chhattisgarh)
    Communist Party of India, 116, 117
    Communist Party of India People's
        War, 114, 116
    ideology and focus, 1960s+, 115
Nehru, Jawaharlal, 69
neoclassical realism (neorealism),
    8–9, 28–29
Niazi, Amir Abdullah Khan, 57
Niyomito Bahini, 55
Nizami, Motiur Rahman, 161
    execution, 37–38
    official charge against, 58
nonstate actors
    activists, 25, 26
    definition, 17–18
    interests, varying, 25
    militia, 17–18
    need, 1–2
    opportunists, 25–26
    origins and proliferation, 7–8
    typology, of allies, 15–23
    violence monopoly,
        illegitimate use, 8

Öcalan, Abdullah, 133
Olağanüstü Hal (OHAL), 136–37
operational collaboration, 19, 20f
  proxies, 21–22, 30, 31
Operation al-Mizan, 105–6
Operation Blitz, 43
Operation Green Hunt, 126
Operation Searchlight, 42, 43–45, 46
opportunist-activist framework,
  10, 11–12
opportunist rebel, 10
opportunists
  balance-of-interests theory, 12
  balance-of-interests theory, new,
    24–30, 27f
  balance-of-interests theory, new, vs.
    activists, 26–28
  coercion, 25–26
  interests, 25
  nonstate actors, 25–26
  state-nonstate alliances, civil war, 12
  state preference, vs. activists, 28
  transactional alliances, 26–28
outsourcing violence. See also specific
    countries, proxy groups, wars,
    and topics
  definition, 16
  as high-stakes gamble, 3
  India, 2–3, 6
  Pakistan, 2–3, 7
  policy recommendations, 161–65
  prevalence, 3, 4f
  problem, 16
  risks, 3, 161
Özal, Turgut, 131, 134

Pakistan
  Pashtun Party, 103–4, 107–8, 111
  Pashtun Party, secular Awami National
    Party, 111
  security implications, 168–69
  state-nonstate alliances, 158–60
Pakistan, 1971 war, 37–63, 163–64
  al-Shams, 56–57, 58
  Awami League, 40
  balance-of-interests framework and
    U.S. relationship, 61–63

Bangladesh, bloody birth, 39–40
Battle of the Belonia Bulge, 47–49
constitution, first, 39
data sources, 41
dates, 38
documentation, lack/suppression, 40
East Pakistan, Pakistan regaining
  control (March-May, 1971), 41–47
East Pakistan, refugees to India, daily
  number entering, 49–50, 50f
Islamist counterinsurgent atrocities,
  U.S. on, 38–39
Islamist parties, rise, 39
Kader Bahini and Abdul Kader
  (Tiger) Siddiqui, 56
Mujib Bahini, 55–56
Mukti Bahini (freedom fighters), 37,
  48–51, 54–55, 55f, 58
Niyomito Bahini and Gano Bahini, 55
Nizami, Motiur Rahman, 161
Nizami, Motiur Rahman,
  execution, 37–38
Nizami, Motiur Rahman, official
  charge against, 58
opportunists and activists, early
  lack, 38
Pakistan–al-Badr activists alliance,
  56–59, 159
Pakistani army–Islamist militant
  alliance, 28, 38–39
Pakistani army–Jamaat-e-Islami
  alliance, 37–38, 45–46
Pakistan political setting, 37–40
Pakistan–Razakar opportunists
  alliance and "volunteers," 25–26,
  51–54, 159
from parity to insurgent dominance
  (June-December), 33–56, 55f
plausible deniability, 61, 63
power and interests, 59–61
rebel groups, 55–56
religion, elective reforms, 39
Sangram Parishads, 55
from state control to parity (May-June,
  1971), 47–51, 50f
Suicide Squads, 55
Toofan Bahini (Storm Troops), 55

Uban Force, 56
war crimes tribunal, Bangladeshi, 37
Pakistan, anti-Taliban tribal
    "awakening," 100–12
    background, 97–100
    conclusions, 127–28
    Federally Administered Tribal Areas,
        105, 106–7
    fundamentals, 100–1
    government policy toward,
        early, 98–99
    interests, context, 101–6
    Inter-Services Intelligence–Taliban
        links, 103–4
    Khassadars (tribal police force), 107
    lashkar, "awakening," 98, 100
    lashkar, weak alliance and
        misalignment of interests, 106–12
    lashkar, withholding support
        for, 98–99
    Malik and Adezai Aman
        Laskhar, 97–98
    Operation al-Mizan, 105–6
    Taliban Movement of Pakistan, 97,
        104–5, 111
Pakistan–al-Badr activists alliance,
    56–59, 159
Pakistani army–Islamist militant alliance,
    28, 38–39
Pakistani army–Jamaat-e-Islami alliance,
    37–38, 45–46
Pakistan People's Party (PPP), 111
Pakistan–Razakar opportunists alliance,
    51–56, 159
    "volunteers," 25–26
Pandits, Kashmir, 31, 66, 69
paramilitary. See militias,
    pro-government
Parrey, Kuka, 73–79, 89, 161
    Awami League and Kashmir Assembly
        elections, 89, 90f
    Ikhwan-ul-Muslimoon, 76, 78–79
Pashtun Party, Pakistan, 103–4,
    107–8, 111
    secular: Awami National Party, 111
Patrullas de Autodefensa Civil,
    Guatemala, 5

People's Liberation Army Militia,
    China, 20–21
piling-on bandwagoning, 66–67,
    130, 139
PKK. See Kurdistan Workers'
    Party (PKK)
plausible deniability
    East Pakistan, 63
    India, 99–100, 158–59
    India's Kashmir war, 65
    nonstate counterinsurgents, 5–6, 165
    Pakistan, 158–59
    paper trail absence, 21–22
    Russia, Chechnya, 132
    weak democracies and aid recipients
        from democracies, 23, 61
policy recommendations, 161–65
power
    battlefield efficacy, 30
    civil wartime state-nonstate alliance,
        10, 11–12
    distribution, alliance formation, 24
    lower power balance, socio-ideological
        links, and state-nonstate alliance
        outcomes, 27f
    operationalizing, 29–30
    perceptions, of punishing defection or
        rewarding collaboration, 30
    territorial control, 29–30
    via guns, 66
process tracing, 32–33
pro-government military. See militias,
    pro-government
proxy, 21–22, 30. See also specific types
    operational collaboration,
        21–22, 30, 31
    strategically viable, 31
Punjab, Cats, 6
Putin, Vladimir, 132–33
    criminal allies, 153–54
    second Chechen war, 150–55

Rahman, Sheikh Mujibur (Mujib)
    arrest, 44
    Awami League leadership, 42, 43–44
Rashid, Ahmed, 103–4
Rashtriya Rifles, 71, 73, 79–80

Razakar–Pakistan alliance, 51–56, 159
"volunteers," 25–26, 51–52
Razakars, Pakistan, 25–26, 159
functions, 30–53
Razakar Ordinance, 29
"volunteer" army, Islamist
believers, 53–54
"volunteer" army, opportunists and
underdogs, 53
"volunteer" army, recruitment and
training, 29–52
realist international relations (IR)
theory, 8
rebel alliances, existing research, 9–10
Reese, Roger, 28
reflexivity, 35–36
relational alliances, activists, 26–28
research, existing, 7–11
Aham, 7–8
Centeno, 7–8
civil war scholarship, 8
militias, pro-government, 11
nonstate actors, origins and
proliferation, 7–8
realist international relations theory, 8
rebel alliances, 9–10
state alliances, 8–9
violence monopoly, nonstate actors'
illegitimate use, 8
violence monopoly, state
legitimate use, 7
warfare as state's domain, 7
research design, 32–34
revisionist state, 8
Revolutionary Armed Forces of
Colombia (FARC), 164
Russia, Chechnya wars, 132–33, 143–55
balance-of-power overview, 129–30
first Chechen war, 143–49
ideology hypothesis, 132
Kadyrov–Putin relationship, 132–33
outsourcing violence rationale, 132
postwar spoils, 132–33
second Chechen war, 149–51
second Chechen war, Russia–
Gantamirov alliance, 152–53

second Chechen war, Russia–
Kadyrovtsy alliance, 153–55
Russia, state-nonstate alliances, 160–61
Russia–Gantamirov alliance, 152–53
Russia–Kadyrovtsy alliance, 153–55

Said, Sheikh, 135–36
Salarzai lashkar, 110
Salarzai tribe, 109–10
Salati, Zafar, 80–81
Salvadoran right-wing death squads, 17
Salwa Judum, Chhattisgarh, 6, 100, 160
"awakening," 112–28 (see also India, anti-
Naxalite "awakening," Chhattisgarh)
chaos from, 126
child recruitment, forced, 123–24
joining, coercion, 125
joining, material and security
benefits, 124–25
Karma, Mahendra (Bastar Tiger),
119–22, 125, 161
leadership, 126
Operation Green Hunt, 126
opportunists, India alliance, 119–27,
123t (see also India, anti-Naxalite
"awakening," Chhattisgarh)
spread and growth, 2000s,
121–25, 123t
Sangram Parishads, 55
Saxena, Girish Chandra "Gary," 69–70
Science of Politics, The (Kautilya), 14–15,
16, 19, 157
security scholarship, 164
self-defense patrol. See militias,
pro-government
shabiha, Syria, 5
Shah, Javaid Jussain, 91
Sheikh, Mona Kanwal, 104–5
Siddique, Bilal Ahmad, 83–84
Siddiqui, Abdul Kader, 56
Smith, Adam, 157–58
South Asia
geostrategic importance, 6–7
outsourced counterinsurgents,
overview, 6
security, 168–70

Special Police Officer (SPO)
  Kashmir war, India's, 91–92
  Salwa Judum, 122, 123–24
standing army, necessity, 7
state. *See also specific states*
  physical force, legitimate use, 7
  standing army, necessity, 7
  warfare as domain of, 7
  Weberian conceptualization, 16
state-nonstate alliances, 16
  balance-of-interests theory, 16, 158
  balance-of-interests theory, Pakistan
    and India, 158–60
  complexity, 1–2
  local-level comparative
    advantage, 16–17
  research, existing, 8–9
state-nonstate alliances, civil war, 12. *See
    also specific countries and wars*
  balance-of-interests approach, 158
  interests and power, 10
  opportunists, 12
  Pakistan and India, 158–60
  Turkey and Russia, 160–61
  understanding, 158
Suicide Squads, 55
SULFA, Assam, 6
Swami, Praveen, 73, 76, 91
Syria *shabiha*, Arab Spring opponents'
    torture, 5

tactics-focused approach, 24
Tagore, Rabindranath, "The Communal
    Award," 37
Taj, Farhat, 106–7, 108–9, 111
Taliban, 78
  Afghan, territorial control, 29–30
  in Kashmir, 78
  Pakistan, anti-Taliban tribal
    "awakening," 100–12 (*see also*
    Pakistan, anti-Taliban tribal
    "awakening")
  Pakistan's Inter-Services Intelligence
    links, 103–4
Taliban Movement of Pakistan (TTP),
    97, 104–5, 111
Tanveer, 84–86

Tehrik-e- Taliban Pakistan (TTP), 97,
    104–5, 111
third actors, 11. *See also* militias,
    pro-government
"Tiger," the, 75, 77–78, 79–80
Tiger Siddiqui, 56
Tolstoy, Leo, *War and Peace*, 167–68
Toofan Bahini (Storm Troops), 55
triangulation, interview, 35–36
tribal "awakening," 99–128. *See also
    specific types*
  India, anti-Naxalite "awakening,"
    Chhattisgarh, 112–28
  Pakistan, anti-Taliban
    "awakening," 100–12
Turkey, Kurdish rebels war, 133–43, 160
  1970s Turkey, 133
  balance-of-power overview, 129–30
  ideology hypothesis, 131–32
  Kurdistan Workers' Party, violent
    campaign, 133–35
  Olağanüstü Hal (OHAL), 136–37
  outsourcing violence
    rationale, 130–31
  piling-on bandwagoning, 130, 139
  rebel relocation, 130
  Turkey–Kurdish clans alliance,
    135–39, 139f
  Turkey–Kurdish Hizbullah
    alliance, 140–43
  Turkish army–Islamist militants
    alliance, secret, 131–32
  Turkish army–nationalist clans
    alliances, 130
Turkey, state-nonstate alliances, 160–61
Turkey–Kurdish clans alliance,
    135–39, 139f
Turkey–Kurdish Hizbullah
    alliance, 140–43

Uban Force, 56
United States
  counterinsurgency field
    manual, 162–63
  Guatemala proxies, 21
US Navy–NYC mafia alliance, World War
    II, 157

Velioğlu, Hüseyin, 141
Village Defense Committees, 92
    activists–India alliance, 92–94
violence, outsourcing. *See* outsourcing
    violence; *specific countries, proxy
    groups, and wars*
Volya, Narodnaya, 29–30
von Clausewitz, Carl, 2, 19, 157, 165, 168

Wagay, Basir Ahmad ("the Tiger"), 75,
    77–78, 79–80

Waltz, Kenneth N., 8
war. *See also specific topics and wars*
    conventional, 18–19
War and Peace (Tolstoy), 167–68
warfare, as state's domain, 7
Weinstein, Jeremy, 10

Yeltsin, Boris, first Chechen war, 144–46

Zedong, Mao, *minbing* militia, 20–21
Zia-ul-Haq, Muhammad, 39